To Jeffrey,

'It aint up yet!'

with love from

Alec Mc

PERSONAL MARK

PERSONAL MARK

by

Alec McCowen

Hamish Hamilton London

First published in Great Britain 1984
by Hamish Hamilton Ltd
Garden House, 57–59 Long Acre, London WC2E 9JZ

British Library Cataloguing in Publication Data

McCowen, Alec
Personal Mark.
1. Bible. N.T.Mark—Commentaries
I. Title
226'.306   BS2585.3

ISBN 0-241-11263-X

Photoset by Rowland Phototypesetting Ltd
Bury St Edmunds, Suffolk
Printed in Great Britain by
Billing & Son Ltd, Worcester

To each generation he speaks in glittering fragments.

Desmond Steward, *The Foreigner*

For
Vivian Matalon
friend and teacher.

ACKNOWLEDGEMENTS

I owe a debt of gratitude to the nine authors of the commentaries used and quoted in this book. I also owe apologies to some of them for contradicting their theories, and for mocking their styles.

In alphabetical order the authors are: William Barclay: *The Daily Study Bible, The Gospel of Mark*; Alan Cole: *Mark*; Robert Crotty: *Good News in Mark*; Manford George Gutzke: *Plain Talk on Mark*; Dr Sherman E. Johnson: *The Gospel according to St Mark*; The Rev. F. Marshall: *The School and College St Mark*; C. F. D. Moule: *The Gospel according to Mark*; D. E. Nineham: *Saint Mark*; and Gerard S. Sloyan: *The Gospel of Saint Mark*.

William Barclay and D. E. Nineham were especially helpful. But, above all, I wish it was possible to thank the Rev. F. Marshall for the great comfort of his homely common sense, and the inspiration of his unquestioning faith.

THE BEGINNING

If there had never been a Christian religion, if Jesus had disappeared from memory, if there was no Matthew, Mark, Luke or John, and, one day, we discovered a little book which opened with the line *The beginning of the gospel of Jesus Christ, the Son of God*; – what would we think?

Our brains are dulled with familiarity.

Even if, from an early age, you have rebelled against the whole idea of God and religion, you will have heard the name of Jesus Christ.

You will have heard the description 'the son of God'.

You will know the word gospel – a dreary word, I think.

And so it is very hard to imagine hearing or reading for the first time 'The beginning of the gospel of Jesus Christ, the Son of God'. Or even an alternative: 'This is the Good News about Jesus Christ, the Son of God.'

But it is probably the most stunning opening line ever written.

It is the start of St Mark's Gospel.

★

'The beginning of the gospel of Jesus Christ, the Son of God.'

What does it mean?

Is it a fantasy?

Is it a dream?

Let us look at the words again.

The beginning

The start

of the gospel

of the good news

(Does that mean that there is more good news – that the good news goes on and on?)

of Jesus

a name – a Hellenised form of Joshua.

Christ

'the Annointed One – equivalent to the Jewish Messiah' (*Enc. Brit.*)

the son of God.

No, I'm sorry! I'm lost!

Who says he is the Son of God?

Does Mark say it?

Does Jesus say it?

Does God say it?

Do they all say it?

Are we expected to agree?

(Commentators say the words should not even be included.)

There is nothing for it but to read on.

That's why it's such a brilliant opening line.

If this story is true, it could be the most important story in the world. It could give us answers to the most nagging basic questions. 'What is life?' 'What is death?' 'What is the universe?' If Jesus *is* the Son of God, maybe he knows the answers to those questions. Maybe God told him.

But where does the story take place?

And what does Jesus look like?

Is he an angel?

Is he a space-man?

Is he a spirit?

Is he Jewish?

2 – 3

'*As it is written in the prophets.*' (What prophets? I am totally ignorant.) '*Behold, I send my messenger before thy face,*' (Before *whose* face?) '*which shall prepare thy way before thee.*' (Perhaps he means Jesus!) '*The voice of one crying in the wilderness, Prepare ye the way of the Lord, make his paths straight.*'

Help!

Where does this prophecy come from?

Isaiah and Malachi.

Is that a help?

No.

'*John*' (Ah! a good straightforward name!) '*did baptize in the* **4** *wilderness,*' – so *he* was the messenger! '*and preach the baptism of repentance for the remission of sins.*'

STOP!

This isn't easy stuff. The writer takes a lot for granted.

Baptism? 'Religious rite of immersing in or sprinkling with water in sign of purification and (with Christians) admission to the church, usually accompanied by name-giving.' (The *Pocket Oxford Dictionary*.)

Yes, but this is pre-Christian.

All right! John the Baptist.

'He baptized Jews and pagans without distinction in the Jordan to the confession and forgiveness of sins, and he connected with this action the proclamation of the approaching kingdom of God as a judgement.' (*J. M. Enc. Brit.*, Fourteenth Edition.)

So evidently John's 'baptism of repentance for the remission of sins' was something new and special. Was it a success?

It must have been.

'*And there went out unto him all the land of Judaea, and they of* **5** *Jerusalem, and were all baptized of him in the river of Jordan, confessing their sins.*'

That must have been a large crowd.

I like the distinction 'and they of Jerusalem' – rather as if the smart Londoners or New Yorkers had joined the ordinary out-of-towners, and been equally eager to repent.

And now we know where we are.

The river of Jordan sets the scene.

'*And John was clothed with camel's hair,*' (Thank you! I won- **6-7** dered.) '*and with a girdle of a skin about his loins;*' (That means a belt.) '*and he did eat locusts and wild honey;*' (Naturally.) '*And preached, saying, There cometh one mightier than I after me, the latchet of whose shoes I am not worthy to stoop down and unloose.*'

Can we imagine what it would be like to be literally waiting for Godot? It seems that most people today ignore God or avoid him, or assume that he is far too remote and grand to trouble with them. John, and all the land of Judaea, and they of Jerusalem, were literally waiting for him in the river of Jordan. And John – who sounds like a nice man – does not rest on his obvious success in the great baptism, but energetically

proclaims his love and loyalty to the long-awaited Messiah. In
the great Jacobean translation the words sound Shakespearean:

7   *'The latchet of whose shoes I am not worthy*
    To stoop down and unloose.

8   *I indeed have baptized you with water;*
    But he shall baptize you with the Holy Ghost.'

What does that mean? The Holy Ghost?

Would it be clearer to say the Holy Spirit?

Yes. At least we get away from images of hoods and
sheets.

Does it mean that John, who baptizes with water, is only an
earthly amateur, but that the 'one mightier than I' has connec-
tions in heaven?

Shall we leave it?

I think we'd better leave it. Something unexpected and
amazing is about to happen.

9   *'And it came to pass'* – I see a dozen exclamation marks!

    'in those days,' I see a dozen more!

    'that Jesus came from Nazareth of Galilee, and was baptized of
John in Jordan.'

Isn't Jesus the name mentioned in the first line, and didn't it
say he was 'the Son of God'? So what's going to . . .

10   *'And straightway coming up out of the water'* – Yes? *'he saw the*
heavens opened,' I don't believe it! *'and the Spirit like a dove*
descending upon him:' ('there is no evidence that an actual bird
was there,' Manford George Gutzke, *Plain Talk on Mark.*)

11   *'And there came a voice from heaven, saying, Thou art my beloved*
Son, in whom I am well pleased.'

Let's take a pause.

Mark does not waste words.

Did John know Jesus? (Manford George Gutzke also tells us
'that these two men humanly speaking were second cousins'.)
When Jesus arrived on the scene did anyone notice him? Was it
anything special?

And then, when 'the heavens opened' – and so on – was
anyone else aware of what was going on?

And who told Mark all this?

Personally, I don't want to believe in special magic effects.
The world is wonderful enough.

Surely it *all* happened inside Jesus's head, and he alone was aware of the Spirit, and he alone heard the voice saying, 'Thou art my beloved Son, in whom I am well pleased.'

And surely all of this was a confirmation of something, a confirmation of a search and a desire and a belief. Surely Jesus had already had a long relationship with God. This could not be a sudden or unexpected voice from heaven. Surely Jesus (even though we know little or nothing about him yet) had a desire for a father that was so strong and powerful that he willed God to choose him as a son.

Jesus heard what he wanted to hear.

Jesus believed what he wanted to believe.

And not only did he want God to claim him as a son, and not only did he want to claim God as his father, he wanted God's love and approval. He was the beloved son; and presumably the *only* son; and presumably the worthy son.

The worthy Son of God.

He was.

Could any human being support such a responsibility? If God spoke to one of us with such approval, could we stand it?

No.

Jesus couldn't stand it either.

Having chosen his father in heaven; having heard himself acclaimed as the beloved; immediately he runs away from the responsibility.

'*And immediately*' – and in Mark if it's not 'immediately' it's   12
'straightway' – 'And immediately *the Spirit driveth him into the wilderness. And he was there in the wilderness forty days, tempted of*   13
Satan; and was with the wild beasts; and the angels ministered unto him.'

Let's go slow again.

And immediately

And straightway

the Spirit

Whatever is the creative force. God himself at work.

driveth him into the wilderness.

There were many wildernesses. It does not have to be a desert. I think this wilderness was Jesus's doubt.

And he was there in the wilderness

This state of doubt.

forty days,

Hebraic speech for 'a long time'.

tempted of Satan;

The adversary, enemy or opposition.

and was with the wild beasts;

Who can know the wild beasts inside Jesus? I do not think they were very different from our own. Surely the wild beasts of lust and greed and a desire for power.

and the angels ministered unto him.

This sounds frightfully Victorian – but I think it simply means 'the good side won'.

This great conflict is compressed by Mark into two verses.

This whole opening of St Mark, the prologue to the gospel, takes only thirteen verses. Two hundred and sixty-one words to introduce the Holy Spirit, Satan, John the Baptist, and a voice from heaven. To set the scene by the river of Jordan. To present the hopes of the people for a Messiah. To introduce Jesus, and describe his baptism by John, and his confirmation from heaven; his temptation to evade responsibility; and – after a long time – his acceptance of the role of the son of God.

I am going to examine the actions of Jesus, and think about the life of Jesus, as if he was an ordinary human being. I do not want a virgin birth, or voices from heaven, or supernatural powers. They diminish his triumph. I want to present – through Mark – a fallible man; sometimes tired, hungry, irritable. Sometimes humorous, cynical, sarcastic. Often compassionate, often reasonable. Always ahead of us. Unpredictable. Unbelievably brave. Understandably frightened.

'What manner of man is this?'

★

14 *'Now after that John was put in prison, Jesus came into Galilee preaching –'* Just a minute!

– after that John was put in prison?

John was put *in prison*?

Who put John in prison?

Why was John put in prison?

Mark is a very impatient writer. Having disposed of his prologue, he cannot wait to get on to the main action. John is put into prison and Jesus comes into Galilee, etc., etc.

Now let *me* dispose of the idea I proposed at the beginning of this book, that this is the first time we have read the gospels, and let us consider the style of Mark.

St Mark's Gospel reads to me like an interview. And indeed it is believed to have been related to Mark by Jesus's disciple Peter. Peter would have been an old man at the time of Mark's interview, and his memory would probably have needed a lot of jogging. I hear this jogging in the writing of the gospel. And, from the questions that Mark asks, we arrive at a portrait of the interviewer.

He is not a sentimental man. He likes facts. He does not linger over second-hand information. This partly accounts for the extraordinary compression of the first verses. They are not the words of an eye-witness. It is not likely that Peter was on the spot when Jesus was baptized by John. It is almost certain that he was not with Jesus during the forty days of doubt. If the gospel was written because of Peter's conviction, and – maybe – Mark's conviction, that Jesus was the Son of God, then it is reasonable to suppose that Mark asked Peter to relate anything pertinent to the divinity of Jesus before the start of his ministry. And we begin with the prophecies that a messenger would cry in the wilderness: 'Prepare ye the way of the Lord, make his paths straight.' And, immediately, Mark introduces John in the wilderness, and tells us in general terms *what* he preached and *who* heard him.

And then I hear the reporter's question: 'What did he look like?' And we get the homely factual details of John's clothes, and the additional information of what he ate. This would either have been common knowledge to the contemporaries of Peter – or else Jesus made the description himself and told his disciples. This is pure Mark – and it is timeless reporting. 'The Queen wore a turquoise hat with ostrich feathers. At the luncheon she ate Oeufs en Cocotte and Suprême de Volaille Kiev, followed by Fraises des Bois.'

But Mark is so determined not to lose his readers, that he actually continues straight on from the description of the clothes and the food, with a quote from one of John's sermons: 'and preached, saying, There cometh one mightier than I' etc. And, having completed the quote, he again continues straight on into the introduction of Jesus. 'And it came to pass . . .' Like a reporter who knows he has a superb story, he is determined to grab his readers and not let them off the hook. 'And it came to pass' (It happened!) 'in those days,' (there and then!) 'that Jesus came' (Where did he come from?) 'from Nazareth of Galilee,' (And what happened?) 'and was baptized of John in Jordan. And straightway . . .'

I was given a little book called *The School and College St. Mark* written by the Rev. F. Marshall, MA. There is no date on it, but it is inscribed to – or autographed by – *Irene Avery 1908*. I think it was given to me as a joke, but it is full of extraordinary information, admittedly some of it useless, but much of it worth far more than many of the modern commentaries. The Rev. F. Marshall is particularly interesting in his comments on 'The Characteristics of the Gospel'. He is also very fond of counting. Here is one of his counting comments: 'The words *straightway*, *immediately*, *anon*, occur forty-one times in the Gospel.' – It would not have surprised *me* if they had occurred four hundred and one times. They are the words of an eager reporter – forever pushing his story forward, determined to engage his readers' interest.

'And *straightway* coming up out of the water, he saw the heavens opened . . .'

'And *immediately* the spirit driveth him into the wilderness . . .'

Perhaps it was Peter who was in the hurry. Perhaps Peter wanted to get to his own entrance in the story as soon as possible, and left Mark to do the best he could with the vision that Jesus saw and the voice that Jesus heard when he was baptized. Did Jesus subsequently try to describe these events to his disciples? How are such things described? We have all heard people talk about what seemed to be supernatural moments: 'It was as if something suddenly came to me!' 'I suddenly knew, clear as day!' These are moments of conviction, moments of decision – usually followed by moments of doubt and indecision. But a mental contract has been signed; an agreement has been settled on. And these moments are forever associated with the time and the place where they occurred. And often they are associated with the physical events which accompanied them.

In Jesus's case, it might have been as if 'coming up out of the water' – after the sudden shock of the cold, and with his eyes blinking in the sunshine – God had put a hand upon his head and given him his blessing and authority to act. Then, after the moment of exhilaration, came the opposing doubts. Perhaps, as became his fashion, Jesus related the temptation in the wilderness to his disciples indirectly, in the form of a parable. This would account for the wild beasts and the angels. But Mark and Peter have neither the time nor information to enlighten us any further. They charge on – 'Now after that John was put in prison, Jesus came into Galilee, preaching the gospel of the kingdom of God . . .'

We will discover that, in his enthusiasm to tell the story of Jesus, Mark puts off giving us further information about John the Baptist until Chapter Six – when the ministry of Jesus is well under way. There are several occasions in the Gospel when Mark gives us information in what seems to be a parenthetical manner. This might account for the earliest recorded review of St Mark's Gospel, by Papias, Bishop of Hierapolis in about AD 130. 'Mark, having become the interpreter of Peter, wrote down accurately all that he remembered of the things done and said by the Lord; *not, however, in order.*' But (apart from the story of John the Baptist and Herod) I do not think this statement means that the main story of Jesus is ever out of sequence. Although it is true that Mark (or Peter) sometimes remembers additions to stories right in the middle of telling them.

My new friend the Rev. Marshall says: 'St Matthew continually groups together similar sayings and deeds.

'St Luke arranges incidents and sermons in artistic order.

'St Mark, on the contrary, reproduces *the chronological order* of the oral Gospel. Hence . . . we can deduce a continuous life of Christ from the Gospel of St Mark.'

This insistence on the accurate continuity of St Mark's story of Jesus is vitally important to me. If I have discovered anything new – and this is mighty unlikely – it is mostly based on the order of Mark's writing, as translated in the King James Version.

Let's get on with it!

'Now after that John was put in prison, Jesus came into Galilee, preaching the gospel of the kingdom of God, and saying, The time is fulfilled, and the kingdom of God is at hand: repent ye, and believe the gospel.'

14
15

I do not have an image of Jesus saying these words in a synagogue, but shouting them in the streets. Shouting them joyfully in the streets. There is a superb simplicity about them. And I do not have an image of the soulful, solemn Jesus most of the great artists have painted, but a buoyant young man in radiant good health – perhaps looking like a thirty-year-old Jon Voigt, or, to keep things equal, a thirty-year-old Muhammad Ali. The words – like the face – are confident and optimistic; the long wait is over and 'the time *is* fulfilled'. It is an assurance. 'And the kingdom of God *is* at hand.' It is waiting to be discovered by anyone with an open heart and an open mind. 'Repent ye.' Change your old ways of thinking. 'And *believe* the gospel.' And acknowledge a new way of life.

The Rev. Marshal says: 'Jesus restores to the phrase (the kingdom of God) the true meaning intended by the prophets, i.e. the Victory of the Spirit of God over the hearts and wills of men.'

What would be the reaction of the people to this joyous proclamation? Probably one of curiosity. Jesus himself was an ordinary working man – he did not look as if he was a king of Israel. He could not have looked like a spokesman for a king of Israel. The people were expecting a new ruler – not a new rule. But Jesus was actually proclaiming a change of heart, a new outlook on life.

Is it likely that he was daunted by the first reaction of people? It is not likely. But it *is* likely that he needed friends.

16-18   '*Now as he walked by the sea of Galilee, he saw Simon*' (this is Peter) '*and Andrew his brother casting a net into the sea: for they were fishers. And Jesus said unto them, come ye after me, and I will make you to become fishers of men. And straightway they forsook their nets, and followed him.*'

Was it that simple?

19-20   '*And when he had gone a little further thence, he saw James the son of Zebedee, and John his brother, who also were in the ship mending their nets. And straightway he called them: and they left their father Zebedee in the ship with the hired servants, and went after him.*'

I do not believe that these were first encounters. I believe that Jesus must have had the most powerful personality in the world, but I do not believe that these young fishermen left their work and their homes on a sudden single command. We are considering a comparatively small community, in which a man like Jesus would have been well known – even though this was not his home. Surely he did not suddenly appear on the scene – as it might seem from Mark's typically sparse account. It is most probable that Simon and Andrew and James and John knew Jesus, and had already heard him speak excitingly about the coming kingdom of God, about his ideas to spread the good news, and about his desire that one day they might join him. They must have been ready for the call. I hear Mark interviewing Peter clearly in these verses. 'What happened when he called you?' 'We were casting a net into the sea.' 'And did you complete the catch?' 'No, we forsook our nets and followed him.' 'And was it the same with James and John?' 'No' – and here is an old man's accurate memory of days long past – 'they were *mending* their nets.' This tiny difference in occupation rings with authenticity. And there must have been something noteworthy in the fact of James and John leaving their father Zebedee in the ship with the hired servants. Perhaps they were younger men. Perhaps they had more to give up in terms of possessions and family. Perhaps Zebedee was a man of importance. Mark mentions him on two other occasions, and one gets something of a sensation that James and John left home.

According to Luke, Jesus was 'about thirty years of age' at the time of his baptism by John. I wonder how old these brothers were, and what was the average age of all the disciples of Jesus. I would think that they were younger than Jesus and probably unmarried. Simon – soon to be called Peter – had a wife, as we shall shortly discover from a story about his mother-in-law. But no other wives are ever mentioned. (Although, in Mark's parenthetical manner, we discover right at the end of the gospel, that women followed Jesus to Jerusalem, and were probably with him and the disciples during most of the ministry.) But certainly from their behaviour, and from Mark's sometimes intolerant attitude towards them, the disciples seem to be young. If they were young, their frequent mistakes and confusion are more forgivable.

The adventure begins.

'*And they went into Capernaum; and straightway on the sabbath*

22 *day he entered into the synagogue, and taught. And they were astonished at his doctrine: for he taught them as one that had authority, and not as the scribes.'*

'And straightway . . .' Jesus, it would seem, could not wait to enter into the synagogue and teach. There is exhilaration in the air. Like a student of law or medicine who has studied for many years and cannot wait to practise; like an actor who has rehearsed his role for what seems an eternity; like a boxer after rigorous training getting into the ring for the great confrontation; Jesus is prepared.

And the people were astonished. One can imagine the pride and the delight of the young fishermen. And, in answer to Mark's request for a description, Peter's great compliment is that 'he taught them as one that had authority, and *not as the scribes*'. The scribes were the establishment scholars, the doctors of the law, the interpreters of the Books of Moses. And the Rev. Marshall tells us (in a tiny footnote) that they were not allowed to teach until the age of thirty. 'Thus our Lord fulfilled the law' – which could be a perfect explanation of Jesus's readiness to begin his ministry at this particular age.

23 *'And there was in their synagogue a man with an unclean spirit; and . . .'* Screech of brakes. We'll have to stop.

This is one of the mysteries of the Gospels. I don't think anybody really knows what is meant by a man with an 'unclean spirit'. And there are many encounters and many mentions of people with unclean spirits. Many descriptions and many cures. Other translators call them people with 'evil spirits', and others call them 'demoniacs'. It seems too simple to divide the sick population of St Mark's Gospel whom we are soon to meet, into the physically sick and the mentally sick because . . .

Well, let's go on for a bit.

24 *'And there was in their synagogue a man with an unclean spirit; and he cried out, Saying, Let us alone; what have we to do with thee, thou Jesus of Nazareth? art thou come to destroy us? I know thee who thou art, the Holy One of God.'*

The man seems to be divided into two.

The Jerusalem Bible translation is 'a man possessed with an unclean spirit, and *it* shouted,' etc. It seems to be the unclean spirit that shouts out and not the man.

'And Jesus rebuked him, saying, Hold thy peace, and come out of him.'

It is as if Mr Hyde is in charge of a struggling Dr Jekyll. And Jesus exorcises Mr Hyde and sets Dr Jekyll free. But, before the exorcism, Mr Hyde recognises Jesus.

Of course, if we were living in that time and place we would probably understand. We lead very sheltered lives today, in a society where the mentally sick are hidden away from us. But much mental illness is caused through a split in personality, and many mad people seem to be dominated by demons they cannot control. The mystery of the cases reported in the Gospels is their recognition of Jesus as the Son of God. And the wonder of these confrontations is Jesus's ability to cast out the devils and release the sick people from their bondage.

Look more closely at the words: 'Let us alone; what have we to do with thee, thou Jesus of Nazareth? art thou come to destroy us? I know thee who thou art, the Holy One of God.'

It is possible that the man with the unclean spirit in the synagogue (and it is interesting that such a man is *allowed* in the synagogue) has listened to Jesus's teaching, hears that he is from Nazareth, and is frightened by the unorthodoxy of Jesus's words. Monsignor Ronald Knox, in his translation of the New Testament, has the man say: 'Why dost thou *meddle* with us, Jesus of Nazareth?' – as if the man is frightened that Jesus may upset the established order of things. We do not know the degrees of intimidation prevalent at that time. Jesus defies the scribes and Pharisees. For many weaker souls – not necessarily with unclean spirits – this must have been terrifying behaviour. Their initial reaction might well have been – like the man in the synagogue's – to beg Jesus to stop, to implore him to 'let us alone'.

But the people with unclean spirits are also drawn to Jesus, and seem to recognise him as a possible saviour. They seem to know that through him they can find release. There are people in the world who live in such terror of themselves that they must always hide their thoughts and feelings. They are people who are unable to cope with their own individuality, or unable to tolerate the surroundings they find themselves living in. Their predicament leads to a life of disguise – which is a form of madness.

At the time and in the place we are considering, there was obviously much spiritual discontent and yearning. We have seen the people flocking to the river of Jordan to repent and confess their sins; and to listen to John the Baptist give his message of hope. Such hope must have been born of great discontent and maybe of despair. There is a climate of tension, perhaps of terror. We will soon discover the scribes and Pharisees lying in wait, listening, watching, criticising anything that does not conform to their rigid rules of conduct. We will soon see how they attack Jesus on the slightest pretence. *He* is able to confront them. *He* is seemingly fearless.

But for many people it may have been like living in a religious Police State. And, when they heard Jesus preaching a new doctrine, the joy and relief must have been enormous. And for the outcasts of society – who were not able to endure the domination of the old teaching – the experience would be almost shocking in its intensity. I think that these cries from unclean spirits are cries for help. The stimulation of the proximity of salvation would shape the strange words. And Jesus, with his huge strength of faith, through his *belief*, is able to cast out and dispel their fear.

The description of the exorcism is accompanied by what some writers have called an epileptic fit.

26 *'And when the unclean spirit had torn him, and cried with a loud voice, he came out of him.'*

Could it actually be the cry of someone coming in out of the cold? the cry of someone reaching home after a long journey? the cry of someone having an open wound healed at last? Relief sometimes makes men shout.

Whatever it was that happened in the synagogue on that sabbath day in Capernaum, it caused a sensation. As well as hearing his teaching – and it is possible that this contained some of the Sermon on the Mount related in St Matthew – the people must have known that Jesus had confidently proclaimed the coming of the kingdom of God; they must have known that Jesus had commanded Simon and Andrew and James and John to leave their work and their homes and follow him; and, after the confrontation with the man with the unclean spirit, Mark tells us:

27 *'And they were all amazed, insomuch that they questioned among*

themselves, saying, What thing is this? what new doctrine is this? for with authority commandeth he even the unclean spirits and they do obey him.'

Despite the fact that his writing is often very spare and to the point, Mark is really an old gossip, and he writes well of gossiping. Here he conveys the chatter of the people and possibly of the disciples. We do not really need the little quotes, but they certainly enliven the story. There are certain people who tell anecdotes full of voices: 'And then she said, "Why are you telling me all this?" And I said, "Work it out for youself, dear! You've had an education!" And so she said, "There's no need to get sarcastic! I only asked!" And then I said, "You only asked because you're too lazy to work it out for yourself!" ' etc., etc. Mark often gives us little quotes, presumably remembered by Peter, and they move the story on. After this first story of healing, the reporter obviously wants the reaction of the onlookers. 'They were all amazed.' 'Yes! But what did they *say*?' 'Well, what do you think they said! They said, "What thing is this? What new doctrine is this?" ' 'Is that all?' 'Well no . . . They said "for with authority commandeth he even the unclean spirits and they do obey him".' 'And so what happened?'

'And immediately his fame spread abroad throughout all the region round about Galilee.'

'Thank you! And what happened after you came out of the synagogue? You must have been tired and hungry.' And Peter told him. And Mark writes:

'And forthwith, when they were come out of the synagogue, they entered into the house of Simon and Andrew . . .'

'What happened to James and John?'

'. . . with James and John. But Simon's wife's mother lay sick of a fever, and anon they tell him of her. And he came and took her by the hand, and lifted her up; and immediately the fever left her . . .'

'Immediately?'

'Yes.'

'. . . and she ministered unto them.'

'How did she minister unto them?'

'Well, I think she made the gravy!'

The mother of a friend of mine often invites us to lunch with her. She lives in a little house in Northfields Road, Acton. She is an extremely lively lady, and, since her husband died, she has taken a lodger. When we arrive she gives us massive drinks, and then tells us her latest news. For lunch she usually makes a steak and kidney pudding. We eat far too much. After lunch we may go for a walk in North Acton Recreation Ground and watch people playing games. Or, if it is a hot summer's day (she even makes steak and kidney pudding in the summer), I will go to sleep in the little garden. Then, at about four-thirty, she makes some tea, and there are home-made cakes. It's a very enjoyable occasion.

If however, when we arrived, we found her lying sick of a fever – with the house uncleaned and the food uncooked – it would be a grave disappointment.

It must have been a disappointment for Simon on that sabbath day in Capernaum, when he was going to entertain Jesus in his house after the amazing time in the synagogue. But Jesus was an unusual guest. He simply came and took Simon's wife's mother by the hand, and lifted her up; and immediately the fever left her. And, if that was not enough, she actually ministered unto them.

Of course, Simon's *wife* may have had everything prepared and under control – unless she was useless – and we do not know how many other members of the family were there. It was certainly a much bigger party than the three of us at Acton, and was probably a very happy, noisy group. And of course it went on for a long time, because Mark tells us:

32-33

'And at even, when the sun did set, they brought unto him all that were diseased, and them that were possessed with devils. And all the city was gathered together at the door.'

The people with unclean spirits seem to move around quite freely. They seem to be an accepted part of society.

34

'And he healed many that were sick of divers diseases, and cast out many devils; and suffered not the devils to speak, because they knew him.'

The news of the cure of the man with the unclean spirit in the synagogue and the cure of Simon's wife's mother must have spread like wild fire. And 'when the sun did set' – which signified the end of the sabbath – it would be lawful for sick people to come to Jesus hoping for a cure. The city, by modern standards, was a very small town, and I think the house would be very small. If Jesus was healing from a little house in Northfields Road in Acton, the neighbours would be stunned by the event – and the crowd would probably spill into the Recreation Ground. What did the family in Capernaum think of having 'all the city' gathered together at their door? Did they mind the sudden notoriety? What did Simon and Andrew and James and John think of Jesus's extraordinary power? *What did Jesus think?* Was the healing of the sick a new discovery, or had Jesus been aware of his powers for a long time? It is likely that he had cured people privately in the past, but that this was the first time he had done it in public and on such a large scale. There is a qualification in 'They brought unto him *all* that were diseased'. and the fact that 'he healed *many*'. This presumbly means that he did not heal everybody. Nevertheless it must have been an astonishing occasion, and must have filled all the people there – and, most of all, Jesus – with wonder and excitement.

How could he sleep after this tremendous manifestation of his powers?

Evidently he didn't sleep for long, and maybe not at all. He needed some privacy after the time spent in the crowded little house. He needed to talk to his father – his chosen father in heaven – and hopefully receive a blessing and further guidance.

'And in the morning, rising up a great while before day, he went out, and departed into a solitary place, and there prayed.' 35

After the voice from heaven, when he was baptized of John in Jordan, and the confirmation that he was God's beloved son, Jesus had the inevitable instinct to run away from his destiny. After this sabbath in Capernaum, and after he had healed many, and cast out many devils, Jesus must have had another reaction. Was he worthy? Could he sustain the demands made on him? And was it right for him to practise mass healing? What did God want from him?

It is easy for us to accept the achievements of great men. We only know the finished result – whether it is a bridge, a cure, a cathedral, or a space-ship. We know nothing of the doubts that accompanied the creation. We do not consider the hours spent working in loneliness. We forget that there was no guarantee that there would ever be an end result. The achievement of

Jesus was his life. He believed that he was the Son of God. In the *Cambridge Bible Commentary*, C. F. D. Moule writes a wonderful sentence. 'The whole Gospel story can be seen as a picture of Jesus working out this sonship day by day in terms of eager obedience to the plan of God – an obedience which, in the end, leads to death.' Jesus had no guarantee, except his own faith and his own desire, that he could or would fulfil this role.

'And in the morning, rising up a great while before day . . .' leaving the sleeping family, and the sleeping town of Capernaum, 'he went out, and departed into a solitary place, and there prayed'. The ministry had only just begun; he had taught with authority; he had effected some cures; and thus he had achieved fame 'throughout all the region round about Galilee'. This could be enough. It would be enough for most men – *more* than enough. Jesus went out that morning to find strength. And strength is found in solitary places.

Did the family hear him get up and leave the house? Did they know where he was going? Did they expect him back? It seems as if they slept till morning and then found people gathering at their door again, hoping to see Jesus, hoping for more cures. The brothers would know the favourite solitary places near Capernaum.

'*And Simon and they that were with him*' (does this include more than Andrew, James and John? Does it include Simon's *wife* perhaps – and *other* friends and relatives?) '*followed after him. And when they had found him,*' (did they call out? 'Jesus! Jesus!') '*they said unto him, All men seek for thee.*' And, by this time, Jesus had found strength from his chosen father; and strength from the rising sun. He was filled with the Spirit; filled with joy and hope. He would not stay in Capernaum. He would not be a big fish in a small pond.

'*And he said unto them, Let us go into the next towns, that I may preach there also.*' And then he adds: '*for therefore came I forth,*' and gives us a tiny glimpse of his knowledge of God's plan.

At this early stage of the story, there are no obstacles, no threats from the establishment, no serious critics of Jesus's teaching or his way of life. And there is a feeling of youth – and even naïveté – in the words and actions of Jesus and his friends.

26

In terms of time and distance, the journey from the first sabbath of the ministry in Capernaum to the last days of Jesus in Jerusalem was not very long. But in terms of experience and personality Jesus seems to age from a young to an old man.

It is natural that Peter should have remembered the first days of Jesus's ministry in detail. But now his memory seems to fade. He can only tell us in a general fashion:

'And he preached in their synagogues throughout all Galilee, and cast out devils.' 39

I don't think this was a long tour. Galilee was a province of Palestine with a maximum length of sixty miles and a width of thirty miles. There was a synagogue in the smallest community. William Barclay in *The Daily Study Bible* writes that 'the law laid it down that wherever there were ten Jewish families there must be a synagogue'; and in the bigger towns and villages there would be many. I think on this first tour Jesus stayed near the Sea of Galilee.

Obviously the factual reporter Mark tried to jog Peter's memory in an attempt to get specific incidents during this period. And Peter remembers an extraordinary occasion which must have impressed them all very much.

'And there came a leper to him, beseeching him, and kneeling down to him, and saying unto him, If thou wilt, thou canst make me clean.' 40

How can *we* imagine this? Lepers do not roam around in our society. The very word leper is usually used to describe an 'outcast'. (The Good News Bible does not even call the man a leper, but uses the cumbersome description 'A man suffering from a dreaded skin disease'.)

How would you or I behave – on our way to the bank or supermarket or cinema – if we were suddenly confronted by a leper? If a leper suddenly knelt down in front of us; would not let us pass; demanded a cure? We certainly could not cure him – but can we even imagine such a thing happening, or what our reaction would be? Or what would be a parallel situation?

Most people have been accosted at some time or other by the outcasts of society, by beggars, drunks, or desperate human beings in distress. How do we behave? I think we dread such encounters. I think we do our utmost to avoid them. It is easy enough to sit at a desk in the privacy of one's home and send a little cheque to some well-organised charity or other. 'Will X pounds be enough? After all, last week I sent a contribution to those other people. I'm not made of money!' But an actual confrontation with the needy, with the desperate, with the disabled, the disfigured, or the maimed, is more difficult.

I have a memory of such an occasion. It also involved my friend Patience Collier. Patience is an actress 'in her middle years' with a uniquely strong personality. Unlike most people, she always knows exactly how she will behave in any situation. She often uses the phrase: 'That's my way!' – or, if someone blithely suggests or supposes that certain alternative actions be taken or certain alternative words might be spoken, Patience will say: 'That's *not* my way!' She will then enlighten everyone as to the correct course of conduct. I do not always agree with her, but I am devoted to her rare clarity of mind, and to her energy and courage.

One evening I was taking Patience out to dinner. She was, as always, beautifully dressed and coiffed. She sat beside me in the car as I drove up Campden Hill Road to the top of the hill where – at that time – the street lighting was very poor. I was not driving fast. A burly man stood in the middle of the road gesticulating for me to stop the car. I stopped. The man stood in front of the car and shouted at us. We couldn't understand what he was saying. He seemed to be very angry. I thought perhaps he was drunk. I called to him to move away. He hit the bonnet of my car with his hand and continued shouting. I leaned out of my window and asked him what he wanted. 'Money!' he said. 'I want some money!' 'Well, come round to the side of the car and I'll give you some,' I said. 'No!' he shouted. 'I'm not moving from here! You'll just drive away!' He continued to strike the car with his hand and shout at us. Patience said calmly, 'Give me some money!' I put my hand into my pocket to find some change. 'No!' she said. 'Give me a note!' I opened my wallet. 'Hurry up!' she said. I gave her a note. She got out of the car and handed the man the money. 'Now let us pass!' she said. He moved away. Patience got back into the car. 'It's always best to do what they want, and do it quickly!' she said. We drove away.

Now, I remember this incident clearly, partly because of my own comparatively feeble behaviour, but mainly because of the speed and certainty with which Patience acted. It is true that she did not act out of compassion. She acted out of expediency. She simply wished us to get to dinner. She was indignant at the delay.

According to many of the translations, when the leper confronted Jesus, 'beseeching him, and kneeling down to him, and saying unto him, If thou wilt, thou canst make me clean', Jesus acted out of 'compassion' – or sometimes they use the word 'pity'.

'And Jesus, moved with compassion, put forth his hand, and 41 *touched him, and saith unto him, I will; be thou clean.'*

But some of the commentators tell us that the word 'compassion' might be better translated as 'anger'. Is this because of the reluctance of the translators to make Jesus appear unsympathetic? There is a lot of difference. (The New English Bible tries to have it both ways: *'In warm indignation* Jesus stretched out his hand.') I *prefer* the word 'anger' to the word 'compassion' in this context. It is more understandable and human. The horror of leprosy makes Jesus angry. The indignity of the disease makes Jesus indignant. The encounter immediately becomes dramatically alive. But whether it is compassion, or anger, or compassionate anger, or warm indignation, Jesus acts with unmistakable speed and certainty. And this speed and certainty is an integral part of the personality of Jesus throughout most of the Gospel. This speed and certainty sets him apart from the rest of us. There is no hesitation; there is no doubt; belief is total. There is no question that the cure will not be effective. There is the challenge: 'If thou wilt . . . make me clean.' There is the acceptance of the challenge. 'I will; be thou clean.' With such direct belief the miracle does not seem mysterious. It seems obvious.

'If thou wilt, thou canst make me clean.'

The arrow is pulled back.

'And Jesus, moved with compassion, put forth his hand, and touched him, and saith unto him, I will.'

The arrow is released.

'Be thou clean.'

The arrow reaches its target.

'And as soon as he had spoken, immediately, the leprosy departed from him, and he was cleansed.' 42

It is as if the man was infected with cleanliness.

We can easily be besmirched by someone else's dirt, or catch someone else's disease, but the leper was infected with Jesus's purity. He caught clean.

To me the miracle is not mysterious; what is mysterious is the passionate faith of Jesus. The power of Jesus's belief and the speed and certainty of his action. Mark emphasises this speed and certainty with the wonderfully colloquial words:

'And as soon as he had spoken, immediately the leprosy departed from him, and he was cleansed.'

What sort of shock was felt by the leper?

What state of amazement was felt by Peter and Andrew, and James and John? But Jesus ignores all this, and now behaves in an unexpected manner.

'And he straightly charged him, and forthwith sent him away; and saith unto him, See thou say nothing to any man.'

This is an instance where the chronological order of the ministry of Jesus in St Mark is important for our understanding of the story.

D. E. Nineham in his *Saint Mark* writes: '. . . it is probably significant that according to the rabbis, the healing of leprosy was "as difficult as the raising of the dead". What, therefore, the Old Testament religion – the Law – could not do was done readily by Jesus.'

This cure of the leper obviously had a sensational effect at this early stage of the ministry. The impact of it certainly remained with Peter. He described in detail Jesus's attitude to the leper and remembered the words he used: 'And he straightly charged him,' – meaning he sternly or strictly charged him – 'and forthwith sent him away' – literally meaning he drove him away – 'and saith unto him, See thou say nothing to any man.'

The Rev. Marshall tells us: 'The priest alone could legally pronounce a leper clean.' This accounts for Jesus continuing:

'but go thy way, shew thyself to the priest, and offer for thy cleansing those things which Moses commanded, for a testimony unto them.'

Jesus was probably anxious on two counts. First that, because of the news of this sensational event, he would be besieged by people wanting cures. And secondly, at this stage of his ministry, that he should stay within the law. This links up with the climate of tension we considered with the story of the man with the unclean spirit, and the degree of religious intimidation prevalent at the time.

The leper had an enormous amount of work to do to fulfil the commandments of Moses. These are described in Chapter 14 of Leviticus, and include offerings of 'two birds alive and clean, and cedar wood, and scarlet, and hyssop': and that he shall 'shave all his hair off his head and his beard and his eyebrows', and make further offerings of 'two he lambs without blemish, and one ewe lamb of the first year . . .' 'And if he be poor, and cannot get so much; then he shall take one lamb . . . and one tenth deal of fine flour mingled with oil for a meat offering, and a log of oil; and two turtledoves, or two young pigeons,' etc., etc.

I have a feeling the leper in our story did not do all this . . . I think he just went out and celebrated. He certainly took no notice of Jesus's stern instructions to 'say nothing to any man'. I have a wonderful James Thurber cartoon image of him careering around the countryside, yelling his head off with joy, scaring the poultry, alarming old ladies, and buying enormous rounds of drinks for all and sundry in the Palestinian equivalent of an English pub.

Mark writes: *'But he went out, and began to publish it much, and to blaze abroad the matter.'*

('Extra! Extra! Jesus's sensational cure!')

'insomuch that Jesus could no more openly enter into the city, but was without in desert places: and they came to him from every quarter.'

I love St Mark! He is not content to let this episode reach a natural end. He will not let us off the hook. He promises us more, much more.

Because of the overjoyed, garrulous leper, Jesus had to hide himself in the country. It also sounds as if he had to travel in disguise. The very thing Jesus must have half dreaded had happened. He was a celebrity. But he was a celebrity because of his powers of healing rather than a celebrity because of his new teaching.

The end of Chapter One ends with a glorious cliff-hanger –

'AND THEY CAME TO HIM FROM EVERY QUAR-
TER' – reminding me of the famous vaudeville phrase: 'You
aint heard nothin' yet!'

CONFRONTATIONS

In St Mark's Gospel the story of Jesus seems so simple until I read the commentaries.

And then I get bogged down and depressed.

Jesus stops being an understandable person – and starts to be someone who can do no wrong. The Jesus whom people have invented has no natural reflexes. He has no age, no stomach, no bowels, no sex, no doubts, no vanities, no exuberance. Except when he is with children he seems unlikeable and forbidding. Does anyone really *like* a man totally without sin? Jesus never makes that claim – indeed at one point in the ministry he actually reprimands a man who calls him 'good'. 'Why callest thou me good? there is none good but one, that is, God.'

But it seems that men have needed to invent a paragon of purity to kneel down before and worship. And the English have created their own particular Jesus: a sort of solemn, bearded schoolmaster who never ventures into the dust of the world. This schoolmaster confiscates dirty books, and frowns upon dirty thoughts. He fasts and is tee-total. He must never be opposed or contradicted. He never smiles or laughs. He doesn't snore or sweat. He reluctantly acknowledges that there is such a thing as sex, but treats it as a gift in plain cover to be unwrapped for the first time in the marriage bed. He abides by the rule book, and there are no exceptions to the rules.

None of this ties up or matches with the Jesus we are now about to meet in St Mark's Gospel. Accepting that the ministry of Jesus in Mark is written in strict chronological order, we now meet an irreverent, impertinent, carefree, fearless young man who puts down and humiliates the local scribes and

Pharisees in no less than five consecutive defiant stories. He is provocative and vain. He is extremely lucky that he is not arrested and locked up there and then, before he affronts and insults more of the establishment.

'And again he entered into Capernaum after some days; and it was noised that he was in the house.

This does not sound as if they were away for long. Perhaps some of the group were quickly homesick for Capernaum. Perhaps it was a short visit back for some domestic matter. Jesus managed to return without being immediately noticed. But then the rumours start. The King James Version gives us the delicious translation: 'and it was *noised* that he was in the house' — which conjures up a small town of whispers and excitement.

Later versions are more prosaic:

'It was reported that he was home.' Revised Standard.

'The news spread that he was at home.' Good News.

'Word went out that he was back.' The Jerusalem Bible.

Oh well . . .

But the fame of Jesus had obviously reached superstar proportions.

'And straightway many were gathered together, insomuch that there was no room to receive them, no, not so much as about the door: and he preached the word unto them.'

Can we hear Mark and old Peter chatting together here? And is old Peter trying to impress Mark? 'There was no room to receive them?' 'No! not so much as about the door.' 'And did he heal many again?' 'Oh no . . . he preached the word unto them.'

Mark and Peter are usually specific about Jesus's actions. If he preached, they say he preached. If he healed people and cast out devils, they tell us that he healed people and cast out devils. We may as well believe them. Peter said it. Mark wrote it down. It is only those who cannot stand the thought of Jesus being an ordinary human being who resist the idea of the story actually being true. If Jesus acts in a reasonable, rational, understandable way, many theologians start to splutter and choke and tell us that St Mark is not a factual document; *not historical*; not to be taken literally. So what are we to do? Take the theologians, the commentators and the clergy literally?

Believe anything except the actual evidence on the printed page?

It would be logical to suppose that after the sensational cure of the leper – and it must have caused a sensation to compel Jesus to live 'without in desert places' – that Jesus would be reluctant to get a reputation exclusively as a miraculous healer. I imagine that, when the people in Capernaum started to gather together again, Jesus made a stipulation: No cures! He was not going to hold another mass surgery. This time he would preach the word unto them. The 'word' being the good news about the kingdom of God. And this is what he starts to do.

But the sick and their loved ones are often desperate. Here, in their midst – in the house up the street – was a man who could cure a leper simply by putting his hand upon him. If you or I had a friend or relative with a seemingly incurable disease, what would we do?

'And they come unto him, bringing one sick of the palsy, which was borne of four. And when they could not come nigh unto him for the press, they uncovered the roof where he was: and when they had broken it up, they let down the bed wherein the sick of the palsy lay.' 3 - 4

This does not mean 'the press' in the sense that newspaper reporters were present – but the press of a crowd. Nevertheless the meaning of the story could be the same. The four men carrying the sick of the palsy were trying out a stunt to get Jesus's attention. And it was a very good stunt, a piece of outrageous behaviour which proved irresistible. (Goodness knows what the long-suffering family of Peter thought about it! I would think it sent the mother-in-law straight back to bed.) Somehow or other the sick man was lowered into the room – perhaps Jesus was forced into helping his progress. Perhaps many hands reached up and helped him down. But, however it was managed, it was an act of tremendous hope on the part of the four carriers, and an act of great courage on the part of the paralytic. As we shortly discover, he was lying on a bed – which the Rev. Marshall helpfully explains was 'a mere pallet or mat, the commonest or poorest kind of bed, just large enough for a man to lie on. It could be spread out in the evening and rolled up and put aside during the day.'

It is possible that the cripple was a boy.

5   *'When Jesus saw their faith, he said unto the sick of the palsy, Son, thy sins be forgiven thee.'* The Jerusalem Bible translation is: 'My child, your sins are forgiven.'

But, whether he was a man or a boy, the commentators now become very complicated and confusing. They seem to be frightened. They cannot possibly accept that Jesus might be congratulating the man or boy on the courage of the manner of his entry into the room, and simply welcoming him with 'Son, thy sins be forgiven thee'. They start to waffle:

'Did Jesus intuitively see, perhaps, that the paralysis, in this particular case, was the psychological result of a sense of guilt?' C. F. D. Moule.

'The man in this story may well have been paralysed because consciously or unconsciously his conscience agreed that he was a sinner, and the thought of being a sinner brought the illness which he believed was the inevitable consequence of sin.' William Barclay.

And even dear Rev. Marshall makes the nervous Victorian observation. 'It may be the man's illness was due to sinful indulgences.'

However, their reluctance to accept a straight-forward narrative about the admiration of Jesus for the courage of a sick man becomes a little more understandable when we read what happens next. This is a very dramatic moment in the Gospel and takes us by surprise.

6
7   *'But there were certain of the scribes sitting there, and reasoning in their hearts, Why doth this man thus speak blasphemies? who can forgive sins but God only?'*

Well! The news has certainly spread abroad! The scribes are sitting there ('on the floor, oriental fashion') watching and listening. The scribes have come to Peter's house to listen to the young teacher. They have heard of his sensational healing – now they hear a sensational blasphemy. Let us consider the importance of the scribes and their place in the community of that time.

The Supreme Council of the Jews at the time of Jesus was called the Sanhedrin. This council consisted of chief priests and elders and scribes. The scribes interpreted and applied the Jewish law. 'The law of Moses was also the civil law of the land, and the Sanhedrin not only decided on questions of religion and ceremony, but tried all the accused persons sent up to them from the local councils. The scribes were, therefore, a necessary and important body and greatly assisted the Sanhedrin in the interpretation of the law.' (Marshall)

They based their teaching on the tradition of the elders. They were therefore not original teachers. Jesus taught 'with authority'. He taught in his own name. 'I say unto you.' 'Verily I say unto you.' And sometimes, as we shall see in a moment, he called himself 'The Son of man'. These scribes who came to the house in Capernaum had obviously been alerted that there was a man going around teaching as if he was an original prophet. It is possible that they were a fact-finding commission. It is possible that they were already collecting evidence for a charge against Jesus. One of the functions of the Sanhedrin was to be the guardian of orthodoxy. '. . . it was the Sanhedrin's duty to deal with any man who was a false prophet.' (Barclay)

But the scribes did not reckon on the personality of Jesus.

Whether or not Jesus meant anything deeper or more complex when he said 'Son, thy sins be forgiven thee'; whether he was displaying the authority of God; whether it was a conscious act of defiance against the establishment; or whether, as we shall consider in a moment, Jesus was actually performing a miraculous act with his forgiveness; the scribes were scandalised. No man had authority to forgive sins. 'Nowhere in the Old Testament does any prophet forgive sins.' (Sloyan) This is God's prerogative. Jesus spoke as if he had the authority of God. He blasphemed by making himself God's equal. He blasphemed by assuming divinity. (This was eventually the reason why he was condemned to death.)

But was any of this in Jesus's mind when he spoke the words? At this early stage of the ministry Jesus speaks with careless confidence; in the happy certainty that he is the beloved Son of God. He does not call himself by this title; he is not ready. But he has no fears; he is seemingly innocent of the dangers he courts with his words and his behaviour.

Nevertheless he is fully aware of the attitude of the scribes.

Mark writes the thoughts of the scribes in his gossiping style: 'Why doth this man thus speak blasphemies? who can forgive sins but God only?' These were probably some of the whispering complaints which followed Jesus throughout the ministry. There are always critics and carpers who complain against an original personality.

8   '*And immediately . . .*'

Of course, immediately!

'*And immediately when Jesus perceived in his spirit that they so reasoned within themselves, he said unto them, Why reason ye these things in your hearts?*'

This was an unexpected move – a direct answer to their unspoken thoughts. The scribes must have been totally nonplussed. Jesus continues:

9–12   '*Whether is it easier to say to the sick of the palsy, Thy sins be forgiven thee; or to say, Arise, and take up thy bed, and walk? But that ye may know that the Son of man hath power on earth to forgive sins, (he saith to the sick of the palsy,) I say unto thee, Arise, and take up thy bed, and go thy way into thine house. And immediately he arose, took up the bed, and went forth before them all; insomuch that they were all amazed, and glorified God, saying, We never saw it on this fashion.*'

It is this speech of Jesus which worries the commentators into writing many pages of explanation. It is this speech which confuses the devout. It could appear that Jesus – stung by the scribes doubting his authority – embarks on a young man's 'dare'. It could appear that he puts on a display of power expressly for the benefit of the Pharisees. It could appear that he is 'showing off'.

But, in order to avoid the thought of Jesus appearing brash, young, and human, interesting theories are presented: that guilt and sickness are related; that disease is a department of sin; and that when Jesus says 'Son, thy sins be forgiven thee' he is actually healing the young paralytic. (It is also claimed that Mark is combining two separate stories here; one story about the healing of a physical ailment, and the other about the forgiveness of sins. But this is not Mark's style. He does not do this anywhere else in the Gospel. His writing is never complex or contrived.)

I think that the theories about sin and sickness being related are valid. I think that a sense of guilt can physically cripple a person. I think that, whenever Jesus casts out sin or casts out devils, it leads naturally to a cure. I think it is possible that when Jesus says 'Son, thy sins are forgiven thee' he is actively healing the sick man. But the devout are still left with a dilemma. The paralytic does not appear to know that he is healed by Jesus's forgiveness. He still lies on his bed. Jesus senses the outrage of the scribes and decides to show them, to prove to them, that he has the right to forgive sins and that he has powers from heaven. He is, in fact, giving them a sign. It is still a display of power.

'But that ye may know that the Son of man hath power on earth to forgive sins, (he saith to the sick of the palsy,) I say unto thee, Arise, and take up thy bed, and go thy way into thine house' – and the young paralytic discovers that he is in fact cured, although he does not know, any more than we do, exactly when the healing occurred.

And so, despite worthy attempts to prevent Jesus from appearing to act in a human way, we are still left with a possible act of vanity. If Jesus meant nothing more than a welcome or a congratulation when he said, 'Son, thy sins be forgiven thee', he embarked on a 'dare' to prove himself to the scribes. But, if Jesus actually healed the man with his forgiveness, we are still left with an act of blatant showmanship.

D. E. Nineham in his exhaustive commentary, *Saint Mark*, at least has the courage to present the case: '. . . the behaviour of Jesus himself raises questions; are we to suppose that, but for the scribes and their criticism, he would not have healed the paralytic?' Yes, I think it is possible. Nineham continues: 'The suggestion that the healing was performed not for the sake of the sufferer, but purely for its evidential value, conflicts with what we learn of Jesus' attitude elsewhere, especially the refusal of just such "signs" as this at Chapter 8, Verse II.' *But that is much later, in the ministry.*

This is another of the episodes where I feel the continuity of St Mark is so important. Nowhere else in the Gospel does Jesus behave in this fashion. But then nowhere else does he feel compelled to prove himself. (And, when he does behave in a contradictory way, there is always a very good reason.)

To me, this episode is a delightful description of a young man. It is a celebration of youth. It is a display of strength. Of course, as Nineham says, it conflicts with what we learn of Jesus's attitude elsewhere. Jesus had no need to behave like this

again. Slowly, as the story unfolds, Jesus's attitude to the
scribes hardens. By the end of the Gospel he is publicly
insulting them in a devastating manner. But at the beginning
of the ministry there is an understandable desire to impress
these scholars; and it would seem from Mark's words that the
scribes *were* impressed: 'they were all amazed, and glorified
God, saying, We never saw it on this fashion.'

Trust Mark.

Trust Peter.

It is when Jesus is talking to the scribes that he first calls
himself 'the Son of man'. The Rev. Marshall tells us that it is
'our Lord's favourite title of himself'; and he has done another
counting job to discover that 'it occurs fourteen times in the
Gospel'.

It is a beautiful name, conjuring up the idea of the representative of man – or, perhaps, the representative of a new
humanity. Evidently the literal translation from the Aramaic is
simply 'man' or 'this man' – which would be an enforcement
of St Mark's presentation of Jesus as an ordinary man with
extraordinary powers.

But the name could also imply the fulfilment of the Mes-
sianic figure as it is used in The Book of Daniel, Chapter 7,
Verses 13 and 14. These are wonderful haunting lines. 'I saw in
the night visions, and, behold, one like the Son of man came
with the clouds of heaven, and came to the Ancient of days,
and they brought him near before him. And there was given
him dominion, and glory, and a kingdom, that all people,
nations and languages, should serve him: his dominion is an
everlasting kingdom, which shall not pass away, and his
kingdom that which shall not be destroyed.' These may well
have been favourite lines of Jesus.

*

13 *'And he went forth again by the sea side; and all the multitude resorted
unto him, and he taught them.'*

We have heard that Jesus preached in synagogues throughout all Galilee. We know that he taught in Peter's house. Now,
for the first time, he gets out of doors and teaches in the open
air by the sea. I think it is easier and more attractive to imagine
such a scene in connection with a personal memory, rather

than to superimpose a Pre-Raphaelite presentation of lifeless dignity. I love the King James Version's use of the words 'by the sea side' and 'resorted unto him' – conjuring up in my mind the sea-side resort of the old town of Hastings, where, when I was a child, I used to watch the fishermen mending their nets. The later translations such as 'to the sea shore', 'to the lake-side' or the Good News' 'Jesus went back again to the shore of Lake Galilee. A crowd came to him, and he taught them' do not have the same nostalgic evocations.

The sea side is still presumably at Capernaum, situated on the western side of the Sea of Galilee. Galilee was ruled by Herod. The territory directly to the east was ruled by Herod's son, Philip. Capernaum was therefore a sort of frontier town, and people leaving for or entering from the eastern territory had to pay import or export taxes. These were collected at a customs centre. One of the tax collectors was evidently known to Jesus:

'And as he passed by, he saw Levi the son of Alphaeus sitting at the receipt of custom, and said unto him, Follow me. And he arose and followed him.'

14

Just as it is probable that Jesus already knew Simon and Andrew, and James and John, before he called them to follow him, it seems equally probable that he knew Levi. Otherwise the command is extraordinarily abrupt. Levi was most likely an old friend. And the fact that he was an old friend tells us a great deal about Jesus.

Tax collectors and customs officers are not popular today. At the time of Jesus, they were hated and feared as cheats and extortioners. They were classed with adulterers, brothel-keepers, flatterers and informers. 'As a rule they were cruel and oppressive, over charged whenever they had the opportunity, and were of the lowest class.' (Marshall) Their work entailed them 'serving heathen masters and mixing with (unclean) non-Jews of all sorts.' (Nineham). Nevertheless, Jesus wanted the company of one of them, and, after the briefest command, Levi gave up his job. One wonders whether Jesus's 'Follow me' was a whisper, a call, or a shout. One wonders whether Levi neatly finished the work in hand, carefully completing a column of figures, or whether he threw his papers into the air – allowing crowds of visitors to enter into

Capernaum scot free – and joined Jesus to the accompaniment of shouts and cheers from the young disciples. I suspect the latter. I suspect that the group of people around Jesus was extremely boisterous.

'And it came to pass, that, as Jesus sat at meat in his house, many publicans and sinners sat also together with Jesus and his disciples: for there were many, and they followed him.'

Just occasionally – very rarely, hardly ever, but just occasionally – the King James Version needs an elucidatory note. It is disappointing to discover that Jesus was not actually eating with the landlords of The Rose and Crown, The Pig and Whistle, and The Spotted Dog but that the word publican (from the Latin publicanus) in St Mark's Gospel means tax collector. It seems that, after throwing up his job and deciding to follow Jesus, Levi gave a great party and invited many of his fellow tax collectors – *and sinners* – to celebrate his new life and to meet Jesus. The lumping together of tax collectors and sinners is an indication of Levi's immediate circle of friends. But we must not take the word in too melodramatic a sense. They were probably not a group of murderers, thieves and rapists, but people who, like Levi, were outside the establishment. People who did not observe the scribal laws; people who were ritually unclean. When I wrote about the terrors which may have beset people with unclean spirits, I likened Palestine to a religious Police State. But there were many people who were completely outside this religious intimidation. William Barclay writes: 'A clear distinction was drawn between those who kept the law and those whom they called *the people of the land*.' 'By the orthodox it was forbidden to have anything to do with these people. The strict law-keeper must have no fellowship with them at all. He must not talk with them nor go on a journey with them; as far as possible, he must not even do business with them; to marry a daughter to one of them was as bad as giving her over to a wild beast; above all, he must not accept hospitality from or give hospitality to such a person.'

It was with a group of these people that Jesus now had a meal. And a meal, we are told by Robert Crotty in his *Good News in Mark*, was 'the closest expression of intimacy known in the Semitic world'.

It sounds as if Levi had a big house, and that it was a big party. It also sounds as if Jesus was very popular. There is one of Mark's delightful parenthetical additions here: after telling us that Jesus is sitting amid a group of publicans and sinners, he remembers 'for there were many, and they followed him'.

The frightening class and caste system of the day is now emphasised further:

16

'And when the scribes and Pharisees saw him eat with publicans and sinners, they said unto his disciples, How is it that he eateth and drinketh with publicans and sinners?'

First, let us appreciate the unmistakable style of Mark with his treble repetition of the words 'publicans and sinners'. Here again he writes in a way that people talk and gossip: 'many publicans and sinners', 'saw him eat with publicans and sinners', 'he eateth and drinketh with publicans and sinners'. In the repetition one hears the scandalized whispers.

And now Mark counterpoints the publicans and sinners with another double-act – the 'scribes and Pharisees'. We have already considered the scribes. Let us consider the Pharisees.

The word evidently means 'separated'. They were the separate people; who followed the law in every detail. At the time of Jesus, they were the most important religious party. The Rev Marshall says that the Pharisees claimed 'more than ordinary sanctity in religious observances, which, for the most part, were merely outward show'. He tells us a Jewish proverb 'that if but two persons were allowed to enter heaven one of them would be a Pharisee'. He also tells us via St Matthew: 'They prayed while standing at street corners, and caused trumpets to be sounded when they engaged in works of charity.'

We now have these perfect people, with their friends the scribes, watching the newly-appeared young teacher eating and drinking with the outcasts of society. The houses were open and it was possible for people to look in during a feast. As well as keeping bad company, Jesus was probably breaking laws by eating from unwashed pots and cups and risking ritual defilement. He was also – according to some versions – drinking. The Greek manuscripts vary. On this occasion,

43

Matthew's Gospel does not mention Jesus drinking, but Luke's Gospel does. The King James Version of Mark gives us 'he eateth and drinketh'. But the Revised Standard, the New English, the Jerusalem and the Good News leave out the drink. The Living Bible leaves out drink – but makes the Pharisees say savagely, 'How can he stand it, to eat with such scum.'

But whatever the correct translation, there is no need to be coy about Jesus drinking. In glorious words reported in Matthew and Luke (but, I greatly regret, not in Mark), he himself talks quite freely about it – wryly comparing himself with John the Baptist: 'For John came neither eating nor drinking, and they say, He hath a devil. The Son of man came eating and drinking, and they say, Behold a man gluttonous, and a winebibber, a friend of publicans and sinners.' (Matthew Chapter II, Verses 18 and 19.)

The scribes and Pharisees could not bring themselves to confront Jesus directly about his behaviour. Perhaps they were nervous amid the din of the celebration. Or perhaps they simply could not get near enough to him. It is certain that Jesus was the centre of attraction, surrounded by the unclean civil servants and other assorted sinners, and the disciples were probably on the perimeter of the party nearer the entrance where the self-righteous snoopers were making their notes. But eventually their complaint 'How is it that he eateth and drinketh with publicans and sinners?' reached him, and he made an unanswerable reply:

'When Jesus heard it, he saith unto them, They that are whole have no need of the physician, but they that are sick: I came not to call the righteous, but sinners to repentance.'

It is interesting that Jesus compares himself with a physician; but in view of the miraculous cures he has already performed, it is not surprising. It is most likely that he was always aware of his extraordinary powers of healing and of the never-ending demands of the sick. In any case there is a similarity between the uncleanliness of the leper and the so-called ritual uncleanliness of these publicans and sinners.

I have heard people complain that Jesus had no interest in good people – but only in sinners . . . It seems a waste of time to be good if Jesus ignores virtue and only concentrates on sin.

But this very thought is sickeningly self-righteous – and the truth of the matter is: 'There is none good but one, that is, God.'

✳

It might have been the 'morning-after' when the next confrontation occurred. It might have been that Levi's feast took place on a fast day – in Galilee, at that time, the devout observed two fast days a week; or it might have been on another fast day that the disciples were again tucking into a little something. Anyway, Mark tell us:

'*And the disciples of John and of the Pharisees used to fast; and they come and say unto him, Why do the disciples of John and of the Pharisees fast, but thy disciples fast not?*' 18

It seems as if this was another indirect attack – unless, at the time, Jesus had an upset stomach and wasn't himself actually eating or drinking. But I suppose what is more likely is that the question was a general one concerning Jesus's teaching and the unconventional conduct of his followers.

'*And Jesus said unto them, Can the children of the bridechamber fast, while the bridegroom is with them? as long as they have the bridegroom with them, they cannot fast. But the days will come, when the bridegroom shall be taken away from them, and then shall they fast in those days.*' 19 20

First of all, who made the attack? I would imagine it was the scribes, since it was made as if on behalf of the Pharisees. (Although Matthew identifies the questioners as the disciples of John the Baptist.) Fasting was an acknowledged form of piety. The Pharisees 'actually whitened their faces, and went about with dishevelled garments on their fast days so that no one could miss the fact that they were fasting and so everyone would see and admire their devotion.' (Barclay)

But whether the question came from the scribes or Pharisees or the disciples of John – or all three – Jesus again makes a totally disarming reply. With a young man's comparison, he likens himself to a bridegroom, and his ministry to a wedding. It is a dazzling and precocious choice of role and situation. It is, needless to say, a starring role; and after the feasting with the publicans and sinners, the choice of a wedding celebration seems to be characteristic.

45

At first, I thought about it in terms of our formal English wedding receptions, which are fitted in between the marriage ceremony and the departure of the bride and groom for their honeymoon. But this was evidently not the same in a Jewish wedding at that time and place. The couple did not go away, but stayed at home. The celebrations continued for at least a week. Friends and relations – who were called 'the children of the bridechamber' – were entertained and feasted. Guests were exempted from religious duties. 'There was actually a rabbinic ruling which said "All in attendance on the bridegroom are relieved of all religious observances which would lessen their joy". The wedding guests were actually exempt from all fasting.' (Barclay)

Jesus likened himself to a host of a new life of celebration. He said, in effect, that everyone should rejoice simply because of his presence among them. He spoke of himself with extraordinary self-love. He seemed to have no respect for the old rules. He then went on to warn that there would be a time for fasting when he has left them. His words and his attitude must have caused total confusion and consternation. And then – suddenly – comes the voice of authority. After he has taunted and teased the solemn, law-abiding, rule-observing, ritual-ridden old order, Jesus suddenly gives warning. He gives warning in two parables; and the unmistakable voice of the master is heard for the first time in St Mark's Gospel.

21
22
'No man also seweth a piece of new cloth on an old garment: else the new piece that filled it up taketh away from the old, and the rent is made worse. And no man putteth new wine into old bottles: else the new wine doth burst the bottles, and the wine is spilled, and the bottles will be marred: but new wine must be put into new bottles.'

There was to be no compromise.

There was no use patching up the old order. There was no use rejuvenating the old order.

For many, the new way of life would be a violent and savage change.

Jesus uses the harsh words 'rent' and 'burst'. The sense of what he says is unanswerable.

The new teaching, the new spirit, would not be contained within Judaism.

★

'And it came to pass, that he went through the corn fields on the
sabbath day; and his disciples began, as they went, to pluck the ears of
corn. And the Pharisees said unto him, Behold, why do they on the
sabbath day that which is not lawful?'

This scene conjures up a golden image; perhaps it is evening.
We have all walked through corn fields on a sabbath day; we
have all, as we went, plucked the ears of corn. There is a feeling
of the fullness of life; a feeling of growth; a sense of the grand
cycle from seed to harvest. Perhaps Jesus and the disciples have
come from the synagogue where he had been teaching; they
are hungry, perhaps they are being followed or accompanied
by many people – friends and foes. It would appear so.

According to Matthew and Luke, the disciples *ate* the corn.
But this was not the offence. The act of plucking the corn was
against the law. It actually counted as work. It counted as
reaping or harvesting – albeit on a tiny scale. And work was
forbidden on the sabbath day.

Where did the Pharisees spring from? They must either have
been in the crowd with Jesus and the disciples, or perhaps they
were watching from a distance. They must have been waiting
for a specific offence to give them a legitimate excuse to attack.
They found the excuse with a few handfuls of corn, idly picked
by the disciples as they walked, and probably talked, their way
through the field. 'Behold!' comes like the pounce of a police-
man on a guilty group of children caught trespassing on a
private estate, or stealing in an orchard.

Jesus cannot believe that they are serious. The offence is so
petty. He ridicules them with a theological counter-attack. He
implies that they are ignorant of their own scriptures.

'And he said unto them, Have ye never read what David did, when
he had need, and was an hungred, he, and they that were with him?
How he went into the house of God in the days of Abiathar the high
priest, and did eat the shewbread, which is not lawful to eat but for the
priests, and gave also to them which were with him?'

Somebody made a little mistake here. According to 1
Samuel 21, the high priest in the story was actually Ahimelech
not Abiathar. (Evidently Ahimelech agreed to give David and
his followers the hallowed bread 'if the young men have kept
themselves at least from women'. And David confidently
assured him: 'Of a truth women have been kept from us about

these three days, since I came out, and the vessels of the young men are holy . . .') But later, unfortunately, Ahimelech was slain for helping David. So, maybe Mark or Peter – or could it even be Jesus? – substituted Ahimelech's son Abiathar as the high priest. Otherwise, if the Pharisees really knew their scriptures, they could have made a nasty come-back with 'and look what happened to Ahimelech!'

Whoever made the mistake – and I can't help hoping it was Jesus – the quotation must have stunned the Pharisees. They don't reply, and Mark tells us that Jesus continued:

27
28
'And he said unto them, The sabbath was made for man, and not man for the sabbath: Therefore the Son of man is Lord also of the sabbath.'

The first part of this is another version of a rabbinical saying: 'The sabbath is delivered unto you, and you are not delivered to the sabbath.' So the Pharisees were even further humiliated by having one of their own sayings thrown at them.

The humanity of Jesus is very clear in this incident. We have the image of him walking through the corn fields with his disciples on the sabbath day; his immediate defence of their petty crime; his daring to argue with the Pharisees on their own terms; his intended or unintended lapse of memory about Abiathar and Ahimelech; and his beautiful and simple affirmation that the sabbath was made for man.

It is sad that – like the Pharisees – people continued to confine and restrict the Christian sabbath with man-made rules. It is sad that the warmth and generosity of Jesus's personality was forgotten, and that people preferred to substitute a stern and intolerant schoolmaster. It is extraordinary that, although Jesus spent much of his time and energy in defying the rigid rules of the contemporary religious establishment, since his death men felt compelled to create a whole new set of rules. Of course the days of the suffocating Victorian sabbath have long passed, and we do not suffer much restriction today. If we wish, we can totally ignore the sabbath. Nevertheless, for many people it is a day associated with guilt rather than joy. It tends to be a day in which you do *not* do things, rather than a day in which you have the chance to live life more abundantly.

When Jesus says that 'the Son of man is Lord also of the

sabbath', he is promising that he, the representative of the new humanity, will bring a new conception of how men can live.

Again, the Pharisees are silenced.

＊

'And he entered again into the synagogue; and there was a man there **1**
which had a withered hand. And they watched him, whether he **2**
would heal him on the sabbath day; that they might accuse him.'

The last of these confrontation episodes reads like a 'set-up' and a 'show-down'. Jesus is 'set-up' by the Pharisees, and he decides to have a 'show-down' with them.

He goes into the synagogue again, presumably to preach; but it seems as if these visits to synagogues were becoming rare. The rulers of the synagogue invited people to speak, and it is possible that in the synagogues in the region around Capernaum Jesus was no longer welcome. However, I think that on this occasion he was expected. It could be that the Pharisees knew that he was coming to the synagogue and that they deliberately planted the man with a withered hand in order to test Jesus. They were probably still smarting from the episode in the corn field where they tried to accuse the disciples of breaking the law on the sabbath over a trivial incident. Now they plan a more serious offence; and an offence which will directly concern Jesus himself.

The sabbath day laws about sickness and healing were very complicated. If someone's life was in danger, people were allowed to give help – up to a point. But, if the sickness could possibly wait until the sabbath was passed, then it was against the law to administer any healing aid. In the case of the man with a withered hand, an affliction he had probably endured for a long period of time, it was obvious that there was no urgency. It must also have been obvious that there was no known cure. There is a tradition that the man with a withered hand was a stone-mason, and that without the use of his hand, he could not do his work.

In St Mark's Gospel, the Pharisees 'watched' Jesus 'whether he would heal him on the sabbath day; that they might accuse him'. But, in St Matthew's account of the story, the Pharisees actually start the proceedings by *asking* Jesus, 'Is it lawful to heal on the sabbath day? that they might accuse him,' lending further weight to the idea that the incident was planned ahead. But in both versions the atmosphere is very tense. 'And they watched him . . .' Perhaps there were long silences. People standing in shadows. Jesus standing between them, looking from one side to the other. It is like a scene in a Western movie. Perhaps a dog barks in the street outside . . . and the voice of Jesus sounds deceptively gentle.

'And he saith unto the man which had the withered hand, Stand forth.' Another silence. The man comes forward. What is Jesus going to do?

'And he saith unto them, Is it lawful to do good on the sabbath days, or to do evil? to save life, or to kill? But they held their peace.'

The questions of Jesus to the Pharisees are loaded. The questions are impossible to answer. They are also, basically, irrelevant to the situation. They open up entirely new arguments. 'Is it lawful to do good on the sabbath days, or to do evil?' Nobody has said anything about doing evil – but Jesus implies that the attitude of the Pharisees and their sabbath laws is evil. He continues: 'to save life, or to kill?' Nobody has said anything about killing. No one is at the point of death. But Jesus implies that the rigidity of the Pharisees is a blasphemy against life. He turns the situation into an attack – the 'set-up' into a 'show-down'. The sordid little plot to trap Jesus misfires. Instead, Jesus hints at the possibility of a new morality; a morality without hard and fast rules of conduct; a morality which implies individual choices about good and evil – rather than the traditions of the elders. And the Pharisees are tongue-tied.

'And when he had looked round about on them with anger, being grieved for the hardness of their hearts . . .'

(The later synoptic Gospels, Matthew and Luke, leave out the anger.)

'. . . he saith unto the man, Stretch forth thine hand. And he stretched it out: and his hand was restored whole as the other.'

After opening up doubts about their religious philosophy, Jesus then defies the Pharisees and performs a dazzling act of healing. It is easy to imagine their fury. Luke writes: 'And they were filled with madness.' They walk out of the synagogue, leaving Jesus with a group of astonished people.

'*And the Pharisees went forth, and straightway took counsel with the Herodians against him, how they might destroy him.*'

6

Matthew and Luke do not mention the Herodians, but in view of Jesus's increasing popularity with the people, it would be an understandable move for the Pharisees to join forces with them. They were unlikely allies for the Pharisees because by their association with the dissolute King Herod they were irreligious, and by their association with the Romans they were unclean. But it would seem, at this stage, to be natural for the Pharisees to hope that the Herodians might rid the country of Jesus, sparing them the inevitable unpopularity that such an action would bring. They hope to persuade the Herodians that Jesus is a political danger, and that he must be destroyed.

These confrontations with the scribes and Pharisees have now led to a situation of great danger. The controversy about the forgiveness of sins with the sick of the palsy; the controversy about eating and drinking with publicans and sinners; the controversy about fasting; the controversy – first with the disciples plucking corn, and then with Jesus healing the man with a withered hand – about the sabbath day laws; have led to what amounts to a declaration of war by the Pharisees. It is early on in the ministry and already we are afraid for Jesus. He seems to have risked everything in order to heal a man with a withered hand. In the claustrophobic atmosphere of the synagogue the Pharisees have been defied and out-manoeuvred. They decide to destroy him.

And suddenly, with masterly narrative cunning, Mark astonishes us. He has led us to believe that the followers of Jesus are entirely local. We assume that Jesus is only known around Capernaum and the Sea of Galilee. After the Pharisees leave the synagogue, Mark tells us:

'*But Jesus withdrew himself with his disciples to the sea: and a great multitude from Galilee followed him,*'

7

And then, as if in a movie, the camera draws back and reveals . . .

'*and from Judaea,*
And from Jerusalem,
and from Idumaea,
and from beyond Jordan;
and they about Tyre and Sidon,'

a great multitude,
when they had heard what great things he did,
came unto him.'

And we realise why the Pharisees are so afraid. And we are reassured about the safety of Jesus. And we are exhilarated by this evidence of his popularity and success. And we wonder if the Pharisees will ever stop him.

The Rev. Marshall helpfully tells us that Judaea and Jerusalem are in the centre; Idumaea is the south; 'beyond Jordan' the east; and Tyre and Sidon the north-west.

And, again as if in a movie, having drawn back the camera to astonish us and reveal the hugeness of the crowds, Mark suddenly zooms in to a close-up of Jesus whispering to the disciples:

9 *'And he spake to his disciples, that a small ship should wait on him because of the multitude, lest they should throng him.'*

There is a sudden practicalness about this specific request; and a wonderful contrast in the writing between 'a great multitude' and 'a small ship'. This is the distinctive homely style of Mark – which suits so well with the personality and behaviour of Jesus. At one moment Jesus is talking impressively about his mission as 'the Son of man', and the next moment he is making practical suggestions for a sensible safety arrangement.

And then we discover that Jesus had thrown caution to the winds, and stopped worrying about his reputation as a healer rather than a teacher.

10
11 *'For he had healed many; insomuch that they pressed upon him for to touch him, as many as had plagues. And unclean spirits, when they saw him, fell down before him, and cried, saying, Thou art the Son of*
12 *God. And he straightly charged them that they should not make him known.'*

It is impossible to tell how much time has passed since Jesus first called Simon and Andrew, and James and John. He has certainly done one tour of Galilee; and the confrontations with the scribes and Pharisees have happened over another unspecified period of time. But, no matter how much time has passed, I am sure that each event is reported in its right order. And we now reach a new peak of success with multitudes from all over the Holy Land – and beyond – crowding in upon Jesus.

This adoration must have made Jesus feel momentarily safe from the threats of the scribes and Pharisees. But, even so, he would not receive the title of 'the Son of God', although his manner of refusal somehow acknowledged the fact that the title was correct. This refusal was doubtless because, in the first place, he was not yet ready to share his belief in his divinity; but it may also have been for the practical reason that a proclamation of his kingship – which is how the Jews imagined their Messiah – would play into the hands of the Pharisees. It would be seen both as a threat to Herod, and to the Romans.

In this scene of mass healing, and in the voices of the unclean spirits recognising Jesus as the Son of God, there is a memory of the first sabbath in Capernaum. On that day, 'all the city was gathered together at the door' of Simon's house, and Jesus 'healed many that were sick of divers diseases, and cast out many devils; and suffered not the devils to speak, because they knew him'. And then, Mark told us that 'in the morning, rising up a great while before day, he went out, and departed into a solitary place, and there prayed'.

It would seem as if this pattern was repeated after the crowded scene of healing by the sea. It would seem as if Jesus had another reaction, and needed to be alone. He needed to talk with his father; to receive further instructions and guidance.

All Mark tells us is:

'And he goeth up into a mountain, and calleth unto him whom he would: and they came unto him.' **13**

But Mark does not tell us how long Jesus was in the mountain before he called his friends. I think that he spent some time alone. St Luke's version tells us: 'And it came to pass in those days, that he went out into a mountain to pray,' – and Luke writes specifically – 'and continued all night in prayer to God. And when it was day, he called unto him his disciples:'

I think it is important to emphasise this version, because it shows the natural pattern and progression of Jesus's personality and behaviour. And the pattern continues. After the first early morning spent in a solitary place, Jesus reached a moment of decision: to continue his ministry and increase the area in which he preached. He told Simon and the others: 'Let us go into the next towns, that I may preach there also.' After the time spent in the mountain, Jesus again reaches a decision to continue: and on this occasion to increase the number of his disciples to twelve. These moments of retreat are followed by greater energy and greater dedication to his task of fulfilling God's plan.

14
15
'And he ordained twelve, that they should be with him, and that he might send them forth to preach, And to have power to heal sicknesses, and to cast out devils:'

There are many reasons why Jesus ordained more disciples at this particular time. First of all, they were chosen when – as we have just learnt – Jesus's life was in danger from the Pharisees plotting with the Herodians. He needed more protection. He needed to safeguard his ministry. But also, with the growth of his popularity, he needed more help, more organisation; and he probably needed the choice of a larger group of friends. (Although we discover, as the journeys continue, that usually only three of the disciples were his constant companions.) Then, there is the idea of what we call in the theatre 'touring companies'. He chooses more disciples 'that he might send them forth to preach'. They would obviously learn from him, and he would rehearse and prepare them for their very own ministries to confirm and proclaim the good news. But perhaps, most of all, they might take the burden of healing from him. It is significant that the ordaining of the twelve 'to have power to heal sicknesses, and to cast out devils' happens after another episode of mass healing. It is certain that these demands created a great conflict for Jesus. He might think that, if the disciples had equal powers of healing, he would have more time to teach people. There might also be the conflict of vanity. It is easy to imagine the gratitude of the sick, and their families and friends. They must often have wanted to repay Jesus, to give him gifts and hospitality; in fact to worship him for being a miraculous physician. But he knew that this was not why he was God's beloved Son. The temptation, in a modern sense, must have been to surrender to the 'glamour' of his reputation as a miracle worker, and the adulation of the crowds.

It is thought that Jesus chose twelve disciples because there were twelve tribes of Israel. The men he chose were – as far as we know – ordinary men; and they must have been relatively poor men, since we discover later in the Gospel that they were impressed by wealth. There were evidently no theologians amongst them.

They were a mixed bunch.

If Mark wrote down the list from Peter's dictation, it tells us something of Peter. He puts himself first:

'And Simon he surnamed Peter.' **16**

Then, interestingly, he lists James and John rather than his own brother.

'And James the son of Zebedee, and John the brother of James; and **17** *he surnamed them Boanerges, which is, The sons of thunder.'*

And only then does Andrew get into the list:

'And Andrew, and Philip, and Bartholomew, and Matthew, and **18** *Thomas, and James the son of Alphaeus, and Thaddaeus, and Simon the Canaanite, And Judas Iscariot, which also betrayed him.'* **19**

The King James Version's 'he *surnamed* Peter' and 'he *surnamed* them' means he gave them fresh names – or, it would seem, affectionate nicknames. The commentators have a field day with the disciples' names, and discover a lot of useless information. I have pilfered some of it.

Peter's name means the rock (derived from the slightly Hellenised form of the Aramaic word Kepha). So we may assume that the modern equivalent of his nickname would be Rock, Rocky, or even Rock-Man.

Then come James and John. They were great favourites of Jesus. As we shall see, they were very likeable personalities, naïve and direct – although sometimes putting their collective foot in things. They must also have been hot-tempered and noisy, since Jesus calls them 'the sons of thunder'. The nickname is not reported in the other Gospels. (And Matthew and Luke put the brothers Simon and Andrew together at the head of *their* list.) Peter and James and John seem to be the most intimate disciples of Jesus. On many occasions he chooses to be with them, and one wonders how the other disciples felt about this; particularly one wonders about Andrew.

Matthew is thought to be Levi, the tax collector.

Bartholomew is thought to be the Nathaniel named in the other Gospels.

Thomas is nicknamed 'the twin'.

Thaddaeus could be called 'Big-Hearted'.

55

Simon the Canaanite is evidently better translated as Simon 'the Zealot' or 'the Keen'.

And Judas Iscariot means either Judas from Kerioth, or Judas 'the dagger-man' – although I am sure the latter nickname was only given after the events which led to the crucifixion.

By their association with Jesus, this group of ordinary men achieved immortality. We know little or nothing about most of them, except that they left their work and their homes to follow a man with revolutionary ideas of a new society, new values, and new behaviour.

The practical arrangements of the group are not explained. They were continually travelling. We do not know how they found places to sleep, or how they found food to eat. One gathers, from the instructions Jesus gave his disciples later, they just asked. After the crucifixion – as I have already mentioned – Mark tells us: 'There were also women looking on afar off;' and that they had followed Jesus when he was in Galilee, 'and ministered unto him'. He also says that there were 'many other women which came up with him unto Jerusalem'.

Perhaps there were already many women accompanying them. Perhaps there was often a much larger group of followers than the chosen disciples. And perhaps this explains why the establishment was afraid to stop Jesus's teaching. Outside of Jerusalem, the sheer size of his followers and admirers must have daunted them.

And from now on in the story there is often a sense of danger from the crowds. On two occasions specific numbers of five thousand and four thousand people are mentioned. Imagine being followed by the entire audience of the Albert Hall! As we shall now see, this state of affairs alarmed his family and friends.

The next episode starts with a deceptively simple piece of information:

'and they went into an house.'

In the King James Version this is not even given a new sentence, but carries on from the naming of the disciples. Later versions give it more weight; and some of them translate 'house' as 'home' – but I do not know what this means unless they think we are back at Peter's house again. At any rate, these six little words are the prologue to a tremendously important scene in the ministry of Jesus. In this scene we see him at the centre of an adoring multitude, and yet in a situation where both the representatives of authority, and his own family, are against him. It is a wonderful episode – and, to me, it seems as if here, in this house, Jesus speaks and behaves with the authority of a great man. It begins:

'and they went into an house. And the multitude cometh together 20
again, so that they could not so much as eat bread. And when his 21
friends heard of it, they went out to lay hold on him: for they said, He
is beside himself.'

These words do not seem to need any great clarification – but there are, nevertheless, various alternatives. 'His friends' are thought to be 'his family' or 'his people' – as opposed to his immediate followers and disciples. And the King James Version's 'He is beside himself' – which is only reported in St Mark, and which has a recognisably contemporary ring – is variously re-translated as 'He must be mad', 'He's gone mad', or 'He was out of his mind'. Manford George Gutzke in his *Plain Talk on Mark* tells us helpfully that they said 'in effect, "Let's take it easy. Go slow. You are going overboard in this matter"'.

But I think the King James Version is sufficiently clear. (It is interesting that the same phrase is used in The Acts Of The Apostles when Paul is accused: 'Paul, thou art beside thyself; much learning doth make thee mad.') It is a typically self-conscious family reaction to one of its members who seems to be making a public spectacle of himself.

It is a serious accusation.

And it is followed by an even *more* serious accusation.

'And the scribes which came down from Jerusalem said, He hath 22
Beelzebub, and by the prince of the devils casteth he out devils.'

Here is another example of the splendid narrative style of St Mark. He has mentioned the scribes several times. Now, for the first time, he mentions 'the scribes *which came down from Jerusalem'*. These are obviously much more important men, and we realise that Jesus is now regarded as a potential national danger. It is another instance of the cumulative power of Mark's reporting.

57

Jesus is publicly attacked by friends and foes. Beelzebub is a contemptuous name for Satan; the name is the equivalent of 'the Lord of the flies' or even 'the Lord of dung' or 'the Lord of filth'.

What does the carpenter from Nazareth do? He is not intimidated by the scribes *'which came down from Jerusalem.'* With the arrogance of a born aristocrat he summons them to his presence.

23   *'And he called them unto him,'*
And he does not make it easy for them.
'and said unto them in parables, How can Satan cast out Satan?'
(He does not deign to use the name Beelzebub.)

24   *'And if a kingdom be divided against itself, that kingdom cannot*
25 *stand. And if a house be divided against itself, that house cannot stand.*
26 *And if Satan rise up against himself, and be divided, he cannot stand,*
but hath an end.'

The scribes have implied that Jesus is inspired by the devil. In fact, as we soon find out, (Mark and Peter being parenthetical again) they actually said that Jesus had an unclean spirit. Since Jesus had the power to cast out unclean spirits – and had done so on many occasions – their accusation is plainly ridiculous. And Jesus, in typical fashion at this stage of the ministry, ridicules them unmercifully. He is not content to refute them once with 'How can Satan cast out Satan?' but goes on and on mocking them, likening himself and his ministry first with a kingdom; and then – in case they do not understand – with a house; and then – in case they do not understand – with Satan again; and then – in case they have still not understood him – he puts it another way:

27   *'No man can enter into a strong man's house, and spoil his goods,*
except he will first bind the strong man; and then he will spoil his
house.'

In those days, if a man was possessed with the devil and was considered to be dangerous, he was tied up. There is an example later in the Gospel when we learn that a man with an unclean spirit was 'often bound with fetters and chains'. Here, Jesus is saying to the scribes – with calculated naïveté – that it is not possible to cast out devils simply by persuasion (which, in fact, he *is* able to do) but that it is necessary to use force. He is giving them no alternative but to consider his divinity. He is driving them to admit that he can change men by conversion rather than by laws and intimidation.

Nevertheless, these are difficult words to understand. It is the argument of a precocious young man. It is a brilliant mockery.

But, then, Jesus stops the mockery. With new and simple authority, he changes his attack into a solemn warning. And for the first time in St Mark's Gospel we hear the words:

'Verily I say unto you . . .' 28

This expression is only used by Jesus on very special occasions. Here, it is used with great effect to signify the end of his teaching the scribes by teasing and parable. Now, everything that Jesus has said before pales into insignificance.

'Verily I say unto you, All sins shall be forgiven unto the sons of men, and blasphemies wheresoever they shall blaspheme: But he 29 *that shall blaspheme against the Holy Ghost hath never forgiveness, but is in danger of eternal damnation.'*

And only then Marks tells us:

'Because they said, He hath an unclean spirit.' 30

Jesus's words are so important that I think we should compare them with another version of the speech in St Matthew. In this version, Jesus is even more specific in his warning. Matthew quotes:

'All manner of sin and blasphemy shall be forgiven unto men: but the blasphemy against the Holy Ghost shall not be forgiven unto men. And whosoever speaketh a word against the Son of man, it shall be forgiven him: but whosoever speaketh against the Holy Ghost, it shall not be forgiven him, neither in this world, neither in the world to come.' (12: 31, 32.)

In this version Jesus makes it clear that he is merely an interpreter or representative of the Holy Spirit, and that personal insults do not matter to him. But the authority of the words in both versions is amazing.

Jesus actually said, 'All sins shall be forgiven unto the sons of men.' How could he say this? Who gave him the authority to say this? And what was the reaction of the scribes, with their countless laws and rules, to these astonishing words?

And then he actually said:

'And blasphemies wheresoever they shall blaspheme.'

Jesus, in one sentence, is erasing the whole of the religious past.

And then he proposes an entirely new outlook:

'But he that shall blaspheme against the Holy Ghost hath never forgiveness, but is in danger of eternal damnation.'

This proposes recognition of a *benificent* life force. It proposes a simple choice of belief or unbelief in the universe of good or evil. It recognises a purpose in creation. It proposes that we should lead positive lives. It challenges us to believe in the Holy Spirit.

In his commentary *The Gospel of St Mark* Gerald S. Sloyan writes: 'What Mark actually says is that the sole exception to the general law of forgiveness is in the case of looking upon the works of light and attributing them to darkness.'

It is here that we realise – vividly – that Jesus is a total revolutionary. It is here that, by his teaching, he releases men from the bondage of the old teaching and preaches a new doctrine. Sins are forgiven; blasphemies are forgiven; but Jesus demands recognition of the Holy Spirit. He not only demands recognition but warns that there is no future for mankind without it. In one stroke, he wipes out the rules and laws invented by well-intentioned men in their busy attempts to organise themselves into a race of obedient civil servants; and he proposes an individual choice of belief or unbelief in the purpose of creation. If one accepts that there is a good purpose in creation, then this belief leads to unwritten rules of conduct and behaviour. Unwritten rules which are dictated by individual consciences.

*

But the episode is not yet over. There is a further release for the sons of men. After disposing of the laws and rules of the old religion, Jesus disposes of the tyranny of the family, and proposes a new relationship.

We are still in the house.

31 'There came then his brethren and his mother, and, standing
32 without, sent unto him, calling him. And the multitude sat about him,
    and they said unto him, Behold, thy mother and thy brethren without
33 seek for thee. And he answered them, saying, Who is my mother, or
34 my brethren? And he looked round about on them which sat about

him, and said, Behold my mother and my brethren! For whosoever shall do the will of God, the same is my brother, and my sister, and mother.'

Again, the narrative progresses. We have read that when 'his friends' heard of his behaviour 'they went out to lay hold on him: for they said, He is beside himself'. And if we understand 'his friends' to mean 'his family' then they must have been the more distant relations; his uncles and cousins perhaps. Now, we have his brethren and – working up to the closest relationship – his mother. Presumably they cannot get into the house because of the crowd; or else they refuse to come into the house because of embarrassment and annoyance. They 'sent unto him, calling him'. An unwise move. The multitude must have been bemused and amused by the situation. They probably had to interrupt Jesus while he was talking. Did they cough politely and put up their hands for permission to speak? Did they expect Jesus to break off immediately and either call his family or go to them?

Let us consider a few examples of Jesus's attitude to the family.

St Luke tells us that, in Jerusalem as a twelve-year-old, Jesus gave his parents the slip and disputed in the temple for three days. And when they found him:

'His mother said unto him, Son, why hast thou thus dealt with us? behold, thy father and I have sought thee sorrowing. And he said unto them, How is it that ye sought me? wist ye not that I must be about my Father's business? And they understood not the saying which he spake unto them.' Luke 2: 48, 49, 50.

Later, when Jesus is calling followers, the family is again put into perspective.

'And he said unto another, Follow me. But he said, Lord, suffer me first to go and bury my father. Jesus said unto him, Let the dead bury their dead: but go thou and preach the kingdom of God.

'And another also said, Lord, I will follow thee; but let me first go bid them farewell, which are at home in my house. And Jesus said unto him, No man, having put his hand to the plough, and looking back, is fit for the kingdom of God.' Luke 9: 59, 60, 61, 62.

Here is a reference to his mother.

'And it came to pass, as he spake these things, a certain woman of the company lifted up her voice, and said unto him, Blessed is the womb that bare thee, and the paps which thou hast sucked. But he said, Yea rather, blessed are they that hear the word of God, and keep it.' Luke 11: 27, 28.

In St Matthew Jesus says:

'For I am come to set a man at variance against his father, and the daughter against her mother, and the daughter in law against her mother in law. And a man's foes shall be they of his own household. He that loveth father or mother more than me is not worthy of me: and he that loveth son or daughter more than me is not worthy of me.' Matthew 10: 35, 36, 37.

And in St Luke Jesus says:

'If any man come to me, and hate not his father, and mother, and wife, and children, and brethren, and sisters, yea, and his own life also, he cannot be my disciple.' Luke 14: 26.

Or alternatively the Good News Bible – which slightly modifies this:

'Whoever comes to me cannot be my disciple unless he loves me more than he loves his father and his mother, his wife and his children, his brothers and his sisters, and himself as well.'

Surprisingly, these sayings of Jesus are not in St Mark. But perhaps they were shocking to the family man, Peter.

They *are* shocking statements; but they are the sayings of a revolutionary.

They are also the statements of one born out of wedlock. I believe that Jesus was an illegitimate child. I believe that he was desperately angry and ashamed of this fact. And I believe that this fact deeply influenced both his life and his teaching.

If Jesus was originally a carpenter from a small town, there must have been good human reasons for his amazing driving force. I think that one of those reasons was his illegitimacy; indeed it could have been the root cause of his ambition. Because he could not bear his illegitimacy, it became necessary for him to invent a father. He invented a father in heaven; he invented the greatest father of them all; and he invented his own role of the beloved son. He then had to fulfil his father's wishes. And his father's wishes – which were of course Jesus's wishes – were, like Jesus's birth, unconventional. They upset an entire establishment. In this sense, Jesus's life was a life of revenge.

Let us return to the crowded house. Here, Jesus rejects his mother and his brethren, electing to join the multitude and inviting the multitude to join him in the family of man.

And now let us balance the quotes about his attitude to conventional family life, with a quote about the larger family. In St Matthew's account of the Last Judgement the Son of man comes as a king, and humanity is divided and set on his right hand and on his left.

'Then shall the king say unto them on his right hand, Come, ye blessed of my Father, inherit the kingdom prepared for you from the foundation of the world: For I was an hungred, and ye gave me meat: I was thirsty, and ye gave me drink: I was a stranger, and ye took me in: Naked and ye clothed me: I was sick, and ye visited me: I was in prison, and ye came unto me; Then shall the righteous answer him, saying, Lord, when saw we thee an hungred, and fed thee? or thirsty, and gave thee drink? When saw we thee a stranger, and took thee in? or naked, and clothed thee? Or when saw we thee sick, or in prison, and came unto thee? And the King shall answer and say unto them, Verily, I say unto you, Inasmuch as ye have done it unto one of the least of these my brethren, ye have done it unto me.

'Then shall he also say to them on the left hand, Depart from me, ye cursed, into everlasting fire, prepared for the devil and his angels: For I was an hungred, and ye gave me no meat: I was thirsty, and ye gave me no drink: I was a stranger, and ye took me not in: naked, and ye clothed me not: sick, and in prison, and ye visited me not. Then shall they also answer him, saying, Lord, when saw we thee an hungred, or athirst, or a stranger, or naked, or sick, or in prison, and did not minister unto thee? Then shall he answer them, saying, Verily I say unto you, Inasmuch as ye did it not to one of the least of these, ye did it not to me.'

THE PARABLE DAY BY THE SEA

Now the story of Jesus, as told by Peter and Mark, changes. We have had three hectic chapters crammed with incident and conflict. Now the pace slackens and the villains disappear. For the next three chapters Jesus teaches and heals, but there are no confrontations with the scribes and Pharisees. The rhythm of the Gospel changes and Mark's terse reporting becomes more conversational.

'And he began again to teach by the sea side: and there was gathered unto him a great multitude, so that he entered into a ship, and sat in the sea; and the whole multitude was by the sea on the land. And he taught them many things by parables, and said unto them in his doctrine, Hearken: Behold, —'

We are in the open air. Jesus evidently decides to become more organised. Earlier, we have overheard him telling his disciples that 'a small ship should wait on him because of the multitude, lest they should throng him'. Now this has been arranged. He enters into a ship and sits in the sea. He is safe from the pushing and shoving of the crowds. He is also relieved of the proximity of the sick. He can teach with a degree of privacy, surrounded in the ship only by his friends and disciples.

What an astonishing sight!

To me, the theatricality of the scene is very appealing.

Was there an announcement that he would teach?

Was it decided at what time he would appear?

Did he wait for late-comers?

Were they selling food and drink in the crowd?

Did men leave their jobs, and housewives their work, to come and listen to him?

Was there a great noise – especially from children and dogs?

Was it a holiday atmosphere – with shouts and calls and singing?

Did the disciples help to control the situation?

Were there other speakers – or was Jesus the sole attraction?

. . . I think he was the sole attraction.

He now begins to illustrate his teaching.

Up till now his actions have hinted at a new concept of behaviour. He has confounded the scribes and Pharisees with their rules and rituals and their strict observance of 'the law', and he has introduced a new attitude to the accepted conventions with regard to publicans and sinners, to fasting, and to the sabbath. He challenges men to make a *personal* choice in their behaviour and in their way of life. Can his teaching even be summarised by the prosaic description of 'common-sense'? The parables will clarify and enlarge upon the thinking of Jesus.

First, he calls for quiet.

'Hearken.'

Then he asks us to exercise our imaginations.

'Behold.'

And the first parable begins. It is deceptively simple.

'*There went out a sower to sow: And it came to pass, as he sowed,* **4 –** *some fell by the way side, and the fowls of the air came and devoured it up. And some fell on stony ground, where it had not much earth; and immediately it sprang up, because it had no depth of earth: But when the sun was up, it was scorched; and because it had no root, it withered away. And some fell among thorns, and the thorns grew up and choked it, and it yielded no fruit. And other fell on good ground, and did yield fruit that sprang up and increased; and brought forth, some thirty, and some sixty, and some an hundred. And he said unto them,* **9** *He that hath ears to hear, let him hear.*'

What does it mean?

The last line seems to be a clue.

Surely the sower is Jesus himself. Surely it means we should listen to him. Surely . . .

All right! No commentator is needed! Jesus explains it all.

'*And when he was alone, they that were about him with the twelve* **10** *asked of him the parable.*'

'And when they were alone' presumably indicates a time jump.

65

According to Mark, Jesus has only just entered into the ship to teach the crowd 'many things by parables'. He has started off with a corker. I am confused. Maybe you are confused. Perhaps Mark was confused. And it's possible that at this point he asked Peter for an explanation. Then Peter recalled the occasion when 'they that were about him with the twelve' actually did the same thing to Jesus.

Perhaps it was lunch-time on the day in question. Perhaps there was a break in the proceedings, and Jesus and his friends and disciples had some refreshment; perhaps something prepared by Simon's wife – or Simon's wife's mother. I think of this chapter of the parables as a single, vividly-remembered day in the early ministry of Jesus. There were obviously many more parables than the reported ones – but the reported ones would be in the correct order – and this parable of the sower would definitely be the first. It is the foundation of Jesus's teaching.

But it must be made clear.

Luckily, at this stage, Jesus was easily approachable. Later on in the Gospel, we sense in the disciples a growing fear and awe. But for now, when 'they that were about him with the twelve' got him on his own, they tackled him fearlessly about his opening parable – and perhaps even complained of unnecessary obscurity in this form of teaching. It's lucky for us that they did so, because we get both a general and a particular explanation from Jesus.

'And he said unto them, Unto you it is given to know the mystery of the kingdom of God: but unto them that are without, all these things are done in parables: That seeing they may see, and not perceive; and hearing they may hear, and not understand; lest at any time they should be converted, and their sins should be forgiven them.'

This is the general explanation – to do with his use of parables as a form of teaching. He tells his friends and disciples that they are privileged to know the mystery of the kingdom of God. Presumably they are privileged because they have made a commitment to him, and have been converted by his teaching. However, this commitment and conversion does not make them master-minds; any more than the members of the crowd on the bank of the Sea of Galilee.

And here we must face a ruthless side of Jesus's personality that will recur throughout the Gospel. On this occasion it is his attitude to 'them that are without'. In St Matthew, Jesus is quoted as saying: 'For this people's heart is waxed gross, and their ears are dull of hearing, and their eyes they have closed.' The tone is contemptuous. These people see – and do not perceive. They hear – and do not understand. And then there is the big 'lest'. 'Lest at any time they should be converted, and their sins should be forgiven them.'

The difficulty with all this is that it sounds as if a true follower of Jesus needs enormous intellect.

I don't think belief requires scholarship. *But it will not come without desire.* And I think it was the people without desire, without longing, without the ambition to understand, who were the real target of Jesus's contempt.

His use of parables is obviously a test of a person's desire for the kingdom of God; for belief in belief.

Now, however, Jesus returns to the specific parable of the sower, and for the first time we are aware of a mild exasperation with the disciples.

'*And he said unto them, Know ye not this parable? and how then will ye know all parables?*' 13

A little intellect might not be necessary for conversion – but it would certainly help in companionship. For the first time Jesus shows awareness of the intellectual gap between himself and his disciples. And, as the Gospel continues, these ordinary men are often utterly bewildered by the mental agility of Jesus.

He slowly explains the parable.

'*The sower soweth the word.*' 14

This simple sentence demands attention. Without understanding this sentence, the parable has no impact.

What is 'the word'?

'The word' is the sum of Jesus's teaching.

'The word' is the inspiration of Jesus.

'The word' is what the New Testament is all about.

'The word' – at this stage – is as fragile as a seed in comparison with the established laws of the land.

'The word' means faith. 'The word' means belief. 'The word' means commitment.

'The word' is eternal life.

67

'The word' is that God is good, and that the Holy Spirit is abroad.

That is the word.

'The sower soweth the word' – and what happens?

15

'*And these are they by the way side, where the word is sown; but when they have heard, Satan cometh immediately, and taketh away the word that was sown in their hearts.*'

Rev. Marshall calls these the *hard hearts* 'on which preaching can make no impression.'

16

'*And these are they likewise which are sown on stony ground; who, when they have heard the word, immediately receive it with gladness;*

17

And have no root in themselves, and so endure but for a time: afterward, when affliction or persecution ariseth for the word's sake, immediately they are offended.'

Note the double use of the word 'immediately'. This part of the explanation of the parable could have been written by Noël Coward. It deals with the superficial people. They remind me of certain first night visitors who come back-stage immediately after a play has ended, throw their arms around you and tell you, 'Darling, it was wonderful!' Then, the next morning, if the critics have given the play unfavourable reviews, they immediately tell their friends, 'Darling, it was terrible!'

18
19

'*And these are they which are sown among thorns; such as hear the word, And the cares of this world, and the deceitfulness of riches, and the lusts of other things entering in, choke the word, and it becometh unfruitful.*'

I wonder if Jesus often repeated these words. I wonder if he often warned his disciples and if they often warned each other, of the magnet of worldly things, and that these words became catch-phrases.

'The cares of this world' can mean providing for a family, or nursing the sick and tending the old. And the cares can claim us completely.

'The deceitfulness of riches' can mean devoting oneself entirely to making money, or attempting to dazzle friends with one's life-style and possessions. And this also can be a full-time occupation.

'The lusts of other things . . .' Was Jesus actually talking about *sex*? I hope so! I have an uncomfortable feeling that Peter and Mark started the clean-up job that has gone on ever since.

(In *his* version of the parable, Matthew leaves out this reference altogether.) Many Christians keep sex out of sight and out of mind. They invent a stained-glass people who never flirt, cuddle or copulate. When I was a teenager my father once startled me by saying, 'Ninety per cent of life is sex.' Inwardly I thought, 'Then why do we never talk about it?' The Good News Bible compounds the cover-up with the coy translation 'all other kinds of desires'; and The Living Bible refers to 'the lure of attractive things'. Do they think that Jesus was talking about a fondness for smelling pretty flowers?

It's certainly possible that Jesus talked about sex. Despite his emphasis on adultery and fornication as sins to be condemned, it's possible that his life-style would shock many of his present-day followers. But the puritans have censored this whole area, and we are bereft of vital advice and teaching. Of course, in this instance, within the parable, Jesus is talking about sex taking us over completely to the exclusion of spiritual things. But at least he is admitting that this is possible; and that much is a comfort.

'And these are they which are sown on good ground; such as hear **20** *the word, and receive it, and bring forth fruit, some thirtyfold, some sixty, and some an hundred.'*

God does not choose *us*.

We choose God.

And in order to choose him – in order to choose 'the word' – 'and the word was God' – we must be receptive to him; we must be receptive to 'the word'.

This seems to be, and always seems to have been, frightfully difficult. The deep pessimism in all of us does not dare to think of salvation. We would prefer to be tempted. To be tempted by Satan; to be tempted by the superficial; to be tempted by our worries; by making money; by self-gratification.

In this first parable Jesus offers us a choice.

This is the new teaching.

There need be no rules, no rituals, no dogmatism, if you are receptive to the word. And the word means eternal life, a benign universe, and joy. If you are receptive to joy your life will increase 'some thirtyfold, some sixty, and some an hundred'.

It is a choice. We must choose the life we wish to live. We are free to do this.

I believe this is the meaning of the first parable. And it is the key to the teaching of Jesus.

Choose to believe. And, *if* you choose to believe, this will dictate the way you behave.

I choose to believe St Mark's Gospel and its correct order of narrative.

I have supposed that Jesus's explanation of the first parable to his friends and disciples took place during a break on this well-remembered day of teaching. Mark reports that Jesus now returns to talking directly to the people on the shore.

'*And he said unto them . . .*' Jesus starts the second parable.

Most of the commentators hold that in this chapter Mark has gathered together a random collection of Jesus's parables and sayings which do not have any connection with each other. William Barclay reminds us that the next verses in St Mark's Gospel are actually scattered *all over* St Matthew's Gospel. Verse 21 is in the Sermon on the Mount; verse 22 is found in Jesus's instructions to his disciples before they set out to teach; verse 24 is in another part of the Sermon on the Mount; verse 25 is in St Matthew's own account of Jesus teaching by parables – and is also spoken another time by Jesus on the Mount of Olives just before the final passover. Ignore the confusion! I choose to believe that they were spoken on the same day, in the order reported by St Mark, and that they are indeed all connected. Matthew and Luke and John gathered together much more material than Mark was able to do – but for sanity's sake let us believe in the order of the first Gospel, and *let us learn from that order.*

Why should we know better than Peter?

21

'*And he said unto them, Is a candle brought to be put under a bushel, or under a bed? and not to be set on a candlestick?*'

Explanations: – 'The "candle" of the Authorised Version has nothing in common with the modern article of that name, but must be regarded as simply another name for lamp.' (Marshall) Nevertheless it would probably have a naked flame. There are various interpretations of a bushel; a two gallon measure; a meal tub; a pudding basin. But again the Rev. Marshall has the most helpful one: 'The poor having no table, would turn the bushel measure upside down and place the lamp upon it.'

So now let's start again.

Is a lamp brought to be put under a table, or under a bed? and not to be set on a lampstand?

And now let's try hearing it for the first time.

Surely it's a joke! Surely it got a good laugh!

There is a wonderful cumulative good humour about Jesus's teaching on this day by the sea.

If you put a lamp under the table you won't be able to see anything; and, if you put a lamp under your bed, the whole thing will soon go up in flames and you'll go leaping into the air like a cartoon cat.

The candle – the lamp – is another substitute for 'the word'. And we know what 'the word' means.

In effect Jesus is saying, 'Don't be afraid of your joy; don't be afraid of your belief. Let it shine for everyone to see.'

He continues:

'For there is nothing hid, which shall not be manifested; neither **22** *was anything kept secret, but that it should come abroad.'*

If our deepest guilts and worst sins will eventually be revealed, it is absurd to hide our joy and our belief.

There is a tremendous sense of relief in these lines; and I think that Jesus shouted out the next sentence. I think he yelled it out to startle the people and make them laugh, to defy the scribes and Pharisees, to proclaim his personal doctrine.

'If any man have ears to hear, let him hear.' **23**

He is a young man, revelling in the intensity of his belief, spreading 'the word' to all and sundry. He is certainly not hiding his candle under a bushel.

★

Then comes a warning. The crowd is in a relaxed and happy mood, and, like an accomplished orator, Jesus takes advantage of their temporary open-mindedness to teach a salutary lesson. He has challenged them good-humouredly with the words 'If any man have ears to hear, let him hear'.

Then Mark reports:

'And he said unto them, Take heed what ye hear.' **24**

His teaching changes from the general to the specific. The crowd's attention is arrested. Jesus now teaches that it is one thing to *believe* 'the word'; it is another thing to *practise* it.

With extraordinary economy he tells us:

'With what measure ye mete, it shall be measured to you: and unto you that hear shall more be given.'

At least he tells it with extraordinary economy in the King James Version. In the Good News he sounds a little less crisp: 'The same rules you use to judge others will be used by God to judge you – but with even greater severity.' I prefer 'with what measure ye mete, it shall be measured to you'. It is more all-embracing. Surely Jesus isn't only talking about judging people. He is talking about human behaviour. He is talking about how much we give and how much we take. He is also talking about generosity of spirit. And with splendid vanity Jesus claims that 'unto you that hear shall more be given'. He claims this on behalf of God.

Unto you that hear *'the word'* shall more be given.

25 *'For he that hath, to him shall be given: and he that hath not, from him shall be taken even that which he hath.'*

This is the Son of God talking. This is the introduction of the new establishment, the new aristocracy; the believers in 'the word', in the kingdom of God, *who practice what they believe.*

The odds are uneven.

The believers will have even more than their due.

The non-believers will not even keep what they started out with.

It sounds wildly unfair. But this is the bait that Jesus held out to the people on the shore. This is the bait he still holds out.

If it is crazy to believe – it is even more crazy to doubt.

Unlike most of us, Jesus was an optimist.

*

Now he goes on promising more and more. The next two parables illustrate the growth, the inevitable increase of the kingdom of God.

The first one is a great comfort.

26
27 *'And he said, So is the kingdom of God, as if a man should cast seed into the ground; and should sleep, and rise night and day, and the seed*
28 *should spring and grow up, he knoweth not how. For the earth bringeth forth fruit of herself; first the blade, then the ear, after that the*

full corn in the ear. But when the fruit is brought forth, immediately he putteth in the sickle, because the harvest is come.'

This parable allows for the fallibility of man. Many of us have moments of enlightenment, moments of elation, moments of commitment, followed by long – sometimes indefinite – periods of doubt, apathy and puzzlement. 'The cares of this world' claim us.

You cannot stand for long on a mountain top; the air is too rarified. You start sneezing.

You cannot always sing alleluias; the cupboard may be bare. Your stomach rumbles.

You may have a clear dream of conversion; but it is forgotten in the morning. A living must be earned. A garden must be cultivated. A journey must be made. And yet . . .

Jesus tells us in this parable that if we have at least accepted 'the word' – which is the Kingdom of God – even though we may cast it away, even though we move on to the demands of the ordinary business of living, 'the word' is still there, growing in strength, increasing in power, waiting for us to recognise it again.

To those of us – most of us – who lapse alarmingly, this parable is of particular comfort.

And, since I am a jealous old fool where St Mark is concerned, I am glad that this parable is contained solely in my favourite Gospel. Matthew and Luke obviously didn't think it worth their while to repeat. Perhaps they imagined that fallibility, or the thought of God giving us a second chance, was not something to talk about. The dehumanising process had begun. But to me, after his teaching, it is the fallibility of Jesus which is his most persuasive feature; and in St Mark's Gospel we find a Jesus who is recognisably human. He understands the cares of this world; he experiences some of them during his ministry. He reacts as we would react to hunger and fatigue. He is overwhelmed by the demands of the sick. He is not always tolerant of the lack of understanding among his disciples. He is sometimes enraged by the scribes and Pharisees. And, at the end, he dies with a protest to God. This was a man.

★

Now we reach the third parable of seeds, and I think that Jesus may have finished the day on a note of laughter.

30 - *'And he said, Whereunto shall we liken the kingdom of God? or with what comparison shall we compare it? It is like a grain of mustard seed, which, when it is sown in the earth, is less than all the*
32 *seeds that be in the earth: But when it is sown, it groweth up, and becometh greater than all herbs, and shooteth out great branches; so that the fowls of the air may lodge under the shadow of it.'*

The parable of the mustard seed – known in Palestine as the smallest seed in the world – growing into a redwood is a glorious exaggeration. It is 'over the top'. Perhaps, accompanied by gestures and mime, Jesus amused the crowd with an imaginary tiny seed thrown into the ground and disappearing from view – and then, slowly, watched a giant tree grow up and up into the sky, becoming a home for all the birds of the air. At least, that's how *I* understand the parable. Most commentators scratch desperately around for a literal explanation; telling us that by the Lake of Gennesaret the actual height of the shrub is about eight or ten feet; telling us that 'the plant referred to is probably a *Sinapsis* (formerly included in the genus *Brassica*); it has a small seed which grows quickly to a considerable height.' (C. F. D. Moule) And about the fowls of the air D. E. Nineham writes: 'Just possibly . . . St Mark interpreted these words allegorically as implying that the preaching of the Gospel would bring all nations within the scope of the kingdom.' 'Just possibly' St Mark did. 'Just possibly' Jesus meant this. Otherwise it's a fairly useless addition.

It is very sad that people should turn themselves inside out in attempts to rationalise a story that cannot actually be rationalised. The mustard seed grows into a plant or vegetable of considerable height – but it is not 'greater than all herbs', and does not 'shoot out great branches', and 'the fowls of the air' do not 'lodge under the shadow of it'. This is Jesus's exaggeration, in order to make us laugh, and in order to make us see his point.

*

33 *'And with many such parables spake he the word unto them, as they*
34 *were able to hear it. But without a parable spake he not unto them;*

74

and when they were alone, he expounded all things to his disciples.'

It seems that nothing more can be specifically remembered of Jesus's teaching on that special day by the sea, but Mark writes in general terms that there were actually 'many such parables' told to the crowd by Jesus – and then adds wryly 'as they were able to hear it'. I always want to substitute a word here and change the line to 'as they were able to *bear* it'. I think it *means* that. I think that Jesus went on until the intellectual capacity of his audience was exhausted. It is probable that the people would have preferred a more direct form of teaching. Although the parables make good stories, it was – and is – hard work to discover what Jesus meant by them. But, as he has already intimated to his disciples, he intended it to be hard work. Jesus told stories which were easily remembered, but which tested the desire of people to understand 'the word' contained within them. This is sometimes a very severe test.

Nevertheless, 'without a parable spake he not unto them'. And then Peter must have admitted to Mark that 'when they were alone, he expounded all things to his disciples'. A pattern is established in this chapter which will be repeated throughout the Gospel; the explanations of things Jesus said and did, given to his disciples. Mark tries to maintain an impartiality in writing about this, but I think his impartiality eventually becomes a comment. Mark is a splendid journalist, and distances himself superbly from his story, but we cannot help wondering what he really thought of the disciples, and whether he sympathised with the occasional impatience of Jesus.

Now, although Peter has had difficulty in remembering all of the parables, he remembers vividly the events of that evening.

This is definitely an eye-witness account. Read it right through!

'And the same day, when the even was come, he saith unto them, **35** *Let us pass over unto the other side. And when they had sent away the multitude, they took him even as he was in the ship. And there were also with him other little ships. And there arose a great storm of wind, and the waves beat into the ship, so that it was now full. And he was in the hinder part of the ship, asleep on a pillow: and they awake him, and say unto him, Master, carest thou not that we perish? And he*

arose, and rebuked the wind, and said unto the sea, Peace, be still.
And the wind ceased, and there was a great calm. And he said unto
them, Why are ye so fearful? how is it that ye have no faith? And
they feared exceedingly, and said one to another, What manner of man
is this, that even the wind and the sea obey him?'

41

This amazing story is told in such a colloquial fashion that it
is easy to accept it without question. Mark has described Jesus
teaching by parables from a ship to the people on the shore. We
do not know how long this has gone on; we do not know how
many more parables there may have been. But it has been a
memorable occasion. Then evidently Peter remembered with
pride: 'And the same day . . .' actually the same day as the
parables; 'when the even was come' – and the shadows were
falling and it was time to put children to sleep – 'he saith unto
them, Let us pass over unto the other side.' Jesus probably said
this quietly and with calculation. The crowd was still there. If
he went ashore they might throng him; miracles might be
demanded; they would follow him wherever he went. It is at
this point in St Matthew's account that Jesus complains, 'The
foxes have holes, and the birds of the air have nests; but the Son
of man hath not where to lay his head.' So, 'when they had sent
away the multitude' – 'That's it! Goodnight! Thank you for
coming!' – 'they took him even as he was in the ship' – without
a change of clothing – 'And there were also with him other
little ships' – he obviously could not shake off his entire
audience; some of them had been listening from neighbouring
crafts. 'And there arose a great storm of wind' – which
evidently happens very suddenly on the Sea of Galilee – 'and
the waves beat into the ship, so that it was now full.' Consternation! Where was Jesus? 'And he was in the hinder part
of the ship, asleep on a pillow' – exhausted from the day's
teaching in the sun; exhausted from the demands of the curious
and the faithful; 'and they awake him' – '*You* do it! No, *you* do
it!' – 'And say unto him' – shout unto him more likely –
'Master, carest thou not that we perish?' Things must have
been very bad; after all, at least four of the disciples were
experienced fisherman. 'And he arose, and rebuked the wind'
– What?! – 'and said unto the sea' – he spoke to the sea?! You
mean he *spoke* to the sea?! What did he say to the sea? – 'Peace,
be still.' What good did that do? 'And the wind ceased, and

there was a great calm.' It was a coincidence! Of course it was a coincidence! It must have been a coincidence! I expect even Jesus was surprised. 'And he said unto them, Why are ye so fearful? how is it that ye have no faith?' Straightway into the attack! No mercy shown! They were about to drown for God's sake! *'Why are ye so fearful? how is it that ye have no faith?* What were they doing with this young preacher? Why had they left their safe jobs? How was it going to end? 'And they feared exceedingly' – of course! 'and said one to another' – muttered more likely – 'What manner of man is this, that even the wind and the sea obey him?' That's just what *I* was muttering.

5

THREE MIRACLES

Chapter Five consists of accounts of three miracles.

Each story is strange, and each miracle is difficult to believe; but then *all* miracles are difficult to believe. Mark spends longer on these stories than he has done on his previous accounts of miracles, and for this reason they assume a slightly worrying significance.

First, Jesus cures a raving madman, who lives in a graveyard and obviously terrorises the neighbourhood. In the course of this miracle, two thousand pigs commit suicide.

Second, a woman who has been bleeding for twelve years creeps up behind Jesus in a crowd, and heals herself by touching his garment.

Third, Jesus is asked to heal a little girl, who lies ill in a nearby house. She dies while he is on his way to her. Then, in front of her parents and three of his disciples, he raises her from the dead.

These are amazing happenings. These are tales of desperate people. In each instance, Jesus shows a rare authority. But I do not think that in themselves these strange stories advance the ministry of Jesus, nor do they, in themselves, help us to love him more. They obviously impressed the disciples, and Peter's memory of them is full of vivid detail. But, apart from the astonishment they caused, these miracles do not seem to me to serve any purpose.

The value of Chapter Five lies in what Jesus *says* during the course of these amazing incidents. He is reported as saying very little, but the few sentences we have certainly further our understanding of his personality; and there are five words – making up two commands – which are perhaps the most precious words in the entire Gospel. And because of these five words this is an important chapter. Here is the first story.

'*And they came over unto the other side of the sea, into the country of the Gadarenes. And when he was come out of the ship, immediately there met him out of the tombs a man with an unclean spirit, Who had his dwelling among the tombs; and no man could bind him, no, not with chains: Because that he had been often bound with fetters and chains, and the chains had been plucked asunder by him, and the fetters broken in pieces; neither could any man tame him. And always, night and day, he was in the mountains, and in the tombs, crying, and cutting himself with stones. But when he saw Jesus afar off, he ran and worshipped him, And cried with a loud voice, and said, What have I to do with thee, Jesus, thou Son of the most high God? I adjure thee by God, that thou torment me not. For he said unto him, Come out of the man, thou unclean spirit. And he asked him, What is thy name? And he answered, saying, My name is Legion: for we are many. And be besought him much that he would not send them away out of the country. Now there was there nigh unto the mountains a great herd of swine feeding. And all the devils besought him, saying, Send us into the swine, that we may enter into them. And forthwith Jesus gave them leave. And the unclean spirits went out, and entered into the swine: and the herd ran violently down a steep place into the sea, (they were about two thousand;) and were choked in the sea. And they that fed the swine fled, and told it in the city, and in the country. And they went out to see what it was that was done. And they come to Jesus, and see him that was possessed with the devil, and had the legion, sitting, and clothed, and in his right mind: and they were afraid. And they that saw it told them how it befell to him that was possessed with the devil, and also concerning the swine. And they began to pray him to depart out of their coasts. And when he was come into the ship, he that had been possessed with the devil prayed him that he might be with him. Howbeit Jesus suffered him not, but sayeth unto him, Go home to thy friends, and tell them how great things the Lord hath done for thee, and hath had compassion on thee. And he departed, and began to publish in Decapolis how great things Jesus had done for him: and all men did marvel.*'*

After the great storm on the Sea of Galilee, Jesus and his disciples land in 'the country of the Gadarenes'. Although this is not an enormous distance from the Capernaum side, it seems as if they have landed on another planet. We do not know if it is late in the evening of the 'parable day' by the sea, or whether they spent the night on board the ship, and went ashore in the morning. I think it is probably dawn.

'And immediately' (of course 'immediately'!) Jesus was confronted by a wild man with an unclean spirit who sprang out from some tombs. According to St Luke he 'ware no clothes'. And according to St Matthew there were actually *two* men. Mark describes the man's existence with more detail than anything else so far in the Gospel. We learn that he had enormous strength, and obviously terrified his countrymen who made frequent attempts to tame him or bind him with fetters and chains. He always broke free. He rushed about the mountains and tombs yelling and trying to wound himself. It was the most extreme case of an unclean spirit taking possession of a person that Jesus had yet met. But what does it mean?

Perhaps a clue is to be found in the location. Mark assumes that we know all about the 'country of the Gadarenes'. Perhaps it was predominantly Gentile country. Perhaps the residents were renowned pagans. We soon learn that there was a huge herd of pigs nearby. The Jews did not keep or eat pigs. Perhaps the unhappy man was a deeply religious person living in an unsympathetic community. In the first recorded encounter with a similarly affected man in the temple at the start of the Gospel, I put forward a theory that these split personalities were perhaps people who could not express their religious feelings openly. If this was difficult for them living among the stern and rigid establishment, perhaps it was even more difficult for the man living among pagans.

This is all surmise; but the wild man in the country of the Gadarenes certainly rushed to Jesus with eagerness and cried for help. He displays the same split behaviour of simultaneously worshipping Jesus, and at the same time begging Jesus to leave him alone – 'torment me not.' His devils want to be left in peace.

Jesus behaves with his usual calm. He directs the devils to come out, and then coolly asks the man his name. Had anyone asked this man his name before? He was probably totally shunned by the populace – except when they tried to tame him or to chain him up. The man makes a wonderful reply; in a passionate attempt to prove to Jesus the strength of his possession, he says that 'my name is Legion'. This was like saying that his body was occupied by six thousand armed men. (I am not fond of the Good News translation: 'My name is "Mob".' It sounds like one of Kipling's Jungle Book animals.)

Now the story becomes totally incomprehensible. The man begs Jesus not to send his devils 'away out of the country'. And the devils themselves suggest that Jesus sends them into the nearby herd of swine.

Jesus agrees. The swine stampede.

And they run straight into the sea.

What on earth happened?

It is possible that the exorcism caused the man called Legion to have an attack similar to the one reported in the first chapter. Mark wrote then that 'when the unclean spirit had torn him, and cried with a loud voice, he came out of him'. Perhaps the Gadarene wild man cried with an even louder voice. Perhaps he scared the pigs. (Perhaps, if he was Jewish, he hated the pigs and *wanted* to scare them.)

But I cannot believe that this is what Jesus intended. It seems totally out of character. Those two thousand pigs were the livelihood of the local people; they weren't doing any harm.

Then, evidently, there followed another stampede. The swineherds, frightened to death, rushed to tell their fellow countrymen what had happened. 'And they went out to see what it was that was done.'

There must be a lapse of time here. When the people arrived, the wild man was not only sitting, 'and in his right mind', he was also fully clothed. Perhaps the disciples had some spare clothing on board the ship. Perhaps the wild man was calmly sitting having breakfast with Jesus and the disciples and telling them his story. But this would hardly have been a comfort to the owners of the pigs. The miracle was not popular. Nobody wanted to risk another. The populace begged Jesus to leave – and it appears that he readily agreed. The wild man seems to have followed Jesus aboard the ship, and then 'prayed him that he might be with him'.

How would Jesus be feeling? The excursion into the country of the Gadarenes had not exactly been a success. He had barely got a foothold into it. Now the people were firmly seeing him off. It was a big contrast to the adulation he usually received. There was only the cure and conversion of the wild man to demonstrate his power. And, for the first and only time reported in the Gospel, Jesus gave instructions to a beneficiary of a cure to go and tell the people what had happened to him. 'Go home to thy friends' (I hope he had some friends!) 'and tell them how great things the Lord hath done for thee, and hath had compassion on thee.' And we learn that the man subsequently became a successful missionary for Jesus.

It is a very strange story.

Why does Mark give it so much space? There are twenty verses devoted to this episode compared to only six verses allotted to the cure of a leper, and five verses given to the first cure of a man with an unclean spirit in the first chapter.

One might think that Mark – and Peter – would have wanted to hush up this story. (Luke shortens it to fourteen verses, and Matthew to seven.) But perhaps it was the fact that this was a foray into pagan country that made it especially memorable. And perhaps it was also the fact that the story is uncharacteristic of Jesus; not only that the cure of the wild man had the unfortunate side effect on the swine, but also, for the first time, Jesus asks that his healing power be made known. It is an exceptional story in the Gospel. It is also partly incomprehensible.

To me, its value lies in its failure. The failure of Jesus to convert the people. Its value also lies in the vanity of Jesus wanting his healing powers to be known in this unsympathetic region. The fact that the ministry was not a complete push-over is a comforting reality, and makes the Gospel all the more believable. The fact that Jesus could sometimes behave in a contradictory manner is also a comfort. It makes him more accessible. The fact that Peter recalled the incident so fully is perhaps because of these reasons. And the fact that Mark included it in his Gospel is perhaps because he liked everything about Jesus.

'What manner of man is this?' A complex one.

*

The next two stories also get a fuller account in St Mark than in St Matthew or St Luke. (Nevertheless, Matthew and Luke retain Mark's surprising order of events.) Here again Peter obviously remembered vividly, and the words come tumbling out in a rush of wonderful narrative.

'And when Jesus was passed over again by ship unto the other side, **21** much people gathered unto him: and he was nigh unto the sea. And, behold, there cometh one of the rulers of the synagogue, Jairus by name; and when he saw him, he fell at his feet, And besought him greatly, saying, My little daughter lieth at the point of death: I pray thee, come and lay thy hands on her, that she may be healed; and she shall live. And Jesus went with him; and much people followed him, and thronged him.

And a certain woman, which had an issue of blood twelve years, **25** And had suffered many things of many physicians, and had spent all that she had, and was nothing bettered, but rather grew worse, When she had heard of Jesus, came in the press behind, and touched his garment. For she said, If I may touch but his clothes, I shall be whole. And straightway the fountain of her blood was dried up; and she felt in her body that she was healed of that plague. And Jesus, immediately knowing in himself that virtue had gone out of him, turned him about in the press, and said, Who touched my clothes? And his disciples said unto him, Thou seest the multitude thronging thee, and sayest thou, Who touched me? And he looked round about to see her that had done this thing. But the woman fearing and trembling, knowing what was done in her, came and fell down before him, and told him in all truth. And he said unto her, Daughter, thy faith hath made thee whole; go in peace, and be whole of thy plague.

While he yet spake, there came from the ruler of the synagogue's **35** house certain which said, Thy daughter is dead: why troublest thou the master any further? As soon as Jesus heard the word that was spoken, he saith unto the ruler of the synagogue, Be not afraid, only believe. And he suffered no man to follow him, save Peter, and James, and John the brother of James. And he cometh to the house of the ruler of the synagogue, and seeth the tumult, and them that wept and wailed greatly. And when he was come in, he saith unto them, Why make ye this ado and weep? the damsel is not dead, but sleepeth. And they laughed him to scorn. But when he had put them all out, he taketh the father and the mother of the damsel, and them that were with him, and entereth in where the damsel was lying. And he took the damsel by the hand, and said unto her, Talitha cumi; which is, being interpreted, Damsel, I say unto thee, arise. And straightway the damsel arose, and walked; for she was of the age of twelve years. And they were *astonished with a great astonishment. And he charged them straightly that no man should know it; and commanded that something should be given her to eat.'*

The words are as fresh as if these stories happened yesterday. The sense of movement, the urgency of the supplicants, the turmoil of the crowds, all these things are wonderfully conveyed. And, in the middle of these highly populated human dramas, five words of Jesus stand out like a grand monument.

As soon as Jesus gets to the other side of the Sea of Galilee, the people gather again. The demands begin again. His reputation must have been very high because 'one of the rulers of the synagogue, Jairus by name', risks the displeasure of the hierarchy by falling at Jesus's feet and humbly begging for help. Jairus's actual words are remembered and quoted. He must have been a desperate man to kneel at the feet of the friend of publicans and sinners. Perhaps Jesus had a moment's reflection before he consented to go with him. Perhaps he reflected on the growth of his reputation. Perhaps there was a slight temptation to refuse. I sense a little hesitation at this point, a hovering of decision before the words 'and Jesus went with him'.

We do not know how far they walked. We do not know how long it took. We learn that the crowds were huge, and perhaps the disciples tried to protect Jesus from them. They didn't have much success. If Peter was recalling these events for Mark, it sounds as if he suddenly broke off his narrative. Another memory came flooding back. 'Wait a minute! It was at this point – I remember now! And a certain woman . . .' This story told within a story has an endearingly natural quality. Nobody could invent this construction. Having embarked on the tale of Jairus and aroused our curiosity about Jesus's association with that desperate ruler of the synagogue and his sick daughter, Mark suddenly plunges into another tale; another desperate human being demands our attention.

'And a certain woman . . .'

Peter's voice is wonderfully clear at this point. He is scandalised by the story he tells; each disgraceful piece of information piles on top of the other:

'Which had an issue of blood twelve years' – can you imagine such a thing!

'And had suffered many things of many physicians' – Oh, those doctors!

'And had spent all that she had' – Poor soul!

And then comes the unbelievable piece of information that clinches the scandal:

'*And was nothing bettered, but rather grew worse!*'

Peter then gets back to the main theme:

'When she had heard of Jesus, came in the press behind, and touched his garment.'

This story, told in parenthesis with the Jairus story, is also full of parenthetical information; information which the woman must have given after the miracle happened.

The reason why the woman behaved in such a furtive manner was probably because of the embarrassing nature of her complaint; but it was also a fact that 'The disease rendered her ceremonially unclean, and thus she was debarred all religious and social life.' (Marshall). She was obviously a brave and determined woman. She was convinced that she could – and would – cure herself by touching Jesus's clothes. She didn't need to speak to him. She needn't bother anybody. Anonymous among the crowd, she caught up with Jesus and touched a fringe or tassel of his outer garment. And she was cured! How did she know this instantly? We cannot tell. But Mark writes – typically using a 'straightway' and an 'immediately' – 'And *straightway* the fountain of her blood was dried up; and she felt in her body that she was healed of that plague. And Jesus, *immediately* knowing in himself that virtue had gone out of him, turned him about in the press and said, "Who touched my clothes?"' The moving crowd comes to a sudden standstill. Probably the people at the back pushed the people at the front. Everybody was touching everybody. The disciples make a bad joke. They are hot, and perhaps irritable. They jeer at Jesus with an authentic familiarity, 'Thou seest the multitude thronging thee, and sayest thou, Who touched me?' Jesus ignores them. Perhaps the crowd senses a drama. Jesus is looking around him. Perhaps the crowd grows quiet. And then, out of the silence, the woman, filled with guilt at her secret action, filled with dread at her sudden notoriety, but also filled with wonder at the sudden miracle of her healing, makes herself known. She falls at the feet of Jesus and tells the story that Mark has already told us.

To Jesus, this incident must have seemed like a reward. We have heard of many demands made on him. We know that at times he had to hide from people for self-protection. Even at this moment he is on an errand of mercy for a man who 'besought him greatly'. This woman had worked her own miracle. She had not troubled him. He recognises her faith and, significantly, addresses her as a relative. 'Daughter' he says, 'Daughter, thy faith hath made thee whole.' She is related to Jesus by faith.

And he blesses her.

Then the Gospel continues at breakneck speed: 'While he yet spake, there came from the ruler of the synagogue's house certain which said, Thy daughter is dead.' We have forgotten Jairus in the drama of the woman. How did he behave during this delay? He must have been very anxious. Now he learns that his daughter is dead. It is a small unimportant detail, but if we read Mark's account literally – and I see no reason not to do this – when Jesus said to the woman, 'Daughter, thy faith hath made thee whole,' it is possible that the messengers from the house heard him and then broke the news to Jairus with the comparative inflexion, '*Thy* daughter is *dead*.' They may also have been embarrassed by the ruler of the synagogue's association with Jesus, and the messenger's next words – 'why troublest thou the master any further?' – could have been spoken in order to get Jairus away. But Jesus overheard them. Jesus had overheard that Jairus's daughter was dead. And he then said the five words which stand like a monument in the midst of these stories. I do not know whether he said them loudly or softly, quickly or slowly, but they have echoed in our ears for two thousand years. He said to a man who had just heard that this daughter was dead: 'Be not afraid, only believe.'

They were still standing by the woman whose faith had made her whole. She had provided an example which might possibly have given Jesus additional power and strength. It is possible that her faith was the inspiration for what happened next. In the midst of the great crowd, Jesus challenged the newly bereft father with two mysterious commands: 'Be not afraid' (be not afraid of death?), 'only believe' (only believe in life?).

And then he started to act with total authority.

He instructed the thronging crowds not to follow him – and it would seem that, like lambs, they obeyed. He took Peter and James and John, and walked with Jairus to the house. There were already many mourners. It may be that some were family and some were professional. ('The Jews hired professional mourners.' Marshall. 'Flute players were essential.' Barclay. 'Even the poorest in Israel should have not less than two flutes and one wailing woman.' (quoted by Sherman E. Johnson.) Jesus looked at them, and then said: 'Why make ye this ado, and weep? the damsel is not dead, but sleepeth.'

The reaction was angry. 'They laughed him to scorn.'

He put them all out.

It would seem that Jairus did not question Jesus as he took complete control of the household.

Jesus led the small group into the room where the little girl lay dead. The mother had joined them.

Jesus knew exactly what he was going to do.

He held the little girl's hand and commanded her to rise. The actual Aramaic words are given only in St Mark. 'Talitha cumi.'

'And straightway' – of course, 'straightway!' – the girl got up and walked. It is then that the parenthetical Mark tells us that she is twelve years old. He also reports the greatest astonishment so far in the Gospel. And then Jesus commands the family not to talk about it, and interrupts their joy with the prosaic reminder, 'Something should be given her to eat.'

It is no wonder that, as well as being an inspiration, Jesus disconcerts and perplexes us. It is natural to want a hero, to want a super-man, to want to worship someone stronger and more powerful than ourselves. We would prefer a separation between fallible mankind and infallible God. It is easier to endure a life ruled by fate rather than by our own choice. We do not like to be reminded that 'the fault, dear Brutus, lies not in our stars, but in ourselves that we are underlings'.

In this staggering story of a girl raised from the dead, Jesus emerges as an ordinary man. He performs the miracle in private; he then asks that it is not talked about; and then, like a general practitioner, he prescribes a little nourishment for the patient.

How are we to understand him?

How are we to emulate him?

He has just told us.

'Only believe.'

This challenge has nagged for two thousand years.

We would prefer to build cathedrals, compose sacred masses, paint the Sistine Chapel. We would prefer to fast or fight crusades. We try to evade the ordinary words.

'Only believe.'

'Stand up!' 'Sit down!' 'Wake up!' 'Only believe!'

Only?

Easier to fly to the moon.

6

HOME; HEROD; AND HIGH SPIRITS

'And he went out from thence, and came into his own country; and his disciples follow him. And when the sabbath day was come, he began to teach in the synagogue: and many hearing him were astonished, saying, From whence hath this man these things? and what wisdom is this which is given unto him, that even such mighty works are wrought by his hands? Is not this the carpenter, the son of Mary, the brother of James, and Joses, and of Juda, and Simon? and are not his sisters here with us? And they were offended at him. But Jesus said unto them, A prophet is not without honour, but in his own country, and among his own kin, and in his own house. And he could there do no mighty work, save that he laid his hands upon a few sick folk, and healed them. And he marvelled because of their unbelief. And he went round about the villages teaching.'

After the exciting events reported in Chapter Five, Jesus decides to go home. It reads as if he was in a hurry. It reads as if he walked right out of the ruler of the synagogue's house and started on his way to Nazareth; 'and his disciples follow him' – perhaps trying to keep up with him. I have an image of Jesus striding in front of the rest – sometimes breaking into a run of impatience; sometimes bounding ahead with high spirits. I dislike the portrayal of Jesus as a dignified, carefully robed, slow-moving figure. I bet Jesus loved running.

And I cannot help having a contemporary Englishman's idea of 'home'. I know it is not correct, but at this point in the Gospel I have a sentimental picture of Jesus returning to his boyhood haven; to his own bed and his own room; seeing his old possessions and old friends; being spoilt by his mother with favourite dishes; being safe and protected from the dangers and demands of the adult outside world. It is unlikely

that Jesus had his own bed or his own room; he probably had
few possessions; but perhaps there were old friends, and
perhaps his mother spoilt him. Or maybe he *hoped* that she
would. Perhaps, according to his time and place in history,
Jesus's thoughts weren't so very different from our own at the
prospect of returning home.

In the report from Nazareth, this sentimental picture is soon
to be shattered. Of course we do not know how Jesus was
received by his mother and the family. It was probably a
mixed reception. When the family had come to the house
where the multitude was so great 'that they could not so much
as eat bread', and had 'sent unto him, calling him', it seems that
Jesus behaved in a very casual manner towards them. We do
not know if he even saw them after he had finished teaching. It
could be that this visit home was partly to make amends.

And where did the disciples live during this time? Did
they stay with relatives of Jesus? How did they behave?
Did they antagonise the family with their admiration for
Jesus? Did they boast about the crowds and the miracles and
the adulation by the shores of Galilee? It would be natural
for them to be possessive. This could have aroused jealousy
and made the family feel like outsiders.

Equally, the disciples could have made themselves unpopu-
lar with the townsfolk. Perhaps even *before* the sabbath there
was a hardening of hearts towards the returning local hero.

In his report of Jesus teaching in the synagogue 'when the
sabbath day was come', Mark uses his gossiping voices again.
At the start of the ministry, in the synagogue at Capernaum,
the voices were full of wonder. Now, they are unsympathetic
and critical. 'From whence hath *this man* these things? and
what wisdom is this which is given unto *him*, that even such
mighty works are wrought by his hands? Then we reach the
heart of the matter: '*Is not this the carpenter . . . ?*

St Mark's is the only Gospel that refers to Jesus as a
carpenter. St Matthew refers to him as 'the carpenter's son'.

There is a splendid entry about Jesus Christ in the 1932
edition of the Encyclopedia Britannica. This is the first sentence. 'The principal problem which is presented by the New
Testament to the historian is the problem of accounting for the
faith of the early Christians in one whom they had known as

Jesus the carpenter's son in Nazareth, and whom they had seen die the shameful death of a criminal outside Jerusalem.'

The faith of the early Christians is not easy to understand. Jesus did not present the expected image and personality of the Messiah. On this visit to Nazareth, Jesus was not making any claims to being the Son of God, but he obviously taught with amazing authority, and the 'mighty works' 'wrought by his hands' were obviously known. The little people of Nazareth knew him to be a carpenter. They could not accept a higher status. There are people today who can only accept his higher status and will not accept the fact that he may have been a carpenter. 'Nowhere in the New Testament is Jesus of Nazareth referred to as the carpenter except here, by people who were unbelievers. If you are prone to refer to Him as 'the man of Galilee', don't do it. You are not honoring Him in either case. The only people in those days who referred to Him in that manner were unbelievers. He is Christ Jesus. Give Him His name and His honour, the Lord Jesus Christ.' That is by Manford George Gutzke who obviously likes titled folk.

But, to the people of Nazareth, Jesus was not only a carpenter, he was also the boy from down the road. His very ordinary relations were well-known neighbours. And, in Mark, the relations are specifically mentioned by the unbelieving people. He is 'the son of Mary'; he is 'the brother of James, and Joses, and of Juda, and Simon'. And finally, as if to clinch the matter, they ask, 'And are not his sisters here with us?'

Jesus must have been disappointed by his reception, but he makes a wry joke about it. I don't know whether he was the first person to coin the saying, 'A prophet is not without honour, but in his own country'. There are many variations of it. But, on this occasion, Jesus sadly adds the words, 'and among his own kin, and in his own house.' These seem like specific complaints.

Let us look at the family.

There is no mention in St Mark's Gospel of a father – except in heaven. There is no mention of Mary's husband Joseph – who is well featured in St Matthew, St Luke, and St John. We do not know for certain whether James and Joses and Juda and Simon were real brothers or half-brothers or step-brothers. As usual Rev. Marshall does his best. He surmises that they could be cousins – on either Mary's or Joseph's side, or that they were the children of Joseph by a former marriage, or that they were the children of Mary and Joseph . . . which covers just about everything. The sisters remain anonymous.

My own conviction is that Jesus was an early child, conceived before Mary married Joseph. I believe that Jesus's feelings towards his family were ambiguous. And it would seem that their feelings towards him were also uncertain. On this visit home he complains that he is not honoured by his own kin, or in his own house; but this could mean that he was simply treated with the cheerful disrespect common in relationships among large families.

Anyway, despite the attitude of his family and the local people, it seems that during this visit he stayed in the neighbourhood for some time, and, presumably, lived at home. It is probable that he had a natural affection for the place where he grew up.

After the adulation of multitudes and the diverse miraculous acts of healing – particularly his sensational success in raising a child from the dead – there might have been a human desire for homely anonymity. There might also have been a need for re-charging. It might be that Jesus was tired.

Certainly the people of his home town defied his powers. There was no return of faith. 'And he could do there no mighty work' – and then Mark adds one of his adorable provisos – 'save that he laid his hands upon a few sick folk, and healed them.' I always think of these as being very minor miracles: mending a broken finger; curing a toothache; perhaps relieving a stubborn constipation.

Jesus was surprised by this resistance: 'And he marvelled because of their unbelief' – but he didn't waste any time over it. He ignored his town's folk, and went round about the local villages – not healing, but 'teaching'.

'And he called unto him the twelve, and began to send them forth by two and two.'

If Jesus stayed in the Nazareth region and lived at his home for any length of time, it is possible that the disciples became restless, and this was why he sent them out on their own. I imagine they arranged to meet up again at a certain place on a certain day, and, as we shall discover, that place would seem to have been somewhere by the Sea of Galilee. It was certainly not back in Nazareth.

Once again we see the practical side of Jesus as he sends them out in pairs. A disciple on his own might be lonely and frightened. Two disciples could support each other. Three might have quarrelled.

'And gave them power over unclean spirits.'

I do not know how he did this, except by the transmission of his faith. The disciples wouldn't dare to fail. Also, they had seen the way in which Jesus behaved with these tormented people; doubtless they would try to emulate his power and authority.

'And commanded them that they should take nothing for their 8
journey, save a staff only; no scrip, no bread, no money in their purse: 9
But be shod with sandals; and not put on two coats.'

Jesus was a hard man. Whatever possessions the disciples owned or acquired had to be left behind – although I imagine that they always travelled light. Nevertheless, on this their first experience of preaching the word, he did not allow them to take food, money, or even a begging bag (scrip). He also instructed them to keep their clothes down to a minimum. The translations vary with this order: 'to wear sandals and not put on two tunics' (Revised Standard Version); 'not even an extra pair of shoes or a change of clothes' (The Living Bible); 'wear sandals, but don't carry an extra shirt' (Good News). Take your pick!

'And he said unto them, In what place soever ye enter into an 10
house, there abide till ye depart from that place. And whosoever shall 11
not receive you, nor hear you, when ye depart thence, shake off the
dust under your feet for a testimony against them.'

Eastern hospitality demanded that strangers were entertained. 'When a stranger arrives in a village or an encampment, the neighbours one after another must invite him to eat with them. There is a strict etiquette about it, involving much ostentation and hypocrisy; and a failure in the due observance of this hospitality is violently resented and often leads to feuds among neighbours. It also consumes much time, causes unusual distractions of mind, and every way counteracts the success of a spiritual mission.' (Marshall quoting Thomson's *Land and the Book*.)

This is presumably why Jesus instructed the disciples to stay in *one house* 'till ye depart from that place'. It was to save time and avoid feuds among neighbours. On the other hand, if the disciples met with a lack of hospitality, and encountered people who were not keen to listen to them, Jesus's instructions were ruthless: 'Shake off the dust under your feet for a testimony against them.' This was a symbolic action which meant that the disciples totally dissociated themselves from the inhospitable people. It was in fact the equivalent of calling them 'heathen'. It is very likely that the disciples protested at this point for Jesus continued with typical insistence:

'Verily I say unto you, It shall be more tolerable for Sodom and Gomorrha in the day of judgment, than for that city.'

When I discovered that this sentence was cut in the Revised Standard, The Living Bible, The Jerusalem Bible, the Good News – in fact all versions except the King James – my libertine blood was aroused. How dare the puritans cut out this beautiful example of the tolerance of Jesus! But the reasons for the later translations leaving out the sentence are evidently because of some manuscript discovery. Since the sentence is still to be found in St Matthew one cannot truthfully expose a nasty cover-up job. But I am very sorry that it should disappear from later translations of St Mark. It is a wonderful indication of the humanity of Jesus of Nazareth. It is like the thrilling news that 'all sins shall be forgiven unto the sons of men, and blasphemies wherewith soever they shall blaspheme'. I take it to mean that sexual excess and general dissipation are not likely to be condemned as much as unkindness or inhospitality. It is Jesus on the side of publicans and sinners. It is perhaps another small indication that Jesus was not only well aware of the tug of war between the spiritual and the physical, he was also very sympathetic towards the physical side.

'And they went out, and preached that men should repent. And they cast out many devils, and anointed with oil many that were sick, and healed them.'

They were obviously a great success.

★

94

Since Jesus prepared the disciples to stay more than one night in various houses in various places, it could be that their travels took several weeks. Mark takes advantage of this time lapse in the ministry of Jesus to bring us up to date with the story of John the Baptist.

This is an entire story on its own; and the contrast of its characters and location, with the journeys of Jesus and the twelve, is startling. While Jesus is taking a less active role in the ministry, the story of John the Baptist, with Herod and his awful wife and step-daughter, makes us aware of the dangers abroad at that time for a religious teacher.

The story is told backwards.

'*And King Herod heard of him (for his name was spread abroad:)*   14
and he said, That John the Baptist was risen from the dead, and
therefore mighty works do show forth themselves in him. Others said,   15
that it is Elias. And others said, That it is a prophet, or as one of the
prophets. But when Herod heard thereof, he said, It is John, whom I   16
beheaded: he is risen from the dead.'

The opening section of the story is important for two reasons. First, it gives us an idea of Jesus's reputation at that time. I am very fond of Mark's typical understatement 'for his name was spread abroad'. This is particularly low-key after we have heard that multitudes from Galilee, Judaea, Jerusalem, Idumaea, from beyond Jordan, and 'they about Tyre and Sidon' have already flocked to see and hear Jesus. The royalty of the time must have led a protected life. They were a bit slower at hearing the country's hot news. Finally, however, the story of Jesus's teaching and healing reached the ears of Herod, tetrarch of Galilee and Peraea.

Secondly, this section reveals Herod's guilt about the murder of John the Baptist. Once again we hear Mark's gossiping voices. This time they are in imaginary conversation with the tetrarch, who immediately makes an association between Jesus and John. Herod thinks that, if someone is going round the country performing miracles and urging the people to repent, it must be John the Baptist 'risen from the dead'. Some of the people, who are not afflicted with any guilt, hopefully imagine that it is Elias. (This is another name for Elijah, of whom it is written in Malachi 4: 5: 'Behold, I will send you Elijah the prophet before the coming of the great and dreadful day of the Lord.') Other people are less specific. They vaguely imagine that Jesus is some *new* prophet. It had been a long time since there had been a major prophet in the land. But Herod replies categorically, 'It is John, whom I beheaded' – he sounds like a man hounded by guilt – and then he adds for the second time, 'He is risen from the dead.'

Today, resurrection is unimaginable. At that time, it was obviously thought of as a possible idea.

Now the story plunges into flashback and starts to lurch about.

'For Herod himself had sent forth and laid hold upon John, and bound him in prison for Herodias's sake . . .'

Who?

'. . . his brother Philip's wife . . .'

Ah!

'. . . for he had married her.'

Gracious!

'For John had said unto Herod, It is not lawful for thee to have thy brother's wife.'

Presumably he said this *after* the event. Rev. Marshall tells us that it was 'not lawful' for three reasons.

(1) The former husband of Herodias was still living.

(2) The former wife of Herod was still living.

(3) Herodias was the niece of Herod.

It was therefore a pretty scandalous affair. Nevertheless it would seem that John was the only person to make an open attack on it. How did the two principals react?

'Therefore Herodias had a quarrel against him and would have killed him . . .'

She was obviously very angry.

'. . . but she could not . . .'

Why?

'. . . For Herod feared John, knowing that he was a just man and an holy . . .'

This must have been when he 'bound him in prison'.

'. . . and observed him; and when he heard him, he did many things, and heard him gladly.'

This scene conjures up a likeable picture of Herod visiting John in his cell, and having long theological discussions; desperately trying to separate the incestuous marriage from the rest of his behaviour. It is probable that Herodias discovered that these private talks were going on, and became even more determined to get rid of John. It does not sound a restful household.

The story takes another lurch forward.

'And when a convenient day was come . . .' 21

Convenient? Convenient for whom?

'. . . that Herod on his birthday . . .'

His birthday!

'. . . made a supper to his lords, high captains, and chief estates of Galilee . . .'

Herod obviously liked a good party. ('Following the practice of the Roman Emperors who kept their birthdays with magnificent banquets.' Marshall)

'And when the daughter of the said Herodias came in . . .' 22

The daughter? Nobody said anything about a daughter! What was she doing?

'. . . and danced and pleased Herod and them that sat with him . . .'

Remember she was his step-daughter, and they were probably all drunk.

'. . . the king said unto the damsel, Ask of me whatsoever thou wilt, and I will give it thee.'

The daughter obviously couldn't believe her ears. So Herod spelt it out for her.

'And he sware unto her, Whatsoever thou shalt ask of me, I will give it thee, unto the half of my kingdom.' 23

He sounds like an intoxicated King Lear.

The daughter, who seems to have had very little imagination, cannot think of anything she wants. She may have been dim-witted.

'And she went forth, and said unto her mother, What shall I ask?' 24

Presumably her mother was longing for all the drunken high captains, lords and chief estates of Galilee to go home. Her daughter's vacuous question gives her a vicious idea. If Herod was drunk, it might just possibly work.

'And she said, The head of John the Baptist.'

The daughter, with surprising obedience, doesn't argue. Probably nobody argued with Herodias. She didn't ask for jewellery, robes, or even a few more dancing lessons.

25   *'And she came in straightway with haste unto the king . . .'*

Perhaps Herodias had told her sharply to get a move on before the king sobered up.

'. . . and asked, saying, I will that thou give me by and by in a charger the head of John the Baptist.'

The charger seems to have been the daughter's idea. At least she got *something* out of it. (I like the Living Bible translation: 'I want the head of John the Baptist – right now – on a tray.' With an order of French fries?)

26   *'And the king was exceeding sorry . . .'*

Well, of course he would be! But, after all, it was his own fault.

'. . . yet for his oath's sake, and for their sakes which sat with him, he would not reject her.'

The events turn sour. No party can ever have fallen so flat. The jerky, colloquial tone of the story changes to factual reporting. The scandal becomes a squalid tale of pettiness, jealousy and greed.

27
28   *'And immediately the king sent an executioner, and commanded his head to be brought: and he went and beheaded him in the prison, And brought his head in a charger, and gave it to the damsel: and the damsel*
29   *gave it to her mother. And when his disciples heard of it, they came and took up his corpse, and laid it in a tomb.'*

This isolated account of John the Baptist and Herod in the Gospel of St Mark is written in a much looser narrative style than the main story of the ministry of Jesus. It is certainly not a first-hand narrative. It has the style of someone struggling to remember the order of events. It has the naturalness of re-corded, unedited story-telling. It is as if someone was suddenly asked on a chat programme to recall a notorious royal or political scandal. It is very intriguing because of the personalities involved. And it is a curious precursor of the great events to come.

★

Now we return to the main story. There is a happy reunion. For the first, and only, time in the Gospel, the disciples are called apostles. What is the difference?

'*"Disciple"* one who receives or professes to receive instruction from another: a learner: a follower.'

'"*Apostle*" one expressly commissioned by Christ to preach the Gospel: an early or first missionary: a messenger.' (Nuttall's Standard Dictionary)

'And the apostles gathered themselves together unto Jesus, and told **30** *him all things, both what they had done, and what they had taught. And he said unto them, Come ye yourselves apart into a desert place, and rest awhile: for there were many coming and going, and they had no leisure so much as to eat. And they departed into a desert place by* **32** *ship privately.'*

As I have already proposed, Jesus must have left his home in Nazareth and joined up with the twelve somewhere by the Sea of Galilee. It may well have been at Capernaum, in order to give some of the disciples a chance to visit *their* homes. It makes a happy picture with them all telling their stories, boasting of their adventures, wanting praise for their successes. But, immediately they returned from their journeys, they found themselves engulfed in massive crowds again. Jesus was well known in Capernaum and the north-east shore of the Sea of Galilee, and he may have gone there before the disciples returned and attracted great attention. The disciples probably groaned and complained at the size of the crowds, and it is likely that Jesus thought that they deserved a rest.

Certainly, for the next few episodes of the ministry, Jesus himself is in wonderfully energetic form. He seems to have gathered strength from his stay in Nazareth. Now he decides it is the disciples' turn to take it easy. The group endeavour to leave without being noticed; perhaps it was in the same ship that they used during the parable day by the sea and the trip to the country of the Gadarenes. The King James Version's 'desert place' would be a 'deserted place' – not somewhere with a lot of sand and a palm tree.

'And the people saw them departing, and many knew him, and ran **33** *afoot thither out of all cities, and outwent them, and came together unto him.'*

William Barclay – who seems to know – writes: 'At this particular place it was four miles across the lake by boat and ten miles around the top of the lake on foot.' He also says that if it was a windless day 'a boat might take some time to make the passage, and an energetic person could walk round the top of the lake and be there before the boat arrived'. Barclay adds with admirable authority: 'That is exactly what happened.'

An energetic person can certainly walk ten miles, but we are shortly to discover that it was actually five thousand men who 'ran afoot thither out of all cities, and outwent them'. And, in *his* version, St. Matthew even adds (for which I am grateful) 'beside women and children'.

There was no holiday for the disciples.

34 *'And Jesus, when he came out, saw much people, and was moved with compassion toward them, because they were as sheep not having a shepherd: and he began to teach them many things.'*

This is another point in St Mark where the writing becomes very clear and personal. Although St Matthew and St Luke also record this story, St Mark's version is much more detailed, and the dialogue has a marvellously authentic ring. (St John also reports it but with a totally different beginning and end.)

Consider the reality of the situation: the disciples are tired from their missions and have been promised a rest; Jesus is fresh from his stay in Nazareth, and characteristically unable to resist the impressive display of faith from 'much people' who have chased him round the lake. He teaches them 'many things'. 'Much people.' 'Many things.'

In the light of this background to the story now read in the frustration of the twelve. Imagine the muttering as Jesus continues teaching, teaching . . . Remember the disciples have been on their own; they have been their own masters. Now they must take a supporting role again, attending on him. The shadows start to lengthen.

35
36 *'And when the day was now far spent, his disciples came unto him, and said, This is a desert place, and now the time is far passed: Send them away, that they may go into the country round about, and into the villages, and buy themselves bread: for they have nothing to eat.'*

This was probably spoken quietly so that the crowd could not hear.

Jesus ignores his disciples' request; he seems blithely unaware of their ill humour. With superb unconcern:

37 *'He answered and said unto them, Give ye them to eat.'*

This is too much for the disciples. It is not what they had in mind. They start to protest. The voices become ugly.

'And they say unto him, Shall we go and buy two hundred pennyworth of bread, and give them to eat?'

Two hundred pennyworth meant two hundred denarii. A denarius equalled a labourer's wages for a day's work. The Living Bible simply writes: 'It would take a fortune to buy food for all this crowd!'

Jesus was probably astonished by this outburst of bad temper from his disciples. He replies calmly, but the tension is apparent.

'He saith unto them, How many loaves have ye? go and see.' **38**

Between the practical question and the next three words, something must have happened. The disciples probably ridiculed Jesus. 'How many loaves have we!' Did Jesus imagine that their small rations would feed this enormous crowd? Was he totally out of his mind! 'And what about our holid . . .' Jesus's next three words suddenly thunder out, as if to naughty children. 'GO AND SEE!'

There is a pause in the proceedings while the disciples go back to the ship and sulkily check on the state of the pantry. When they return, the answer is taciturn.

'And when they knew, they say, Five, and two fishes.'

Jesus hadn't asked about any other food than the loaves. I think that the disciples added the news of 'two fishes' out of sheer impertinence.

Imagine hearing this story for the first time. Wouldn't one think that this was the end of the matter?

The writing now becomes impersonal. It is routine reporting. We are given a few facts and figures. We are almost lulled into thinking that nothing extraordinary is going to happen.

'And he commanded them to make all sit down by companies upon **39** *the green grass. And they sat down in ranks, by hundreds, and by fifties. And when he had taken the five loaves and the two fishes, he* **41** *looked up to heaven, and blessed, and brake the loaves, and gave them to his disciples to set before them; and the two fishes divided he among them all.'*

After this rather dull statistical information, Mark gives us four tremendous shocks. It is as if he explodes four firecrackers in our faces. Mark himself seems to be amazed by the reverberations of the miracle.

'And they did all eat . . .' **42**

First shock.

'and were filled.'

Second shock.

43 *'And they took up twelve baskets full of the fragments, and of the fishes.'*

Third shock.

44 *'And they that did eat of the loaves were about five thousand men.'*

('beside women and children.' St Matthew.)

Fourth shock.

For some reason which I do not understand, this miracle has a greater impact than any of the others reported in the Gospel. Perhaps it is the quality of the writing; perhaps it is the unexpectedness of the event; perhaps it is the fact that no one would dream of such a happening. St Mark himself pays tribute to it in an unexpected intrusion of his own feelings which we shall reach very soon.

The most puzzling part of the miracle is perhaps the twelve baskets full of fragments. This is reported in all four Gospels, and some commentators make great play with the numbers. Alan Cole has a surprising flight of fancy: 'Of the twelve, each disciple had gathered a basket full of pieces, and we may be sure that this was to be their food for the next day.' Robert Crotty writes: 'There were five books in the law of Moses and there were twelve tribes that constituted Israel.'

But I don't think that this has any relevance.

Was it an act of showmanship? – Is there a prosaic explanation?

Of course, we cannot comprehend it.

And of course it isn't necessary that we should.

Far better to read St John's Gospel, Chapter 6, 27–59.

And far better that we should hear the very human altercation between Jesus and the disciples echoing in our ears.

45 *'And straightway he constrained his disciples to get into the ship, and to go to the other side before unto Bethsaida, while he sent away*
46 *the people. And when he had sent them away, he departed into a mountain to pray.'*

Many things happen here. This is Mark at his most abrupt. *How and why* did Jesus constrain his disciples to leave him immediately after the feeding of the five thousand? Could it be that, by now, in addition to feeling harassed by the crowds, the disciples were utterly confused by the miracle? Having been fed, did it seem as if the multitude would settle down for the night? Was Jesus feeling sorry for the twelve? Or was he irritated by them? In most of the later translations it is simply written that Jesus 'made' the disciples get into the ship. I do not know why they changed the King James Version's beautiful word 'constrained'.

' "*Constrain*" to urge by force, either by impelling or restraining; to urge with irresistible power.'

I would think that the disciples were extremely reluctant to abandon Jesus to the five thousand. Whether or not there was still bad feeling, the disciples would probably need a lot of persuading to leave him. But Jesus, who seems at this time to be brimming with energy and power, preferred them to go. Whether from loving consideration, or from irritation, he 'constrained' them, he urged them with irresistible power, to get into the ship. And then, with equally irresistible power, he managed to disperse five thousand men – 'beside women and children'. Instinctively I feel that all of this was done by Jesus with enormous good humour; that his persuasion of the disciples, and then his persuasion of the crowd, was done with overwhelming charm.

Although it was a generous and no doubt welcome action, the miracle of the loaves and fishes was not vital. Immediately afterwards Jesus sent the crowd away; they could have gone home to eat, or bought themselves food 'in the country round about'. Jesus's *next* miracle is *totally* unnecessary. He seems to me, at this time, to be in uncontrollably high spirits. Having manipulated the disciples, and then the crowd, to leave him, he climbs a hill to pray, to 'find a place to be alone with heaven', to speak to his chosen father.

'*And when even was come, the ship was in the midst of the sea, and he alone on the land. And he saw them toiling in rowing; for the wind was contrary unto them: and about the fourth watch of the night he cometh unto them, walking upon the sea, and would have passed by them. But when they saw him walking upon the sea, they supposed it had been a spirit, and cried out: For they all saw him, and were troubled. And immediately he talked with them, and saith unto them, Be of good cheer: it is I; be not afraid. And he went up unto them into the ship; and the wind ceased: and they were sore amazed in*

47

*themselves beyond measure, and wondered. For they considered not
the miracle of the loaves: for their heart was hardened.'*

Before the miracle of the loaves and fishes Mark wrote,
'And when the day was now far spent;' and then the disciples
reminded Jesus, 'Now the time is far passed.' In this passage
we hear, 'And when even was come . . .' It seems to be a
protracted day. Rev. Marshall, with his store of information,
writes: ' *"Even"* – the Jews had two evenings – the first began
at 3 p.m. the second at sundown.' So that clears up that
problem.

Now consider the scene: 'The ship was in the midst of the
sea, and he alone on the land. And he saw them toiling in
rowing . . .'

Was Jesus unable to concentrate on praying?

Did he watch the disciples rowing against the wind for a
long time?

The fourth watch of the night started at 3 a.m. This is when
Jesus began to walk on the water going towards the ship. And
then Mark writes: 'and would have passed by them.'

D. E. Nineham, in his meticulously researched commentary on St Mark, writes: 'These words have never been really
satisfactorily explained.'

What on earth was Jesus doing?

What on earth is this story all about?

Of course it is cheap and blasphemous to suggest that Jesus
was playing the fool.

But that is what I *do* suggest.

The disciples, who have already had a terrible day, were
now in their ship battling with frightful weather. Jesus starts
walking upon the sea, catches them up, 'and would have
passed by them'.

'These words have never been really satisfactorily explained . . .'

George Eliot wrote: 'It is an uneasy lot at best, to be what we
call highly taught and yet not to enjoy: to be present at this
great spectacle of life and never to be liberated from a small
hungry shivering self – never to be fully possessed by the glory
we behold, never to have our consciousness rapturously trans-
formed into the vividness of a thought, the ardour of a passion,
the energy of an action, but always to be scholarly and

uninspired, ambitious and timid, scrupulous and dim-sighted.'

I do not know if George Eliot's words are apposite. I do not know what is going on in this section of St Mark. I do not know if we are permitted to think of our Lord as a clown. But this seems to me the best explanation. And this seems to me the most likeable explanation.

Try it in another version.

'About three o'clock in the morning he walked out to them on the water. He started past them, but when they saw something walking along beside them they screamed in terror, thinking it was a ghost, for they all saw him. But he spoke to them at once. 'It's all right,' he said. 'It is I! Don't be afraid.' Then he climbed into the boat and the wind stopped.' (Living Bible)

Now read Jesus's words accompanied by his laughter. If there had been a schism between Jesus and his disciples, mightn't this be a way of making friends again?

Did it succeed?

We learn that the disciples were 'sore amazed in themselves beyond measure, and wondered' – which, like being 'asto-nished with a great astonishment', would seem to mean more amazed then usual. They were also puzzled.

Then Mark adds – and this is not reported in the other Gospels – 'For they considered not the miracle of the loaves: for their heart was hardened.'

It always sounds to me as if the disciples were completely bowled over by the walking on the water, but didn't think much of the miracle of the loaves and fishes. It also sounds as if Mark himself was more impressed by the first miracle, and that he was highly critical of the disciples' insensitivity. But this interpretation may be wrong.

There is confusion in all translations of St Mark at this point. The New English and The Jerusalem Bible's version of the disciples' reaction is 'their minds were closed.' These two miracles of Jesus – the loaves and fishes, and the walking on the water – are more difficult to comprehend than all the miracles of healing. One is provoked into finding rational explanations for two utterly bizarre events. Did the crowd already have food of its own? Or did each member eat only a tiny portion of the loaves and fishes? Was the crowd actually much less than five thousand? Was their hunger satisfied because of some sort of mass suggestion? Were the baskets filled with the debris of the whole day? When Jesus walked on the water was it because 'the shore is shallow because of silt brought down from Mount Hermon?' (Sherman E. Johnson) And haven't we forgotten something? There is a second calming of a storm. When Jesus went up into the ship 'the wind ceased'. This piece of information is just thrown away in the writing.

But then I wonder what is the point of all this agonising if one does not wish to believe in the miracles in the first place?

I believe that at times – and this was certainly one of the times – Jesus was so full of power that he could do anything he wanted. I also believe that he was sometimes tempted into playing jokes.

I don't care much about these miracles. But I desperately want a human being.

And I'd prefer a humorous one.

*

As a footnote, if we believe that Peter related these things to Mark, it is particularly interesting that St Matthew's version of the last miracle contains a delightful story of Peter asking Jesus whether he could join him walking on the sea. After Jesus has reassured the disciples, 'Be of good cheer; it is I; be not afraid,' Peter says, 'Lord, if it be thou, bid me come unto thee on the water.' Jesus agrees, and Peter sets off. It is impossible to tell how far he got, 'But when he saw the wind boisterous, he was afraid; and beginning to sink, he cried, saying, Lord, save me.' Jesus saves Peter – and then, typically, tells him off for his lack of faith.

Why is this not reported in St Mark?

Was Peter ashamed of his lack of faith?

Or was Mark ashamed for Peter?

Whatever the reason, it is a pity the story was omitted.

Also, in Matthew's version, at the end, it would appear that the disciples were *not* 'sore amazed in themselves beyond measure, and wondered', or that 'their heart was hardened', or that their minds were closed. When Jesus gets into the ship,

Matthew writes that the disciples 'came and worshipped him, saying, Of a truth thou art the Son of God'. This is a much happier ending to the story than Mark's description of the grumpy group. And, for once, I would prefer to go with another version. It looks as if our man might have been doing a cover-up job.

'And when they had passed over, they came into the land of Gennesaret, and drew to the shore. And when they were come out of the ship, straightway they knew him, And ran through that whole region round about, and began to carry about in beds those that were sick, where they heard he was. And withersoever he entered, into villages, or cities, or country, they laid the sick in the streets, and besought him that they might touch if it were but the border of his garment: and as many as touched him were made whole.'

53

56

With this short description of Jesus's successful tours in the highly populated area south of Capernaum, we reach a climax in the first part of the ministry. It is a false climax – but Mark doesn't let us know that yet. It could have been a perfectly happy ending to the whole story. Jesus not only seems to be functioning with amazing energy, he also seems to be completely untroubled. This time of healing appears to have been uneventful. I think that Jesus reached a very human decision during his stay in Nazareth; a decision to let things take their own course; a decision to respond without question to the demands of the people. And, from the two beautiful sentences describing what happened after his arrival in Gennesaret, it would seem that the demands made on him were solely for acts of healing. He was loved; probably idolised. The impact of his personality and his extraordinary power attracted unqualified adulation. A lesser man would have been content with this.

But long did it go on? How long could Jesus accept this way of life? There was other work for him to do. He couldn't go on indefinitely being simply the adored servant of the people. Eventually he must take the road for Jerusalem.

THE TURNING POINT

The next two chapters are the most fascinating in the entire Gospel as far as the personality of Jesus is concerned. One detects self-disgust, fear and doubt. The combined pressure of the idolatry of the people, and his mounting guilt, force him into increasingly unsympathetic behaviour.

The trouble starts with a tiny speck of criticism from the scribes and Pharisees – who reappear on the scene after a long absence.

'Then came together unto him the Pharisees, and certain of the scribes, which came from Jerusalem. And when they saw some of his disciples eat bread with defiled, that is to say, with unwashen, hands, they found fault. For the Pharisees, and all the Jews, except they wash their hands oft, eat not, holding the tradition of the elders. And when they come from the market, except they wash, they eat not. And many other things there be, which they have received to hold, as the washing of cups, and pots, brasen vessels, and of tables.'

In this opening of Chapter Seven, Mark once again makes the distinction of 'certain of the scribes, which came from Jerusalem', ensuring that we are aware of their importance. What had the scribes and Pharisees been doing during this period of time? Had they been plotting with the Herodians? Were they waiting for Jesus to do something politically or legally wrong? It is a measure of Jesus's strength that, when the scribes and Pharisees emerge again, they do not criticise him. They find a point of order against the disciples; and for that particular time, it was a fairly minor point. And here Mark makes another distinction. He writes that only 'some' of the disciples ate bread with unwashen hands – presumably to let us know that not all of them were slobs.

Then Mark gives his Gentile readers a little lecture on some of the traditions of the elders; traditions which had been handed down for centuries by Oral Law.

Hands must be washed before eating – up to the wrist so that there was no defilement.

Hands must be washed after a visit to the market which was a public place where there was always the risk of contamination from pagans and other 'unclean' people.

Cups and pots, cooking vessels, and even tables must all be washed.

When these facts are clearly understood, Mark is ready to begin the story. (It is possible that Mark did not actually write this little lecture, and that it was a later addition. But whoever did it loved Mark, and wrote in a similar style.)

'Then the Pharisees and scribes asked him, Why walk not thy disciples according to the tradition of the elders, but eat bread with unwashen hands?'   **5**

I like to think that this was spoken pleasantly and quietly. The Pharisees and scribes had the law on their side, and they would be too clever to antagonise the crowd. There would be no need to raise their voices – unless Jesus ignored the question. They asked merely for information.

Jesus did not ignore their question. The Pharisees and scribes didn't know what was about to hit them. This petty point of law was the springboard for Jesus to make not one but three consecutive speeches of growing anger and intensity. Dramatically, this is a dazzling crescendo of indictment.

The King James Version starts with the weighty:

'He answered and said unto them . . .'   **6**

which warns us that something special is about to happen.

'Well hath Esaias prophesied of you hypocrites, as it is written, This people honoureth me with their lips, but their heart is far from me. Howbeit in vain do they worship me, teaching for doctrines the commandments of men.'   **7**

I like to think that this was also quietly spoken – the surprise of Jesus calling them hypocrites is more dangerous that way.

Esaias is Isaiah; and the quote comes from Chapter 29, verse 13. It is not literal, but the meaning is the same.

Jesus continues:

'For laying aside the commandment of God, ye hold the tradition of   **8**

9 *men, as the washing of pots and cups: and many other such like things ye do. And he said unto them, Full well ye reject the commandment of God, that ye may keep your own tradition.'*

Note the relentless repetition of the words 'commandment' and 'tradition'. There is also a splendid interpolation. Earlier, in the little lecture, we were told, among other things, that the Pharisees washed their 'cups and pots'. Now, the King James Version has Jesus turn the words round to 'pots and cups' – which sounds much ruder.

Jesus used an old trick in this passage. Because of their criticism of the disciples' unwashed hands, he started off by accusing the Pharisees and scribes of 'teaching for doctrines the commandments of men'. Now he accuses them of rejecting the commandments of God – although they haven't actually said anything else. Nobody had mentioned the commandments of God. But now Jesus does. He gives an example of them rejecting a commandment of God, and extends his attack.

10 *'For Moses said, Honour thy father and thy mother; and, Whoso curseth father or mother, let him die the death: But ye say, If a man shall say to his father or mother, It is Corban, that is to say, a gift, by whatsoever thou mightest be profited by me; he shall be free. And ye*

13 *suffer him no more to do ought for his father or his mother; Making the word of God of none effect through your tradition, which ye have delivered: and many such like things do ye.'*

This sounds difficult, but I think that Jesus is talking about a sort of religious tax dodge. A sum of money could be declared 'Corban' which meant that it was a gift dedicated to God. But this seemingly good practice could be misused, and when a debt was owed – even to needy parents – because the money was declared sacred, a son was excused from paying it. The Living Bible by-passes the word 'Corban' altogether with the following breezy piece of writing: 'For instance, Moses gave you this law from God: "Honour your father and mother." And he said that anyone who speaks against his father or mother must die. But you say it is perfectly all right for a man to disregard his needy parents, telling them, "Sorry, I can't help you! for I have given to God what I could have given to you." '

When Jesus has given the Pharisees and scribes this example

of their rejection of God through their tradition, one might expect that his attack was over. But by now Jesus seems unable to stop. He carries on with the moody generalisation 'and many such like things do ye' – and then calls a public meeting.

'*And when he had called all the people to him, he said unto them,* *Hearken unto me every one of you, and understand: There is nothing* *from without a man, that entering into him can defile him: but the* *things which come out of him, those are they that defile the man. If* *any man have ears to hear, let him hear.*' 14 15 16

We have moved on to a more important subject. Here, Jesus starts to pit the rigid Jewish laws about 'clean' and 'unclean' food against his own moral laws about behaviour. He says, in effect, that it doesn't matter what we eat, that nothing we eat can defile us; we can only be defiled by the things we do. To understand the revolutionary nature of his words, it is necessary to be aware of the extent and intricacies of the Jewish rules concerning food.

In The Third Book of Moses, called Leviticus, there are countless rulings on what is considered 'clean' or 'unclean'. (It was from this book that I quoted the requirements for a cured leper.) These rules sound very quaint to some of us, but it is vital that we consider them seriously, otherwise we will not understand the impact of Jesus's words.

As far as meat is concerned, the Lord told Moses and Aaron to instruct the children of Israel: 'Whatsoever parteth the hoof, and is cloven-footed, and cheweth the cud, among the beasts, that shall ye eat.' This meant that they could not eat camels, coneys, or hares, because they were not clovenfooted; and they could not eat swine because, although they were clovenfooted, they did not chew the cud. They must not eat any fish without fins or scales. There are detailed rulings on birds. Among others, they may not eat the eagle, the vulture, any kind of kite or raven, the owl, the swan, the pelican, the stork, any kind of heron, 'the lapwing, and the bat'. The Lord told them that 'flying insects with four legs must not be eaten, with the exception of those that jump; locusts of all varieties – bald locusts, crickets, and grasshoppers – may be eaten.' And so on. There are also strict warnings of defilement from touching dead animals, from clothing, and from ovens.

Now Jesus is saying: 'There is nothing from without a man, that entering into him can defile him.'

There is a terrifying story in The Second Book of the Maccabees. Seven brothers were savagely tortured and put to death because they refused to eat pork. Their mother 'marvellous above all . . . when she saw her seven sons slain within the space of one day, she bare it with good courage, because of the hope she had in the Lord'. She actually encouraged them to accept torture and death. Then, 'Last of all after the sons the mother died.'

Now Jesus is telling people that their priorities are wrong.

Then he adds provocatively – surely for the benefit of the scribes and Pharisees – 'If any man have ears to hear, let him hear.'

Open war has been declared.

At this point in St Matthew's version his disciples come to Jesus and – probably whispering frantically in his ear – say, 'Knowest thou that the Pharisees were offended, after they heard this saying?' – or in today's words, 'You know they didn't like what you just said!' Jesus replies with superb arrogance: 'Every plant, which my heavenly father hath not planted, shall be rooted up.' He goes on: 'Let them alone: they be blind leaders of the blind. And if the blind lead the blind, both shall fall into the ditch.'

But in St Mark's version it reads as if Jesus simply made a grand exit.

'*And when he was entered into the house from the people, his disciples asked him concerning the parable.*'

This was unfortunate. Jesus might have calmed down. Instead of which, the disciples now get the full blast of his fury. Again in St Matthew's version the actual disciple who asked for an explanation is named. It was Peter . . . Has Mark covered up again? Nobody would want to be identified as the fool who cued the following outburst:

'*And he saith unto them, Are ye so without understanding also? Do ye not perceive, that whatsoever thing from without entereth into the man, it cannot defile him; Because it entereth not into his heart, but into the belly, and goeth out into the draught, purging all meats? And he said, That which cometh out of the man, that defileth the man. For from within, out of the heart of men, proceed evil thoughts,*'

112

adulteries, fornications, murders, Thefts, covetousness, wickedness, deceit, lasciviousness, an evil eye, blasphemy, pride, foolishness: All these evil things come from within, and defile the man.'

23

Remember the first question? In fact, the *only* question? 'Why walk not thy disciples according to the tradition of the elders, but eat bread with unwashen hands?' We have progressed from Jesus's refutation of this niggling point of law, to a condemnation of man's worst sins. The Pharisees and scribes purported to be shocked by the disciples' unwashed hands. Jesus is shocked by man's capacity for evil. He distinguishes between a man's heart and a man's belly. He says that all food is harmless and 'goeth out into the draught' – which means into the sewer, the drains, or the latrine. 'Purging all meats' is clarified in later translations as 'He declared all food clean'. He says that real dirt comes from within us.

And then there is that list.

After 'evil thoughts' – which presumably means the *intention* to behave badly – it is interesting that, according to Jesus, the first two things that defile men are adulteries and fornications. They are put before murder and theft. This seems excessively severe.

Commentators write that: 'The list is not in completely logical order' (Sherman E. Johnson) and 'The thirteen types of vice are somewhat different in the Greek text than the Latin from which the above translation was made' (Gerald S. Sloyan). And the various translations have different orders to the list – although they nearly all start with fornication. But we are considering the personality of Jesus according to St Mark in The King James Version, and adulteries and fornications head the list. It is as if adulteries and fornications are the first sins. I think that this is another indication of Jesus's horror of his parentage.

But now he is speaking for his father in heaven. He is confronting the people with the real sins of the flesh. He pours scorn on the old laws and speaks for God.

How could Jesus sustain this role? How could he live with this self-imposed responsibility?

When he was baptized of John in Jordan, and heard his father in heaven speaking to him, he reacted by running away and spending forty days in the wilderness.

Now, after this open attack on the Old Law; after declaring his own original views of behaviour; after speaking up clearly for his chosen father, he retired again. We do not know how long this retirement lasted.

24

'And from thence he arose, and went into the borders of Tyre and Sidon, and entered into an house, and would have no man know it:'

We do not know how long this retirement lasted because Mark rushes on with the story. As ever, the reporter is afraid of losing his readers. If there was a lull in the ministry at this point – as is believed and which seems very likely – Mark, and perhaps Peter, do not consider this interesting. Perhaps they thought that any indication of doubt or hesitancy on Jesus's part would be detrimental to their story.

Why did he travel far away from the region round about the Sea of Galilee where his ministry had always been conducted? Tyre is forty miles from Capernaum, and Sidon is twenty-six miles beyond Tyre. They are the farthest places from Jerusalem visited by Jesus. Is this significant? Why did he go into Gentile territory away from his own people? Why did he enter into an house, 'and would have no man know it'? Not long ago he was healing all and sundry in 'the land of Gennesaret'. Now he attempts to become a recluse – according to some calculations for six to eight months. In this tight little Gospel the lapses of time are difficult to judge; but it seems likely that the time of healing in Gennesaret exhausted Jesus both physically and mentally. The recurring argument of healing or teaching must eventually have troubled him. He must finally have realised that his decision in Nazareth to let things take their own course was not the right one.

If we put this state of mind and mood in perspective with the recent clash with the Pharisees and scribes, and his anger and impatience with his disciples, this journey to the north becomes more understandable.

There was possibly great danger for Jesus after his reckless attack on the old laws. It may have been necessary for him to disappear. Mark never again reports Jesus teaching openly in Galilee; and, although he and his disciples return once to the house in Capernaum for a memorable domestic scene, we are told that, as they went through Galilee, Jesus 'would not that any man should know it'.

But it seems even more likely that Jesus was going through a time of indecision. He was disgusted with himself. He was disgusted with the people. He was ashamed of his easy success as a healer. He was saddened by the stupidity of his disciples. He was maddened by the rigid religious hierarchy. Nothing pleased him. And he was afraid to listen to his voices, the voices in his head. He was frightened by the demands of his chosen father. He was frightened of his destiny. He was frightened of the road to Jerusalem. And he may also, quite simply, have been physically frightened, frightened of pain. He 'entered into an house' – we do not know whose house – 'and would have no man know it': and Mark carries on with breakneck speed:

'but he could not be hid. For a certain woman, whose young **25** daughter had an unclean spirit, heard of him, and came and fell at his feet: The woman was a Greek, a Syrophenician by nation; and she besought him that he would cast forth the devil out of her daughter. But Jesus said unto her, Let the children first be filled: for it is not meet **27** to take the children's bread, and to cast it unto the dogs.'

What!

'And she answered and said unto him, Yes, Lord: yet the dogs **28** under the table eat of the children's crumbs.'

The children in this story are Jesus's own people, the children of Israel. The 'dogs' in the story are the Gentiles. It is a term of contempt frequently used in the Old Testament – sometimes 'dog'; sometimes 'dead dog'; sometimes 'dog's head'. It is still a much-used insult in the East. It is on a par with our own use of 'yids' and 'kikes'. It is not a pleasant expression.

Many people try to excuse this rudeness of Jesus. They try to believe that it was a test of the woman's faith. They try to imagine it was said with warmth. 'Perhaps . . . something depends upon the tone of voice in which he made the protest and the look in his eye at the time.' (C. F. D. Moule) 'Jesus's tone took all the poison out of the word.' (William Barclay) Or there are other attempts at softening the insult by changing dog into diminutives like little dogs or puppies. But D. E. Nineham will have none of it. He concludes his notes on the word: 'He will have said "dogs", not "puppies", still less, as has been suggested, "doggies"!'

If we continue to believe in the correct order of St Mark's

Gospel, then this bad temper of Jesus makes absolute sense. He was being hounded by the scribes and Pharisees. He was trying to evade his role of the Son of God. He was feeling unworthy of the idolatry of the unthinking multitude. He was in hiding. And then he was discovered by this Gentile woman. She fell at his feet. She besought him. And he called her a dog. But the woman, who was not only determined, but also quick-witted, agreed with him. She flattered Jesus by saying, 'Yes, Lord:' – or, in some translations, 'That's true, sir!' And then she mitigated his insult with a very good joke. She said in effect that Gentile dogs can surely have any unwanted crumbs of nourishment left over by the children of Israel. Jesus liked the joke. He liked it so much that he healed the woman's daughter.

29) 'And he said unto her, For this saying go thy way; the devil is gone out of thy daughter.'

He did it by remote control.

30 'And when she was come to her house, she found the devil gone out, and her daughter laid upon the bed.'

If we accept Jesus's humanity, if we accept his bad temper and his lapse into downright rudeness, the story becomes a delight. If we try to cover up the unsympathetic side of it, the story is insipid and coy.

How do we know the story? According to Matthew, the disciples were still with Jesus during this period of exile. According to Matthew, the woman made two attempts to get Jesus's help. The first time he wouldn't even speak to her. 'But he answered her not a word. And his disciples came and besought him, saying, Send her away; for she crieth after us.' And it was after this that the woman made the approach reported in Mark.

Although Mark and Peter do not tell us that 'there were also women . . . Who also, when he was in Galilee, followed him, and ministered unto him' until the very end of the Gospel, and although they omit his harsh references to family life, they have no qualms about revealing the impatience and bad temper of Jesus. In this episode with the Greek woman – and in the later story of the withering of a fig tree when Jesus is outside Jerusalem – the Son of God is certainly more recognisable as the Son of Man.

★

'*And again, departing from the coasts of Tyre and Sidon, he came unto the Sea of Galilee, through the midst of the coasts of Decapolis.*'

I think we'd better try that journey again in a modern version.

'Returning from the district of Tyre, he went by way of Sidon towards the Sea of Galilee, right through the Decapolis region.' (The Jerusalem Bible)

That sounds even more complicated.

'On his return from Tirian territory he went by way of Sidon to the Sea of Galilee through the territory of the Ten Towns.' (The New English)

Ignore the geography! It has been pointed out that this journey is like travelling from London to Cornwall via Manchester. Actually, Jesus left the Gentile region in the north and travelled south to another Gentile region on the eastern side of the Sea of Galilee. Decapolis (or the Ten Towns) is near the country of the Gadarenes. It was where Jesus had sent the cured wild man, and instructed him to 'tell his friends how great things the Lord hath done for thee'.

The journey was part of Jesus's exile from his own people, and may well have been slow and erratic; partly because of Jesus's mood at this time, and partly to avoid confrontations with enemies.

The Gadarene swine-man may have done a good promotion job, because it seems that Jesus was surrounded by a multitude again.

'*And they bring unto him one that was deaf, and had an impediment in his speech; and they beseech him to put his hand upon him.*'

The deaf man with the impediment was unable to speak for himself, and must have been brought to Jesus by friends or family.

'*And he took him aside from the multitude, and put his fingers into his ears, and he spit, and touched his tongue; And looking up to heaven, he sighed, and saith unto him, Ephphatha, that is, Be opened. And straightway his ears were opened, and the string of his tongue was loosed, and he spake plain.*'

As reported by Mark, Jesus's behaviour was different from usual. He took the man *away* from the multitude. He performed the miracle in private. This indicates an attempt to break away from public healing, and ties up with the troubled mood of Jesus. It is true that Matthew reports *many* miracles of healing here, and he tells us 'that the multitude wondered, when they saw the dumb to speak, the maimed to be whole, the lame to walk, and the blind to see: and they glorified the God of Israel.' But let us stay with Mark. Let us avoid confusion. As Mark tells it, Jesus did not wish to be seen by the multitude when he performed this miracle. And, as Mark does not report any other miracles 'on the coasts of Decapolis', I assume this was a special case.

36

'*And he charged them that they should tell no man:*'

This must have been to the friends or family.

'*but the more he charged them, so much the more a great deal they published it;*'

And everybody was talking again.

37

'*And were beyond measure astonished, saying, He hath done all things well: he maketh both the deaf to hear, and the dumb to speak.*'

Nothing had changed.

8

*

Now Mark reports another miracle of loaves and fishes.

This story begins with a charming snatch of dialogue between Jesus and the disciples.

1

'*In those days the multitude being very great, and having nothing to eat, Jesus called his disciples unto him, and saith unto them, I have compassion on the multitude, because they have now been with me three days, and have nothing to eat: And if I send them away fasting to their own houses, they will faint by the way: for divers of them came from far. And his disciples answered him, From whence can a man*

5

satisfy these men with bread here in the wilderness? And he asked them, How many loaves have ye? And they said, Seven.'

In the first miracle of the loaves and fishes the crowd was with Jesus for only one day. And when that day was 'far spent', the disciples had come to Jesus and begged him to 'send them away, that they may go into the country round about, and into the villages, and buy themselves bread: for they have nothing to eat'. Jesus then made the disciples look foolish. It is not certain that they even understood what happened; 'they considered not the miracle of the loaves: for their heart was hardened.'

On this next occasion, although the multitude had been

with Jesus for three days, the disciples said nothing. They were obviously not going to try helping the Master again. This time it was Jesus who was practical. In the friendliest manner, he called them to him and asked their advice. We learn that some of the people had come great distances and would have a long walk home. The disciples replied in dull fashion. They made no helpful suggestions. Then, just as he had done the time before, Jesus asked them 'how many loaves have ye?' Was the question asked impatiently, or with a little smile? Was he quietly challenging them? They replied, simply, 'Seven.' Perhaps *they* were quietly challenging Jesus . . . Or perhaps they thought that seven loaves would be easier than five.

This little piece of dialogue is very revealing about the relationship between Jesus and the disciples at this time. It seems to be in a state of stalemate. Jesus obviously needed the disciples to be with him; and they continued to be loyal. But there is a sense that the next important step in the ministry should be taken. Questions are forming. What was Jesus doing in these Gentile territories? Were he and the disciples going to tour the distant provinces forever? As readers of the Gospel, we are not surprised by the next miracle. We expect it. After all, Jesus was repeating himself.

'And he commanded the people to sit down on the ground: and he took the seven loaves, and gave thanks, and brake, and gave to his disciples to set before them;' 6

And here, Mark makes it quite clear that the disciples were involved in the distribution of the loaves; there was no help from the multitude.

'and they did set them before the people.'

And haven't we forgotten something?

'And they had a few small fishes:' 7

That's right!

'and he blessed, and commanded to set them also before them.'

No shocks this time.

'So they did eat, and were filled: and they took up of the broken 8 *meat that was left seven baskets. And they that had eaten were about* 9 *four thousand:'*

In fact this doesn't seem such an impressive miracle. Seven loaves, four thousand people, and only seven baskets full of the fragments. But evidently the baskets were bigger on this occasion. The Greek words are different. Ronald Knox translates the baskets for this second miracle as 'hampers' – which gives an impression of a huge Edwardian picnic. (Where did all the hampers come from?)

It is argued that this is another version of the first miracle. Despite the difference in dialogue and the difference in numbers, it is argued that both these miracles of the loaves and fishes are one and the same. Another theory is that Jesus performed the first miracle for his own people, and the second for the Gentiles. (Rather like doing the same act at the Palace Theatre, New York, and then at the Palladium Theatre in London.) This seems to me a possible idea. Although I am not convinced by Robert Crotty who writes: 'The numbers four and seven that occur are typically Gentile numbers.'

But the reason for the inclusion of the second miracle of the loaves and fishes must simply be that it happened. It seems that nobody was amazed beyond measure, or astonished with a great astonishment – or, if they were, Mark didn't think it worth reporting. Sadly, as we shall soon discover, the disciples didn't 'consider' the second miracle either. The four thousand ('beside women and children,' St Matthew again) ate the loaves and fishes and were filled. The baskets or hampers were filled with the leftovers.

9   'And he sent them away.'

Nothing had changed.

★

10   *'And straightway he entered into a ship with his disciples, and came into the parts of Dalmanutha.'*

Nobody has any certain idea where abouts this is – but it is thought to be back on the western side of the Sea of Galilee. It seems to be an attempt by Jesus to return to his own people.

11   *'And the Pharisees came forth, and began to question with him, seeking of him a sign from heaven, tempting him. And he sighed deeply in his spirit, and saith, Why doth this generation seek after a*
13   *sign? verily I say unto you, There shall no sign be given unto this generation. And he left them, and entering into the ship again departed to the other side.'*

It was a very short trip. The attempt to return to his own people failed. The Pharisees were waiting for him – news travelled fast around the lake – they were waiting for him with a typical request. Miracles of healing did not impress them. Multiplying loaves and fishes, and walking on the water might be tricks of illusion. They wanted something spectacular. Rev. Marshall says: 'They demanded heavenly confirmation of His mission.' And he gives us five spectacular examples from the Old Testament: '*Moses* – Manna from heaven. *Joshua* – stayed the sun and the moon. *Samuel* – called forth thunder and hail. *Elijah* – fire and rain came at his word. *Isaiah* – caused the sun to go back on the dial of Ahaz.' The Pharisees wanted something comparable.

'And he sighed deeply in his spirit' – which is a beautiful way of writing that he groaned; and Jesus definitely refused to give them a sign. He re-enforced this with a 'verily I say unto you' so that there should be no misunderstanding. And, twice, he rudely referred to them as 'this generation' – which sounds a little strange to modern ears. When Jesus said 'this generation' he meant specifically that particular group of people.

Although it reads like a scene from *The Wizard of Oz*, The Living Bible reports the exchange in the following manner:

'Do a miracle for us,' they said. 'Make something happen in the sky. Then we will believe you.' His heart fell when he heard this and he said, 'Certainly not. How many more miracles do *you people* need?'

I like the use of the words 'you people' for 'this generation'.

In this short description of the trip to Dalmanutha, we discover that the Pharisees are still trying to trick Jesus. And Jesus will not have anything to do with them. He does not attack them, or even criticise them. He just snubs them, and leaves.

Nothing had changed.

*

Jesus had entered into the ship again, and once more they were on their way to the other side of the Sea of Galilee.

'*Now*' –

Meaning on this occasion.

'the disciples had forgotten to take bread, neither had they in the ship with them more than one loaf. And he charged them, saying, Take heed, beware of the leaven of the Pharisees, and of the leaven of

14

16 *Herod. And they reasoned among themselves, saying, It is because we have no bread.'*

This is a classic case of cross purposes.

Let the Rev. Marshall help us. First, with a definition:

'*Leaven* or *yeast*, which permeates the dough and alters its character. Used metaphorically to describe that which permeates and determines the character of the teaching.'

It is nearly always used as a symbol of evil.

The Rev. also tells us that the leaven of the Herodians was 'worldliness', and the leaven of the Pharisees was 'hypocrisy'. He gives a wonderful quote from Latham about the Pharisees' hypocrisy: 'It killed all that is spiritual in religion by reducing everything to a matter of dry proof and dead authority.'

But the disciples thought that Jesus was simply talking about bread. They took Jesus's words literally, and guiltily imagined that they were in the wrong because they had left Dalmanutha without sufficient provisions.

Jesus had just endured the Pharisees demanding a sign from him; sceptical of his power. Now he has the disciples misunderstanding his teaching – and worrying about their lack of bread. All this, after two miracles when he has increased their food.

There is a slow build of fury. In your mind, wait for the disciples to reply after each question.

17 '*And when Jesus knew it, he saith unto them, Why reason ye, because ye have no bread?*

perceive ye not yet, neither understand?

have ye your heart yet hardened?

18 *Having eyes, see ye not?*

and having ears, hear ye not?

and do ye not remember?'

He continues mercilessly. The questions become specific.

19 '*When I brake the five loaves among five thousand, how many baskets full of fragments took ye up?'*

Imagine the disciples, unable to look at him, shuffling on their feet. The reply comes slowly.

'*They say unto him, Twelve.'*

And Jesus goes on:

20 '*And when the seven among four thousand, how many baskets full of fragments took ye up?'*

Would he ever forgive them? Would this moment ever pass?
'And they said, Seven.
And he said unto them, How is it that ye do not understand?' 2₁
The disciples had failed again.
Nothing had changed.

★

In the last episode Jesus echoed words of the Lord from The Book of the Prophet Jeremiah. 'Hear now this, O foolish people, and without understanding; which have eyes, and see not; which have ears, and hear not:' Perhaps he was also thinking of the following words from the same lamentation. 'A wonderful and horrible thing is committed in the land; The prophets prophesy falsely, and the priests bear rule by their means; and my people love to have it so: and what will ye do in the end thereof?'

And what will *he* do in the end thereof?

★

Now we come to the saddest little story in the Gospel.

'And he cometh to Bethsaida; and they bring a blind man unto him, 22 *and besought him to touch him. And he took the blind man by the hand, and led him out of the town; and when he had spit on his eyes, and put his hands upon him, he asked him if he saw ought. And he looked up, and said, I see men as trees, walking. After that he put his hands again upon his eyes, and made him look up: and he was restored, and saw every man clearly. And he sent him away to his* 26 *house, saying, Neither go into the town, nor tell it to any in the town.'*

There are interesting parallels in the writing of this story with the healing of the deaf man with an impediment in his speech. Once again Jesus took the supplicant away from the people, and performed the healing in private. In the previous story Jesus 'took him aside from the multitude'. This time he 'led him out of the town' – which sounds as if he made an even more determined effort at privacy. In both instances the healing is described in detail. In the first, Mark writes that Jesus 'put his fingers into his ears, and he spit, and touched his tongue'. This time, Jesus's technique is described again: 'and when he had spit on his eyes, and put his hands upon him, he asked him if he saw ought.' And later: 'he put his hands again upon his eyes, and made him look up.'

Why are we given these facts? None of the previous miracles of healing has had such detailed description. And why are these two miracles only reported by Mark? Matthew and Luke do not include them in their Gospels. Nineham writes that some scholars think that St Matthew and St Luke had read these descriptions, 'but deliberately omitted them from a feeling that the use of physical means to effect cures was not consonant with the Lord's dignity'. This is very likely.

It seems to me that Peter was describing Jesus at this point with less and less wonder. Even at a distance of two thousand years, there is a sense of disillusion here in the attitude of the story-teller to his hero. And if, at this time – as I am proposing – Jesus was reluctant to accept the challenge of his destiny, if he was shirking his self-imposed responsibility, if he was running away from his role as the Son of God, then, perhaps, it was natural for Peter to emphasise these undignified details and the effort required by Jesus to heal these people. And it was natural for Mark to include this reality in his Gospel. Previous miracles of healing have been described as if they happened by divine magic. Now Mark describes Jesus putting his fingers into ears, and using spit to perform his work.

And then we reach the really extraordinary feature in the healing of the blind man.

At first it did not succeed.

I think we should be grateful for the courage of Peter and Mark to report this fact. The healing took two attempts, 'and this may have been an additional reason for its omission by Matthew and Luke, if it was taken to imply that the first laying on of hands was not successful'. (Nineham)

It was obviously *not* successful the first time – and the implications of this are very great. Of course it is possible that there were many failures of healing during the ministry. There may have been many failures, and also many attempts which only half-succeeded. And it is possible that Peter and Mark decided to ignore this in their Gospel. But then why did they include this sad little tale of the blind man at Bethsaida? There have been occasions during this first part of the ministry when Jesus 'healed many' – in the house of Simon and Andrew in

Capernaum; by the sea when Mark first reported that crowds from all over the country 'came unto him'; and lately in Gennesaret. It is probable that the actual miracles reported in detail were only the most colourful or memorable. Nevertheless, here, we are confronted with a story of Jesus's fumbling. Here, Mark and Peter thought it necessary to record a less than perfect miracle. Jesus asked the man 'if he saw ought' after the first attempt. 'And he looked up, and said, I see men as trees, walking' – which meant that he was not totally cured. Assuming he was an eye-witness, was this a shock for Peter? He certainly didn't forget it.

Perhaps there were many failures at this time. If there were many failures, Mark must have thought it only right and proper to record *one* of them. I think it is possible that the inclusion of this flawed miracle was a brave decision by the writer in order to let us know that at that particular time Jesus's belief in himself was failing. And, if his belief was failing, that meant that his powers were failing.

I think that Jesus *knew* his powers were failing – and that he *wanted* them to fail. For a combination of reasons, made up of disgust with himself, disgust with humanity, and fear of the eventual consequences of his ministry, Jesus did not want to continue.

After this, instead of turning south towards Jerusalem, Jesus again turned to the north. Since the short attempt to return to their own people – which was thwarted by the Pharisees – the group had sailed to the north-eastern corner of the Sea of Galilee. Now, after the encounter with the blind man at Bethsaida – finishing with Jesus desperately imploring him to 'neither go into the town, nor tell it to any in the town' – they travelled to Caesarea Philippi, which is as far north as the borders of Tyre and Sidon.

Nothing had changed – except that now we find that Jesus's powers are beginning to fail.

'And Jesus went out, and his disciples, into the towns of Caesarea 27
Philippi: and by the way he asked his disciples, saying unto them, Whom do men say that I am? And they answered, John the Baptist: but some say, Elias; and others, One of the prophets. And he saith 29
unto them, But whom say ye that I am? And Peter answereth and saith unto him, Thou art the Christ.'

This is the place, historically, where Christianity was born.

This is the place, psychologically, where Jesus decided to go ahead with his chosen father's work.

This is the place where Peter, by his faith, became the rock on which the church was founded.

This is the place where the second part of the ministry of Jesus begins.

What sort of place was it? Why did Jesus decide that this was the place to accept his role of the Christ? What was it about this place that prompted him to challenge his disciples? What was it about this place that challenged *Jesus*?

Geographically, what was this place?

Caesarea Philippi lay at the foot of Mount Hermon. This is by far the most imposing mountain of the region; for much of the year it is snow-covered.

Caesarea Philippi was close to a source of the Jordan.

Jesus was near a high mountain.

Jesus was near to a source of the river in which he had been baptized.

These could be factors which influenced the timing of his decision.

Historically, what was this place?

'In the oldest days it was called Balinas, for it had once been a great centre of the worship of Baal.'

'To this day it is called Banias, which is a form of Panias. It is so called because up on the hillside there was a cavern which was said to be the birthplace of the Greek God, Pan, the god of nature.' (Barclay)

Jesus must have known of these associations with Baal and with Pan. They could also be factors which influenced the timing of his decision.

At that particular time, what was so special about this place?

The territory was ruled by Herod's son, Philip. 'Philip the Tetrarch enlarged and embellished the town, naming it Caesarea after Augustus and adding Philippi to distinguish it from the Caesarea (Palestinae) of his father.' (Enc. Brit. 14th Ed.)

'. . . up on the hillside rose a gleaming temple of white marble which Philip had built to the godhead of Caesar, the

Roman Emperor, the ruler of the world, who was regarded as a god.' (Barclay)

A high mountain; a source of the Jordan; a centre of worship of Baal; the birthplace of Pan; and a temple to Caesar.

Jesus was challenged.

He was challenged by his insignificance.

There must have been a human jealousy. There must have been a necessity to compete.

'Who do men say that I am?'

'John the Baptist, Elias, one of the prophets . . .'

No!

'Whom do ye say that I am?'

'Thou art the Christ.'

Caesarea Philippi was put into perspective.

★

The most stimulating piece of writing that I know about the life and ministry of Jesus is Bernard Shaw's Preface to his play *Androcles and the Lion*. Shaw cuts through the mythology and the religion invented by men to suit themselves, and with buoyant irreverence he reveals the revolutionary teacher. But, in his writing about Jesus, Shaw makes one extraordinary error of judgement. He attributes entirely to Peter the idea that Jesus was the Christ. He writes that 'nobody connects him with that hope until Peter has the sudden inspiration which produces so startling an effect on Jesus'. I think this is ridiculous.

As we have surely realised from his words and actions in the first part of the Gospel, Jesus knew who he was.

Jesus demanded an answer that he had known for many years – since the time when he himself decided it, probably when he was a child. But it had to be acknowledged. Jesus believed he was the Son of God. Now, there had to be a parallel act of faith. In a sense, Jesus demanded that Christ was christened. And Peter christened Christ.

It is also ridiculous to imagine that the idea had not occurred to anyone else. In a land where nearly everyone was in the cast of *Waiting for Godot*, the thought that Jesus was the Messiah must have occurred to *some* members of the crowds. In the company of a man who healed the sick, who cast out devils, who stilled storms, who multiplied loaves and fishes, who walked on water, the idea must have occurred to *some* of the disciples. But there was a conflict here. The Messiah would be a king. Jesus was a man; a carpenter, who ate and drank with publicans and sinners. Jesus was the disciples' companion, with all the ordinary problems of everyday living. Although, undoubtedly, he had great powers, he did not help *himself*. Like them, he suffered heat, cold, hunger and fatigue. Could this be the Messiah?

It was because of this that Peter's words were a great act of faith. And it was because of this that, in St Matthew's version, we learn that Jesus blessed Peter and told him 'upon this rock I will build my church'; and promised to give him 'the keys of the kingdom of heaven'. It was also because of this that, immediately after the acknowledgement of his title, Jesus ordered the disciples to be silent.

30   *'And he charged them that they should tell no man of him.'*

Then, for the first time, he revealed his future.

31   *'And he began to teach them, that the Son of man must suffer many things, and be rejected of the elders, and of the chief priests, and scribes, and be killed, and after three days rise again.'*

I hope that he did not actually reveal all this in just one sentence as reported by St Mark, otherwise the disciples must have been reeling with shock. It is a great deal of information to take in and comprehend. And it would appear that the disciples never did take in or comprehend the last part – that three days after dying Jesus would rise from the dead. This was something that Jesus repeats to them many times at regular intervals. But the early part of the teaching, that the Son of man must suffer many things, was not something that they would expect about the Christ; that he must be rejected of the elders, the chief priests and scribes, was not something they would expect about the Christ; and that he would be killed, was something unthinkable if he was the Christ. It was all too paradoxical and confusing. With wonderful contradictory humanity, after calling him the Christ, Peter was compelled to take Jesus on one side and tell him to stop talking nonsense.

32   *'And he spake that saying openly. And Peter took him, and began to rebuke him.'*

But, although this was understandable, it was not a wise

move. Through Mark we discover that Peter recalled not only Jesus's next words, but also his physical movement.

'But when he had turned about and looked on his disciples, he **33** *rebuked Peter, saying, Get thee behind me Satan: for thou savourest not the things that be of God, but the things that be of men.'*

The disciples were obviously going to need very clear instructions. After this long time of aimless wandering, after the reluctant healings, the repeated requests for silence, the repeated miracles; after his criticism of the scribes and Pharisees and his rejection of the old laws, Jesus now starts to teach affirmatively. The real ministry begins.

Everything had changed.

*

'And when he had called the people unto him with his disciples also, **34** *he said unto them . . .'*

There is a thrilling inevitability about this calling together of the people 'with his disciples also' – and we should hear the ordinary little phrase 'he said unto them' as if for the first time. These will be the first public words of the Christ. When they come, the words are simple; they are also almost impossible to understand. And yet, it is as if one knew them all the time.

'Whosoever will come after me, let him deny himself, and take up his cross, and follow me. For whosoever will save his life shall lose it; **35** *but whosoever shall lose his life for my sake and the gospel's, the same shall save it. For what shall it profit a man, if he shall gain the whole* **36** *world, and lose his own soul? Or what shall a man give in exchange* **37** *for his soul?'*

These last two sentences can be related to Jesus himself. Surely he was partly talking of his own dilemma. With his magnetic personality, and with his astonishing gifts of healing, surely *he* could have gained the whole world. Surely he could have manipulated the society of his time into any shape or form he wanted. Instead of this, he discarded the world and – through his defiance of the accepted religion, and through his insistence on his death and resurrection – gave us a conception of faith as something alive.

He threatened:

'Whosoever therefore shall be ashamed of me and of my words in **38** *this adulterous and sinful generation; of him also shall the Son of man*

be ashamed, when he cometh in the glory of his Father with the holy angels.'

And he promised:

'And he said unto them, Verily I say unto you, That there be some of them that stand here, which shall not taste of death, till they have seen the kingdom of God come with power.'

This is breathtaking.

After the uncertainty, and after the evasion, Jesus now avers – he publicly avers – that he will be seen in the company of his Father with the holy angels.

And he promises – with a 'Verily I say unto you' – that the kingdom of God will happen during the lifetime of some of his hearers.

It didn't – but his faith that it would happen has endured through the centuries.

INTERVAL

GOING SOUTH

'And after six days Jesus taketh with him Peter, and James, and John, and leadeth them up into an high mountain apart by themselves: and he was transfigured before them. And his raiment became shining, exceeding white as snow; so as no fuller on earth can white them. And there appeared unto them Elias with Moses: and they were talking with Jesus. And Peter answered and said to Jesus, Master, it is good for us to be here: and let us make three tabernacles; one for thee, and one for Moses, and one for Elias. For he wist not what to say; for they were sore afraid. And there was a cloud that overshadowed them: and a voice came out of the cloud, saying, This is my beloved Son: hear him. And suddenly, when they had looked round about, they saw no man anymore, save Jesus only with themselves.'

What actually happened? We will never know.

'There are certain indications in the story that symbolism is involved.' (Crotty)

'It is sometimes thought that there is no historic kernel.' (Johnson)

'It is not very profitable to ask exactly what happened.' (Moule)

'. . . the possibility should not be ruled out that by the time the story reached the Evangelist, some of it was already obscure to him.' (Nineham)

'What happened we cannot tell. We can only bow in reverence as we try to understand.' (Barclay)

This clutch of quotes is a comfort, as this is one of the most difficult episodes in the life of Jesus to understand. Some people take it absolutely literally: they only worry about details such as why Mark and Matthew say it happened after six days, and Luke says it happened after about eight; and

131

conclude that it actually happened after about a week. And they point out that Mark does not mention that anything happened to Jesus's face, whereas Matthew says, 'His face did shine as the sun,' and Luke says, 'The fashion of his countenance was altered.' And they note that only Mark makes the homely description that his garments became 'exceeding white as snow; *so as no fuller on earth can white them*' – which always sounds to me like a commercial for washing powder.

However, they do not take any notice of the fact that, halfway through his description of the scene, Luke tells us that 'Peter and they that were with him were heavy with sleep'; and that 'when they were awake, they saw his glory, and the two men that stood with him'. This seems like a clue to what happened. My theory is that the transfiguration was a vivid dream.

Once more, let us consider the continuity, and examine what happened before the event.

Jesus had challenged his disciples about his identity. After a long period of wandering and uncertainty, Jesus demanded of the disciples, 'Whom say ye that I am?' And Peter boldly stated that Jesus was the Christ. We do not know whether this statement had unanimous support from the others. Despite his miraculous powers of healing, and despite the mysterious events of stilling storms and feeding thousands and walking on water, the disciples knew Jesus to be a man like themselves; indeed it is likely that they knew him to be the bastard son of an ordinary family in Nazareth. This was a paradox. Then Jesus began to teach them many things about his future. Having accepted his title of the Christ, he warned them of the suffering he must endure, and of his rejection by the religious leaders of the land. This was a paradox. He promised that he would rise from the dead. This was incomprehensible. And, when Peter rebuked him for talking recklessly, Jesus turned his back on Peter and savagely accused him of being in league with the devil.

Then he called the people together – 'with his disciples also' – and made a staggeringly paradoxical speech.

For the first time he mentioned the cross – and invited the people to join him in denying themselves and taking up this symbol of a shameful death.

He taught that a life devoted to self was a lost life; but a life devoted to the kingdom of God was a life of fulfilment.

He put the life of the soul or the spirit before all material possessions.

He called the people adulterous and sinful.

He warned them that if they did not follow him he would be ashamed of them; and then, in the same speech which had begun with a reference to taking up the cross, he suddenly talked about coming 'in the glory of his Father with the holy angels'. The rejected, criminal carpenter was suddenly up there in the sky with his father, God, and the angels.

Finally, he promised that the kingdom of God would come in the lifetime of some of his hearers.

How could the disciples digest all this?

How could they begin to understand it?

How could they reconcile their friend and companion, the revolutionary teacher, the wonderful healer, with the man who warned them of shame, suffering and death – and also promised that he would appear with God and his angels?

After six days, eight days, or a week, Jesus took Peter and James and John, the privileged three disciples, the favourites, 'up into an high mountain'; probably Mount Hermon. We know that Jesus liked to go to a mountain to pray; but this was the first time he had taken any of the disciples. Were they puzzled or frightened by him? Because of his acceptance of the title of the Christ, because he had specifically foretold his future, because he had taught with total originality and implied publicly that he was the Son of God, were the disciples suddenly in awe of their old companion? Did Peter, and perhaps James and John – because they must have wished it, because it would have been much simpler – *dream* that the carpenter became magically transfigured, that his travel-worn clothes became shining white garments? Did they dream that Elijah (Elias) and Moses came 'and they were talking with Jesus' because the prophet and the law-giver would obviously be more able to converse with the Christ than ordinary fishermen from Galilee who 'wist not what to say; for they were sore afraid'? Did they desperately wish to show their love and loyalty to Jesus, and made the only contribution which seemed humanly possible – a contribution which did not need any intellectual prowess – by offering to make three tabernacles in honour of Moses, Elias and Jesus? Did Peter – and James and John – desperately need confirmation from a higher authority that Jesus was the anointed one? And did they dream that God spoke to them out of the cloud and confirmed that 'this is my beloved Son'; and instruct them to 'hear him'? Did they dream these things because they wanted them to happen, because they could not absorb the paradox of Jesus's teaching and personality, and yearned for simple heavenly magic? I think that, on the mountain, Peter and James and John yearned for a dream which would take the responsibility of acceptance from them. I think it was a necessary dream, which might quite reasonably have occurred after the events in Caesarea Philippi.

If Peter dreamed these things he would have told James and John; or, if they all had a similar dream, it is most likely that they told each other, and then told Jesus.

'And as they came down from the mountain, he charged them that they should tell no man what things they had seen, till the Son of man were risen from the dead. And they kept that saying with themselves, questioning one with another what the rising from the dead should mean.'

If my theory is correct, it would mean that Jesus charged them not to talk about their *dream* of Elijah and Moses – and God speaking to them out of a cloud – until after his death. It also implies perhaps that Jesus hoped that they *would* talk about these things. It implies that Jesus was aware that the dream would be taken for reality, and that he was not averse to the invention and spreading of a legend. He did not mind being seen in the company of Elijah and Moses, and he accepted that his chosen father would wish to speak to his friends. Nevertheless, he did not want them to talk about these things until after his death – or rather, as Jesus put it, 'till the Son of man were risen from the dead'. And with these words the disciples were thrown into confusion again.

First, if he was the Christ, they must have been confused by Jesus referring to himself as the Son of man; and then they must have been confused by the certainty of his belief in resurrection. They must have wondered what form this resurrection would take; how long it would last; and whether Jesus

134

would finally appear as a king. But something about the personality of Jesus prevented these three favourite disciples from asking him direct questions about his prophecy of resurrection. The faith of Jesus must have been an awesome thing.

However, the disciples were able to ask him a more academic question. It was firmly believed that the prophet Elijah (Elias) would return to earth again, to proclaim the coming of the Messiah. In the last verse but one in the Old Testament, Malachi 4: 5, it is written: 'Behold, I will send you Elijah the prophet before the coming of the great and dreadful day of the Lord.' The disciples decided to get this matter cleared up once and for all.

'And they asked him, saying, Why say the scribes that Elias must 11-13
*first come? And he answered and told them, Elias verily cometh first,
and restoreth all things; and how it is written of the Son of man, that
he must suffer many things, and be set at nought. But I say unto you,
That Elias is indeed come, and they have done unto him whatsoever
they listed, as it is written of him.'*

These verses are confusing. They are confusing in all the translations, and are evidently equally confusing in the original Greek.

Jesus starts off by talking of Elias; then he starts to talk about himself; then he returns to Elias again.

For the moment, let us concentrate on Elias.

St Matthew explains that 'the disciples understood that he spake to them of John the Baptist' – meaning that Jesus was stating categorically that John the Baptist was Elias returned to Earth again. Jesus said that 'Elias verily cometh first, and restoreth all things'. If John the Baptist was Elias, what did he restore? Could this refer – as Rev. Marshall seems to believe it does – to the last verse in the Old Testament, Malachi 4: 6; the verse that follows the words 'Behold, I will send you Elijah the prophet before the coming of the great and dreadful day of the Lord'? the prophecy continues: 'And he shall turn the heart of the fathers to the children, and the heart of the children to their fathers, lest I come and smite the earth with a curse;' or in the Good News translation: 'He will bring fathers and children together again; otherwise I would have to come and destroy your country.' Could we relate this – as I am sure the Rev.

Marshall would *not* wish to do – to Jesus's own personal conflict about his parentage – and consider that through John the Baptist Jesus was brought together with his true father, God? Did John the Baptist restore the legitimacy of Jesus? Could this be what *Jesus* believed? And did he believe it so strongly that the alternative was to 'smite the earth with a curse' or 'to come and destroy your country'?

The rest of Jesus's words to the disciples, as they came down from the mountain, are better expressed in Matthew's version. 'But I say unto you, That Elias is come already, and they knew him not, but have done unto him whatsoever they listed. Likewise shall also the Son of man suffer of them.' This version *concludes* with Jesus warning the disciples yet again of his future rejection and death, instead of inserting it – as Mark does – in the middle of the lines about Elias. Jesus was saying, in fact, that like John the Baptist, he too would suffer an ignominious end.

*

14-15 *'And when he came to his disciples, he saw a great multitude about them, and the scribes questioning with them. And straightway all the people, when they beheld him, were greatly amazed, and running to him saluted him.'*

Presumably it was still in the region of Caesarea Philippi when Jesus, with Peter and James and John, joined up with the other nine disciples. I am tempted to think that, after Jesus made his great speech about the necessity of losing one's life in order to save it, and his warning and promise about the future when he would be seen in the company of his father with the holy angels, he went into hiding in order to meditate and pray. I think that this meditation and prayer lasted for the six days – or eight days – before he went up into the mountain with Peter and James and John. During his absence, word must have spread about this astonishing man who spoke with such unusual authority and passion. The disciples were left to their own devices, and presumably continued the master's work. They would have preached and cast out devils and healed the sick. They would also have talked about Jesus. They would most likely have *boasted* about Jesus, and the news reached the ears of some scribes who happened to be visiting that northern region. I think the whole neighbourhood was probably in a state of excitement about their mysterious visitor; so that when Jesus and his three companions joined the other disciples it caused a sensation. There is a feeling of a visiting celebrity in the description: 'all the people, when they beheld him, were greatly amazed, and running to him saluted him.' His legend had gone before him.

But we are now going to meet a different man. The character of Jesus changed after the challenge of Caesarea Philippi and after his decision to fulfil his father's work and take the road to Jerusalem. Jesus was at peace with himself. But this peace certainly did not mean passivity. Jesus's acceptance of the challenge of his mission gave him new courage and new authority. Now, *he* challenged the world.

In his last encounters with scribes and Pharisees, Jesus contradicted them, he rejected their ideas, he snubbed them. On his return from the mountain, when he discovered them questioning with his disciples, he challenged them. Without waiting for them to question him, he challenged them.

'And he asked the scribes, What question ye with them? And one of 16-17 *the multitude answered and said, Master, I have brought unto thee my son, which hath a dumb spirit.'*

The writing surprises us. There is no confrontation with the scribes, but at least we are aware of Jesus's new attitude. Now, in the following detailed account of a desperate father begging for help to cure his epileptic son, Mark gives us further evidence of the change in the man newly called the Christ.

The father continued his plea – with words that seem mischievously translated in the King James Version.

'And wheresoever he taketh him, he teareth him: and he foameth, 18 *and gnasheth with his teeth, and pineth away: –'*

(Counting 'teeth', that's six 'eths' in nineteen words!)

'and I spake to thy disciples that they should cast him out; and they could not.'

The Rev. Marshall has a charming idea about why the disciples failed to perform a cure. 'Their spiritual life might have been weakened by the absence of Jesus, or by desire for personal display in the cure. They may have been desirous to exhibit their powers in pride before the scribes.' This might be true, although from the ensuing description it seems that this

137

was a particularly difficult case. But Jesus did not sympathise with the disciples or with the father. He chided them for their lack of faith. He was immediately articulate.

'He answereth them, and sayeth, O faithless generation, how long shall I be with you? how long shall I suffer you?'

This does not sound like despair – but more like impatience or anger. He continued with the practical command:

'Bring him unto me.'

And Mark balances his command with the words:

'And they brought him unto him.'

In their accounts of this miracle, St Matthew and St Luke now cut straight to Jesus rebuking the unclean spirit and curing the boy. Only Mark gives us the following fascinating dialogue between Jesus and the distraught father. Believing in the continuity of Mark, we clearly detect the change in Jesus, and the change in the ministry.

'and when he saw him, straightway the spirit tare him; and he fell on the ground, and wallowed foaming. And he asked his father, How long is it ago that this came unto him? And he said, Of a child. And ofttimes it hath cast him into the fire, and into the waters, to destroy him: but if thou canst do anything, have compassion on us, and help us. Jesus said unto him, If thou canst believe, all things are possible to him that believeth. And straightway the father of the child cried out, and said with tears, Lord, I believe; help thou mine unbelief. When Jesus saw that the people came running together, he rebuked the foul spirit, saying unto him, Thou dumb and deaf spirit, I charge thee, come out of him and enter no more into him. And the spirit cried, and rent him sore, and came out of him: and he was as one dead; insomuch that many said, He is dead. But Jesus took him by the hand, and lifted him up; and he arose.'

It seems that there were going to be no more easy miracles. Jesus was no longer going to agree to every man's request. He demanded belief. He demanded that men should heal themselves. His behaviour in this episode was very tough. Even after the father had 'cried out, and said with tears, Lord, I believe; help thou mine unbelief' it appears that Jesus was not going to heal the boy. It was only when the altercation and the drama of the situation had attracted even larger crowds – one can imagine the immediate bystanders calling out to their townsfolk that something sensational was going to happen and 'the people came running together' – that Jesus performed the cure.

Twice during this scene Jesus referred to faith or belief.

This sets the tone for the second part of the ministry.

The man who 'healed many that were sick of divers diseases, and cast out many devils' had changed. He would no longer be manipulated. There would be no more mass surgeries. There is, in fact, only one more recorded miracle of healing by Jesus in St Mark's Gospel. Perhaps the disciples continued this work. Although after their failure with the epileptic boy they were obviously very troubled.

'*And when he was come into the house, his disciples asked him* 28 *privately, Why could not we cast him out? And he said unto them,* 29 *This kind can come forth by nothing, but by prayer and fasting.*'

I like the continuation of the pattern of behaviour between Jesus and the disciples as reported in this section of St Mark. 'And when he was entered into the house from the people, his disciples asked him concerning the parable.' 'And when he was come into the house, his disciples asked him privately . . .' 'And in the house his disciples asked him again of the same matter.' The disciples were careful not to be seen in any confusion or doubt in public. They asked him 'privately'. On this occasion Jesus recommended more prayer, but the words 'and fasting' are evidently a later addition – which is a relief. Certainly Jesus does not mention fasting in any other episode – except as a mark of respect for his death. It would be sad to have to equate greater faith with greater hunger; and this was not, I think, what Jesus would have demanded.

★

Now let us consider two examples – apart from the sudden plethora of 'eths' – of the language of the King James Version in this story.

When the boy was brought to Jesus we are told that 'he fell on the ground, and *wallowed foaming*'. Those two words are nothing if not evocative. More recent translations tell us 'he fell on the ground and rolled about, foaming at the mouth' (Revised Standard); or 'he fell to the ground and lay writhing there, foaming at the mouth' (The Jerusalem Bible).

These translations are certainly acceptable – but I don't think that they quite convey the horror of 'he fell on the ground, and *wallowed foaming*' – and they certainly require more words.

When Jesus challenged the father's belief, we hear the man's agonising cry, 'Lord, I believe; help thou mine unbelief.' In the Good News this is translated: 'I do have faith, but not enough. Help me to have more!' Or in The New English Bible: 'I have faith,' cried the boy's father; 'help me where faith falls short.'

These translations are certainly clear and concise, but they lack the glorious poetic drama of the King James Version. Somehow the passion of the father's cry is diminished. And again – even though they are concise – they both take more words. The more words, the less the impact of the drama.

There are two cumbersome attempts to explain the words 'Lord, I believe; help thou mine unbelief' by well-intentioned commentators.

'I believe,' he cried. 'If there is still some discouragement in me, still some doubts, take them away and fill me with an unquestioning faith.' (Barclay)

'Help me, although such belief as I have must be counted as complete unbelief in comparison with what is demanded.' (Nineham)

Words, words, words . . .

'I believe; help thou mine unbelief' is matchless, and needs no help or explanation.

*

Now the journey south begins.

30 - 32 'And they departed thence, and passed through Galilee; and he would not that any man should know it. For he taught his disciples, and said unto them, The Son of man is delivered into the hands of men, and they shall kill him; and after that he is killed, he shall rise the third day. But they understood not that saying, and were afraid to ask him.'

It would either appear that they travelled by night, or else that they avoided people by travelling across country. This was not only to let Jesus teach his disciples, but also, as I have previously written, because it is likely there was danger in the region where he had spoken strongly against the old laws.

We now have a sense of a very close-knit group of people. Although the disciples sometimes blundered and Jesus reprimanded them, there is a wonderful warmth and loyalty between them in the next part of the Gospel as they journey together. Jesus knew that he must suffer a painful death. He knew that he would have to demand that death. He knew that he had to fulfil his chosen father's wishes, and demonstrate forever the power of faith.

In this warning to his disciples, his prophecy was more specific. He said, 'The Son of man *is delivered into the hands of men*' – which was the first hint of a betrayal. And again he spoke of his resurrection – and again the disciples did not understand. If they had any vision of the future, it would have been a happy and triumphant one. They would not want it to involve suffering and death.

The emphasis on the 'third day' is a problem. In his commentary, Alan Cole makes a useful suggestion that 'the third day could be used vaguely and metaphorically for "subsequently"' – which would certainly make it sound a little less like a resurrection time-table.

'And he came to Capernaum: and being in the house he asked them, **33-37** *What was it that ye disputed among yourselves by the way? But they held their peace: for by the way they had disputed among themselves, who should be the greatest. And he sat down, and called the twelve, and saith unto them. If any man desire to be first, the same shall be last of all, and servant of all. And he took a child, and set him in the midst of them: and when he had taken him in his arms, he said unto them, Whosoever shall receive one of such children in my name, receiveth me: and whosoever shall receive me, receiveth not me, but him that sent me.'*

This would be Jesus's last visit to Capernaum. Perhaps, since they did not know what would happen in Jerusalem, it would be the last visit for some – or even all – of the disciples. Did they talk about this? Could they express their feelings? Was there an awareness of the heartbreak in the heart of things? Or were they filled with excitement at the challenge ahead of them?

Jesus's gloomy predictions about himself certainly do not seem to have dashed the spirits of the twelve. Along the way they had argued about their future status. It would be surprising if this was the first time it had happened. Even before the revelation that Jesus was the Christ, the disciples probably talked about their relative positions in his affections. They were a mixed group of personalities, and Jesus must have loved them for various reasons; and his need for any one particular disciple must have depended on circumstances of time and place. This is Peter's remembrance of the ministry, and he and James and John certainly appear to have been closest to Jesus. But for all we know – and perhaps for all Peter knew – Jesus may have been equally close to some of the others.

Serious people express horror at this crass behaviour of the disciples disputing who should be the greatest; they cannot believe their simplicity and lack of sensitivity – but as usual they leave out the possibility of humour. It may well have been a game that the disciples played to pass the time as they trudged through the countryside. We cannot expect that they kept silent, or that they always talked of religious things. It would be understandable in such a large group – just as it would be in a football or rugger team – that they sometimes joked and teased, that they would speculate about who was in and who was out, who had succeeded and who had failed, and who would be next season's captain. And, although they apparently did not have these discussions in Jesus's hearing, he must have known that they went on. Perhaps, on this occasion, the game turned into a violent argument overheard by Jesus, and this was why he decided to face them with it; or perhaps it was simply part of his teaching as they passed through Galilee. I think he used this game of the disciples to enlighten them and make a useful point. I do not think the tone was heavy with reproof; on the contrary, it was surely humorous and affectionate.

Was it evening? Were they tired? Was it the house of Simon and Andrew? Was Simon's wife's mother ministering unto them? Had there been laughter and embracing? Was the house bursting with the unexpected visitors? Had they eaten – and drunk – and was it after an improvised meal that Jesus asked his question? 'What was it that ye disputed among yourselves by the way?' Was there a sudden silence of embarrassment – with perhaps a single muffled laugh – before Jesus 'sat down, and called the twelve'? Did the rest of the family watch and listen, fascinated by the situation? And Jesus 'saith unto them. If any man desire to be first, the same shall be last of all, and servant of all. And he took a child . . .' Whose child? Were there many children? Apart from the twelve-year-old girl Jesus raised from the dead, this is the first mention of a child in the Gospel. With a child – or children – present, could there have been solemnity?

I think this was a very young child, perhaps a staggering little boy, that Jesus set 'in the midst of them'. He was suddenly the centre of attention – something most children do not find objectionable. 'And when he had taken him in his arms' – with a delighted squeal? – 'he said unto them, Whosoever shall receive one of such children in my name, receiveth me.' Another paradox: Where were the elders, the chief priests, the scribes, the rulers of the synagogue in Jesus's new order of things? They were of less importance than a child. And then – just in time, Jesus remembered his own chosen father: 'and whosoever shall receive me, receiveth not me, but him that sent me.'

In this relaxed atmosphere (forget the commentators who say that here Mark collected stray sayings of Jesus that he couldn't fit in anywhere else!) John, the brother of James, the son of Zebedee, one of 'the sons of thunder', was emboldened to ask a question that had been troubling him. 38 – 41

'And John answered him, saying, Master, we saw one casting out devils in thy name, and he followeth not us: and we forbad him, because he followeth not us. But Jesus said, Forbid him not: for there is no man which shall do a miracle in my name, that can lightly speak evil of me. For he that is not against us is on our part. For whosoever shall give you a cup of water to drink in my name, because ye belong to Christ, verily I say unto you, he shall not lose his reward.'

Note the repetition of 'in my name'.

This little passage again confirms the feeling of togetherness. John regards the group as a small exclusive club. Jesus has visions of a much bigger club. Anyone who performs a miracle 'in my name' – anyone who offers them a cup of water 'in my name' is automatically a member. And, in one of those wonderfully comforting statements that undercut all the dogma and all the squabbles of the churches that have been built in his name, he assures them – and us – that 'he that is not against us is on our part'.

How did Christianity get so complicated? What did an obscenity like the Holy Inquisition have to do with this Jesus? Who can explain our obsession with rules? Who can explain our love of titles and orders? Jesus proclaimed a child his equal. He proclaimed the gift of a cup of water as a qualification for discipleship. John's question was answered.

Jesus continues:

42

'And whosoever shall offend one of these little ones that believe in me, it is better for him that a millstone were hanged about his neck, and he were cast into the sea.'

I think this was a direct reference to the child Jesus had taken into his arms. I think the child was still there. (Forget the commentators who deny the continuity of the scene and say that 'little ones' refers to 'immature Christians' or 'disciples of little faith' or 'weaker brethren'. Of course the meaning could apply to such-like poor folk – but let's stick with the child!)

Now the writing becomes formal and poetic. The words are terrifying, but the rhythm of the speech seems to modify the harshness of its instructions. It might have been spoken with Jesus rocking the child in his arms. Although the meaning is deadly serious, it might even have been delivered as a game, with Jesus illustrating the words with the child's hand and foot and eye. Try reading it that way – and hear the frequent interruption of a small boy's laughter.

43 - 48

'And if thy hand offend thee, cut it off: it is better for thee to enter into life maimed, than having two hands to go into hell, into the fire that never shall be quenched: Where their worm dieth not, and the fire is not quenched. And if thy foot offend thee, cut it off: it is better for thee to enter halt into life, than having two feet to be cast into hell, into the fire that never shall be quenched: Where their worm dieth not, and the fire is not quenched. And if thine eye offend thee, pluck it out: it is better for thee to enter into the kingdom of God with one eye, than having two eyes to be cast into hell fire: Where their worm dieth not, and the fire is not quenched.'

The game finishes.

'When he says, "If thy hand offend thee, cut it off" it may sound rather sharp,' writes Manford George Gutzke. Yes, it does . . .

The speech is open to various interpretations. I incline to equate the hand, the foot and the eye to loved ones, friends or relations. If a friend offends us, if a friend attempts to undermine our faith, we should terminate that friendship. If our closest friend or closest relation offends us, we should end that relationship. Jesus warns that to offend the faith of a child warrants punishment by drowning with a millstone round the neck. In *this* passage, I think he instructed his disciples to be fiercely protective of their faith, and to resist any attempts to destroy it.

The verse 'where their worm dieth not, and the fire is not quenched' (which is a quote from Isaiah 66: 24) occurs three times in the King James Version, but only once in nearly all the later translations. According to the Revised Standard, this is because the verses are 'omitted by the best ancient authorities'. It seems a pity; the repetition is splendid, and gives this section a special colour and individuality. There is also the contrast between the formality of the words, with the informality of Jesus sitting with a small child in his arms – perhaps a wriggling child.

Now we come to the 'salt sayings'. These may be the leftovers of Peter's memory of the evening's teaching.

First, Jesus warns them:

'For every one shall be salted with fire . . .' 49

Which I take to mean that at some time all of us will have our faith severely tested.

'. . . and every sacrifice shall be salted with salt.'

Which I take to mean that any sacrifice we make will be judged strictly on its merit.

'Salt is good: but if the salt have lost his saltness, wherewith will ye 50 *season it?'*

Don't lose the intensity of your faith.

'Have salt in yourselves.'

Have courage and determination and individuality.

'. . . and have peace one with another.'

The evening finishes with a blessing; and Jesus's words 'one with another' emphasise the equality of the child with the disciples.

Perhaps Jesus put the child down and patted it towards them . . . before Simon's wife's mother packed it off to bed.

★

1   *'And he arose from thence, and cometh into the coasts of Judaea by the farther side of Jordan; and the people resort unto him again; and, as he was wont, he taught them again.'*

This is another piece of foggy geography. It helps a lot to translate 'coasts' as 'borders', but it's impossible to say which side of the Jordan Jesus was on. If Capernaum and Galilee were regarded as home – and they were where Jesus had just come from – then it is most likely he was now in Peraea – near the banks of the Jordan and the borders of Judaea. Anyway, he was going south. And he had started to teach in public again. There is no mention of healing.

Now the Pharisees have another question for him – and he has another splendid answer for the Pharisees.

2-10   *'And the Pharisees came to him, and asked him, Is it lawful for a man to put away his wife? tempting him. And he answered and said unto them, What did Moses command you? And they said, Moses suffered to write a bill of divorcement, and to put her away. And Jesus answered and said unto them, For the hardness of your heart he wrote you this precept. But from the beginning of the creation God made them male and female. For this cause shall a man leave his father and mother, and cleave to his wife; And they twain shall be one flesh: so then they are no more twain, but one flesh. What therefore God hath joined together, let not man put asunder.'*

If Jesus was in Peraea, he was still in the territories of Herod. The Rev. Marshall wonders: 'Did the Pharisees wish to make Him offend Herodias as John the Baptist had done and by this means bring about His destruction?' It is possible that this was their intention, but I think it is unlikely. The answer Jesus gave would certainly have upset Herodias – but Mark gives no indication of any reaction from the royal household.

From their past experience with Jesus, the Pharisees probably expected a totally different response from him. He had already expressed shockingly unconventional views on clean and unclean food and the Old Laws about defilement. He had broken the sabbath, and spoken slightingly of fasting. He ate and drank with publicans and sinners, and associated with Gentiles. It is likely that the Pharisees expected him to express utter contempt for marriage. They certainly didn't expect Jesus to turn the tables and teach them basic theology.

At that time, divorce was a much discussed question. In The

146

Fifth Book of Moses, called Deuteronomy, it is written: 'When a man hath taken a wife, and married her, and it come to pass that she find no favour in his eyes, because he hath found *some uncleanness* in her: then let him write her a bill of divorcement, and give it in her hand, and send her out of his house.'

The interpretation of 'some uncleanness' caused confusion. There were two schools of thought. The school of Shammai limited divorce to moral delinquency. But the other school – of Hillel – allowed it for the most trifling reasons. Barclay tells us 'They said that it could mean if the wife spoiled a dish of food, if she spun in the streets, if she talked to a strange man, if she spoke disrespectfully to her husband's relations in his hearing, if she was a brawling woman, (who was defined as a woman whose voice could be heard in the next house).' I think it is likely that – at the very least – the Pharisees expected Jesus to belong to the second school; or even, that he would not recommend marriage at all.

Instead, Jesus began by forcing the Pharisees to state their own position. 'What did Moses say about divorce?' Jesus asked them. 'He said it was all right,' they replied. 'He said that all a man has to do is write his wife a letter of dismissal' (The Living Bible). Jesus then started into the attack. With breath-taking nerve, he excused Moses, and informed them that the great law-giver's words were only a concession to the hard-ness of their hearts. Jesus recognised that poor old Moses had problems, and he put the blame firmly on the people. Then he led the Pharisees back to God and Adam.

In the first Chapter of Genesis it is written: 'So God created man in his own image, in the image of God created he him; male and female created he them.' And, in the second Chapter, Adam says: 'Therefore shall a man leave his father and his mother, and shall cleave unto his wife: and they shall be one flesh.'

After an approximate quote of these words, Jesus continued – like a strict arithmetic master with backward children – 'So then they are no more twain, but one flesh,' and then said, on behalf of his chosen father: 'What therefore God hath joined together, let not man put asunder.' 'Jesus takes the Pharisees back to the creation of man, and the primary law of marriage thus referring them to a higher and more absolute law than that of Moses' (Marshall).

It was another humiliation; it was another piece of original teaching; and it is somewhat unexpected. If Jesus only intended to disconcert the Pharisees he certainly succeeded; but I wonder if his real views were as rigid as they appear in this version. I suspect the editing hand of the puritanical Mark, and the family man Peter.

Jesus now goes on to reiterate his views to the disciples, in another of those after-the-event lectures.

10 – 12 *'And in the house his disciples asked him again of the same matter.'*
Hear Mark's voice with the word 'again'!

'And he saith unto them, Whosoever shall put away his wife, and marry another, committeth adultery against her. And if a woman shall put away her husband, and be married to another, she committeth adultery.'

St Matthew's arrangement of this episode is different. Here, Jesus says: 'Whosoever shall put away his wife,' and then adds, '*except it be for fornication,*' before he goes on, 'and shall marry another, committeth adultery.' (In this version Jesus says this to the Pharisees and not to the disciples.) But with their omission of Jesus's harsh references to his mother and to conventional family life, and their reluctance to mention the women who followed Jesus – until the end of the Gospel – it is characteristic of Mark and Peter to leave out this rider of a wife's fornication as grounds for divorce.

(Even with this rider, in St Matthew's version the disciples then complain – in The New English Bible translation – 'If that is the position with husband and wife, it is better not to marry.' And Jesus tells them that 'some are incapable of marriage because they were born so, or were made so by men, there are others who have themselves renounced marriage for the sake of the kingdom of Heaven. Let those accept it who can.' This is a much more considered and believable answer that St Mark's abrupt version.)

★

13 – 16 *'And they brought young children to him, that he should touch them: and his disciples rebuked those that brought them. But when Jesus saw it, he was much displeased, and said unto them, Suffer the little*

children to come unto me, and forbid them not; for of such is the kingdom of God. Verily I say unto you, Whosoever shall not receive the kingdom of God as a little child, he shall not enter therein. And he took them up in his arms, put his hands upon them, and blessed them.'

It is good that this little story of Jesus and the children was remembered by Peter – even though the disciples' behaviour appears to be unsympathetic. It is good that this episode is greatly loved by Christians – even though the second part of it does not always seem to be understood.

'It was a common practice with Jewish mothers to bring their babes to Rabbis for a blessing.' (Marshall) It also seems to have been common practice for the disciples to protect Jesus from the people. If this appears to be unsympathetic, it was surely well intentioned. It may also have been an attempt to carry out Jesus's orders. In St John's Gospel (Chapter 12: v. 21, 22) there is a description of 'certain Greeks' who want to meet Jesus: 'The same came therefore to Philip . . . and desired him, saying, Sir, we would see Jesus. Philip cometh and telleth Andrew; and again Andrew and Philip tell Jesus.' This reminds me of those old musicals where the young composer and lyricist have to make huge efforts to see the producer. Often they only manage to do this as the great man is entering his office. Perhaps it was the same with the mothers and children. Perhaps Jesus caught the disciples rebuking the eager mothers as he returned from other business. And the children immediately won his approval – without any further auditioning.

Jesus used the situation to teach the disciples a lesson. After being 'much displeased' (one wonders how much was 'much') and calling the children to him, he claimed, 'Of such is the kingdom of God.' Perhaps not all of the children were natural choices for the kingdom of God – perhaps some of the children were screaming their heads off. Perhaps some of the disciples protested. But Jesus re-enforced his words with a 'Verily I say unto you', and then made the wonderful statement: 'Whosoever shall not receive the kingdom of God as a little child, he shall not enter therein.' This surely doesn't mean that one has to *be* a child to enter into the kingdom of God, but that as adults we should retain the open-mindedness, the receptivity,

10

the wonder, the joy, the simplicity, the candour and the eagerness of a child.

With the child in the house in Capernaum, Mark wrote: 'And when he had taken him in his arms;' and in this episode he wrote: 'And he took them up in his arms.' This lifting up of the children is only described in Mark's Gospel – presumably it was specifically remembered by Peter. It gives us a picture of an affectionate and demonstrative man.

And, in both stories, Jesus used the children to make special points to the disciples. First, that the child was his equal and their equal in importance; and, second, that the innocence of a child is necessary for entry into the kingdom of God.

Jesus now uses another encounter to teach them. This charming episode develops into a sort of outdoor version of the domestic scene in Capernaum – with an illustrated lesson followed by another little debate.

17 *'And when he was gone forth into the way, there came one running, and kneeled to him, and asked him, Good Master, what shall I do that I may inherit eternal life?'*

They have started on their travels again. Suddenly, in a cloud of dust, a man rushed up to Jesus – had he been running for miles? – knelt at his feet and begged instructions for avoiding death and living forever. (Matthew's version tells us he was a *'young* man' – in case we didn't guess.) Oddly, Jesus doesn't seem to be surprised by the sudden arrival – did the young man nearly knock him over? – or outraged by the baldness of the request; but he disliked being flattered. First of all he corrected the young man's 'Good Master'.

18 *'And Jesus said unto him, Why callest thou me good? there is none good but one, that is, God.'*

Here again he must have confused his disciples. If Jesus was the Christ, Jesus must be good. It should be natural for Jesus to be good. But it seems that Jesus had the same struggles – the failures and the successes – with his behaviour that we all have. It is a relief to imagine a lazy Jesus, a greedy Jesus, a careless Jesus; Jesus with impatience, with envy, Jesus occasionally with spite. He may have had some of these faults. From the evidence of St Mark's Gospel he *did* have some of these faults. He also had knowledge of them. When the young man called him 'good', I think there was immediate irritation – not

150

necessarily with the young man, but with himself. 'Why callest thou me good?' The correction takes us all in: 'There is none good but one, that is, God.' Then, perhaps, there was a reaction against the irritation. Kneeling at his feet, a young man recklessly, publicly, unselfconsciously, expected a formula for eternal life – as if eternal life was the equivalent of becoming a company director, a high-ranking officer, the top of the form; as if eternal life was the equivalent of winning an award, a prize, or a diploma. Did the naïveté of the request and the humour of the situation appeal to Jesus? He tried to be practical. Like a schoolmaster enquiring whether the young man had done all his home-work he asked:

'Thou knowest the commandments, Do not commit adultery, Do not kill, Do not steal, Do not bear false witness, Defraud not, Honour thy father and mother.'

These commandments are found in Exodus 20: V. 12–17 and also in Deuteronomy 5: V. 16–21. In both Books the list starts with the commandment 'Honour thy father and thy mother'; and then the commandment 'Thou shalt not kill.' The commandment not to commit adultery comes third. But Jesus puts it first again. (This order is altered in later translations.)

Also, 'Defraud not' is a much abridged version of 'Thou shalt not covet thy neighbour's house, thou shalt not covet thy neighbour's wife, nor his manservant, nor his maidservant, nor his ox, nor his ass, nor any thing that is thy neighbour's'. (Exodus 20: V. 17)

Evidently the young man had not committed adultery, or killed anyone, or stolen anything, or been a false witness, or defrauded anybody, and he had always been a model son to his parents. The reply comes with irresistible candour:

'And he answered and said unto him, Master, all these things have I observed from my youth.'

If he was in fact a *very* young man, the reply is even more charming. Anyone into their twenties and upwards is likely to have had the experience of exchanges with youngsters who make boastful assertions of their grand experience of life. One is temporarily stunned to learn that a nineteen-year-old has given up drinking, or that an eighteen-year-old is politically disillusioned, or that a seventeen-year-old has decided against

151

any more emotional entanglements. For a moment, the weight of years lies very heavy on us and we are unable to react. We, who have given up drinking so many times; who have wavered politically from right to left and back to right again; we, who – even now – are probably once more involved in some ridiculous emotional entanglement. The wisdom of the very young is both touching and slightly comic. In a protective way, one longs to hug them – to keep them always safe from the dust of the world. This seems to have been Jesus's reaction to the young man.

'Then Jesus beholding him loved him . . .' – 'loved him' is only to be found in St Mark's Gospel. Nineham writes that 'here we should perhaps think rather of some definite outward gesture of affection – 'caressed him' or 'put his arms round him'; and he adds that 'many modern commentators take the same line'.

After the gesture of affection came the test. Jesus determined to find out just how far the young man's perfection would extend.

'. . . and said unto him, One thing thou lackest: go thy way, sell whatsoever thou hast, and give to the poor, and thou shalt have treasure in heaven: and come, take up the cross, and follow me. And he was sad at that saying, and went away grieved: for he had great possessions.'

Jesus's unequivocal instructions to 'sell whatsoever thou hast, and give to the poor' make many people nervous. The Rev. Marshall, in his dear old-fashioned way, arrives at two 'lessons' to be learnt from Jesus's words.

'Lessons –

(1) To be benevolent, but not to follow the injunction 'to sell all' literally in all cases.

(2) To abandon everything – wealth, position, ambition, if these stand in the way of our soul's salvation.'

I think the Rev. Marshall could be absolutely certain of his 'soul's salvation' – I hope he settled for benevolence. However, I am not certain of my own soul's salvation – and I am definitely not willing 'to sell all literally'; and that goes for most of us. So *my* view of Jesus's instruction is that he was teasing the young man – teasing being a light-hearted form of testing. There have been a few good men who have sold all 'literally' – but they are called saints, whether officially or unofficially – and Jesus knew full well that they would always be very few and far between. Did the running and kneeling young man look like a saint? I doubt it. Was he ready to sell everything. Not yet. Was he humbled by Jesus's question? Evidently. He appears to be suddenly tongue-tied – perhaps there was a muffled 'Oh dear!' or a stammered 'Excuse me!' Mark only tells us: 'And he was sad at that saying, and went away grieved: for he had great possessions.'

(More praise for the King James Version! Have the construction and wording of that verse ever been bettered? 'At these words his face fell and he went away with a heavy heart; for he was a man of great wealth.' 'When the man heard this, gloom spread over his face, and he went away sad, because he was very rich.' As a good friend said to the architect of the Taj Mahal when he started to tinker: 'Leave it!')

Now the debate begins.

'And Jesus looked round about, and saith unto his disciples, How hardly shall they that have riches enter into the kingdom of God!' 23

(The King James Version is very sparing with exclamation marks. There is one in Chapter Three after 'Behold my mother and my brethren!' when Jesus ignores his family and indicates the multitude sitting about him. This is only the second one in the Gospel.)

'And the disciples were astonished at his words. But Jesus answereth again, and saith unto them, Children, how hard is it for them that trust in riches to enter into the kingdom of God!' 24

(This is the third!)

'It is easier for a camel to go through the eye of a needle, than for a rich man to enter into the kingdom of God. And they were astonished out of measure, saying among themselves, Who then can be saved? And Jesus looking upon them saith, With men it is impossible, but not with God: for with God all things are possible.' 25-27

Two exclamation marks! Camels and needles! The disciples astonished out of measure! We are obviously at a very worrying place in the ministry. This is revolutionary extremist talk. Does Jesus mean what he says? Help us please, Rev. Marshall!

'This discourse is not a denunciation of the rich' (Ah! Thank goodness!) 'but rather a commiseration of them owing to the peculiar and insidious temptations to which they are incessantly exposed.' (Poor things!) 'Riches in themselves are not wrong' (Of course not!) 'but they are a temptation and a snare, inducing lives of idleness, luxury and vice.' (And very nice too!)

No, but seriously . . .

'And Jesus looked round about, and saith unto his disciples' – 'looked round about' implies that Jesus had watched the young man as he 'went away grieved;' perhaps watched him till he disappeared, and then turned to his disciples as if to challenge them to discussion. He started off with a statement that surprised: 'How hardly shall they that have riches enter into the kingdom of God!' It surprised because the disciples would have grown up believing that riches were a sign of God's favour. They would have believed that wealth and prosperity were the mark of a good man; of a man who had been blessed. Mark reports no actual protest from them, but their reaction must have been strong enough for Jesus to confirm his words. 'Children,' he said ('of such is the kingdom of God') and this is an indication of the warmth of his affection for them, and the level of their relationship with him; 'Children, how hard it is for them that trust in riches to enter into the kingdom of God!' And then Jesus made the extraordinarily vivid remark about a camel going through the eye of a needle. Perhaps it is even more extraordinary to us who rarely see a camel in the High Street. There are attempts to rationalise this saying by translating the word for camel as a rope – or interpreting needle as the name of a postern gate in the city wall. But it is more attractive to think that Jesus made a colourful metaphor of wild improbability. (Jesus was fond of the camel for making a strong point. In St Matthew he lays into the scribes and Pharisees with 'Ye blind guides, which strain at a gnat, and swallow a camel'.)

The disciples 'were astonished out of measure' – which, for them, was very astonished indeed – at the exclusion of rich men from the kingdom of God. And one has a sense of the naïveté of this little group of working men. We must remember that, until they met Jesus, they probably had little experience of life. They would have grown up with certain fixed ideas. They would, until they met Jesus, have accepted the caste systems of their day – one of which was that to be rich was to be blessed and honoured. It is true that by now they had travelled with Jesus for some time, but it seems that the subject of riches had never previously been discussed. With his customary abandon ('All sins shall be forgiven unto the sons of men, and blasphemies wherewith soever they shall blaspheme . . .') Jesus debars the rich from the kingdom of God. It seems that the disciples do not dare to argue – but they say 'among themselves, Who then can be saved?' And then Jesus goes even further. 'With men,' he says, 'it is impossible, but not with God: for with God all things are possible.' I think that Jesus was saying that salvation is only to be gained by spiritual means; that it cannot be achieved by riches – that it cannot be achieved by building churches or acts of charity, that men cannot *buy* their way into the kingdom of God. We are back to the Holy Spirit. We are back to belief. We are back to the challenge of making a choice.

But the ruthlessness of Jesus's words evidently upset the disciples. It must have seemed to them as if their own sacrifice of leaving their work, their homes, and – possibly – their families, might go unrewarded by God. They wanted confirmation that they were close favourites for salvation.

'Then Peter began to say unto him, Lo, we have left all, and have 28–31 *followed thee. And Jesus answered and said, Verily I say unto you, There is no man that hath left house, or brethren, or sisters, or father, or mother, or wife, or children, or lands, for my sake, and the gospel's, But he shall receive an hundredfold now in this time, houses, and brethren, and sisters, and mothers, and children, and lands, with persecutions; and in the world to come eternal life. But many that are first shall be last; and the last first.'*

They needed confirmation that they were favourites – and they got it. Peter, the most outspoken and articulate of the disciples, 'began' to protest (note the 'began'!) and it seems that before he could even finish his words Jesus 'answered and said' – just 'answered and said,' *not* answered and said unto them – 'Verily I say unto you', and the words of comfort come pouring out. This is wonderfully warm and human stuff. It is like a sudden, unexpected love scene between Jesus and the disciples – although, typically, in the middle of his affectionate outpouring, while offering the disciples 'an hundredfold now in this time, houses, and brethren, and sisters, and mothers, and children, and lands', he suddenly inserts the knife and adds *'with persecutions'* – just to remind them that life will never be a bowl of cherries, and that they have not yet arrived somewhere over the rainbow.

Then, after confirming that through their faith they now belong to the larger family of God, Jesus warns the disciples of the dangers of pride and complacency. In words of caution for every archbishop and cardinal, every king and queen, every president and prime minister, every judge and general; and, in words of comfort for the anonymous host of the undistinguished and unrecognised, the unemployed and unemployable, Jesus says: 'But many that are first shall be last; and the last first.'

These words are still revolutionary.

These words partly explain the attraction of the man of Galilee, and the spread of Christianity throughout the world.

I need to quote George Eliot again. '. . . for the growing good of the world is partly dependant on unhistoric acts; and that things are not so ill with you and me as they might have been, is half owing to the number who lived faithfully a hidden life, and rest in unvisited tombs.'

★

32 *'And they were in the way going up to Jerusalem . . .'*

The music of the last movement begins.

Since leaving Caesarea Philippi, Jesus and his disciples have been travelling towards the south; they 'passed through Galilee'; and 'he came to Capernaum'; and then he 'cometh into the coasts of Judaea by the farther side of Jordan'; but Mark has not mentioned their actual destination. Now, as if accompanied by a roll of drums and a fanfare of trumpets, he reveals it; and within the next fifty verses the name 'Jerusalem' is thrillingly repeated.

'And they were in the way going up to *Jerusalem* . . .' Chapter 10: 32.

'Behold, we go up to *Jerusalem* . . .' 10: 33.

'And when they came nigh to *Jerusalem* . . .' 11: 1.

'And Jesus entered into *Jerusalem* . . .' 11: 11.

'And they come to *Jerusalem* . . .' 11: 15.

'And they come again to *Jerusalem* . . .' 11: 27.

The challenge of the Holy City is unmistakable. Of course it is possible that Jesus had visited Jerusalem before. St Luke records the twelve-year-old Jesus disputing in the temple. And St John tells the whole story of the ministry in a quite different order. But, dramatically and psychologically, Mark's version – as if this was the first visit – seems right.

And, dramatically and psychologically, Mark's description of Jesus walking – perhaps running – ahead of the disciples, hurrying towards Jerusalem, eager to please his chosen father, eager to fulfil his role of the beloved son, determined to challenge the establishment, determined to die and rise again and achieve immortality, seems absolutely right.

The road was in the valley of the Jordan below sea level. Jerusalem is 2,500 feet above sea level. That was why they were in the road '*going up* to Jerusalem.'

'*and Jesus went before them: and they were amazed; and as they followed, they were afraid.*'

Once again, only Mark gives us a precious eye-witness account – with details missing from the other Gospels. Only Mark – and Peter – tells us that 'Jesus went before them'. Only Mark – and Peter – tells us that the disciples – and probably many other followers – were 'amazed; and as they followed, they were afraid'. The Son of man, the Son of God, the carpenter, the Christ, had prophesied that terrible things would happen to him. He had quite recently prophesied betrayal and rejection and a shameful death – and yet he rushes ahead of them as if to greet his fate, as if to embrace his destiny. No wonder they were amazed, and as they followed, they were afraid. No wonder they were sometimes confused, and 'they understood not that saying', and they dreamed of a transfigured creature all in white who could be safely and simply worshipped and obeyed.

Instead, they trailed behind this phenomenally energetic, magnetic, paradoxical young man, who astonished, astounded, and terrified them with his courage and the originality of his mind.

They were unable to protect him. Once again he attempts to protect *them*. He makes the third or fourth warning.

'*And he took again the twelve, and began to tell them what things should happen unto him, Saying, Behold, we go up to Jerusalem; and* **33**

*the Son of man shall be delivered unto the chief priests, and unto the
scribes; and they shall condemn him to death, and shall deliver him to*
34 *the Gentiles: And they shall mock him, and shall scourge him, and
shall spit upon him, and shall kill him: and the third day he shall rise
again.'*

In this prophecy the delivery to the Gentiles is mentioned
for the first time. (Once, in New York, after I had given a
recital of St Mark's Gospel, a fierce young Jewish student who
had been in the audience and who had never heard the whole
story before, rushed at me in a great state of excitement. 'We
didn't do it!' he shouted. 'It was the Romans! *They* killed him!
They killed Jesus! We didn't do it! Why do we get all the
blame?') And Jesus not only foretells his delivery to the
Gentiles by the chief priest and the scribes, he also makes
specific prophecies of his suffering. The words come with the
remorseless rhythm of a whipping – and there is the first
repetition of the word 'him' (which Mark – and the King
James Version – uses again during the report of the actual
scourging by the Roman soldiers). 'And they shall mock *him*,
and shall scourge *him*, and shall spit upon *him*, and shall kill
him' – and then, mercifully, the rhythm changes from the
sound of the whipping to the balm of 'and the third day he shall
rise again'.

This little passage of prophecy is a poem. Read it once more.
'And he took again the twelve,
And began to tell them what things should happen unto
him,
Saying,
Behold,
We go up to Jerusalem;
And the Son of man shall be delivered unto the chief priests,
and unto the scribes;
And they shall condemn him to death, and shall deliver him
to the Gentiles:
And they shall mock him,
And shall scourge him,
And shall spit upon him,
And shall kill him:
And the third day he shall rise again.'
Whenever the Gospel reaches any beautiful or dignified

climax, Mark usually brings us back to earth, returning to his more characteristic gossipy style of writing. He has a fear of pretentiousness. After the mystery and solemnity of Jesus's prediction, we now have a chatty, human story. I hear it told in scandalised whispers.

'And James and John, the sons of Zebedee, come unto him, 35 *saying . . .'*

With a careful look backward to make sure they were far away from the other disciples.

'Master, we would that thou shouldest do for us whatsoever we 36 *shall desire. And he said unto them . . .'*

Quietly, in sympathy with their obvious need for secrecy.

'What would ye that I should do for you? They said unto him . . .' 37

With another quick look backward.

'Grant unto us that we may sit, one on thy right hand, and the other on thy left hand, in thy glory.'

Did he try not to laugh?

'But Jesus said unto them . . .' 38

Perhaps forgetting to be quiet.

'Ye know not what ye ask . . .'

Did they shush him? And did Jesus then continue quietly again?

'Can ye drink of the cup that I drink of? and be baptized with the baptism that I am baptized with? And they said unto him, We can.' 39

Did Jesus then shush *them?* Surely he had to look away for a moment to hide his face.

'And Jesus said unto them, Ye shall . . .'

Note the balancing of James's and John's 'We can' with Jesus's 'Ye shall'.

'Ye shall indeed drink of the cup that I drink of; and with the baptism that I am baptized withal shall ye be baptized: But to sit on 40 *my right hand and on my left hand is not mine to give; but it shall be given to them for whom it is prepared.'*

Somehow or other, despite their secrecy, all of this got back to the other disciples. With typical throw-away technique Mark writes:

'And when the ten heard it . . .' 41

A little pause for us to imagine their reaction . . .

'they began to be much displeased with James and John.'

One hopes that this incident did not actually occur im-

mediately after Jesus's prediction of his death and resurrection.
But it is quite possible that it was Jesus's prediction which put
the idea of preferential treatment into the heads of James and
John. Jesus had foretold his resurrection three times. In
Caesarea Philippi he had also described the Son of man coming
'in the glory of his Father with the holy angels'. The disciples
have seemed to ignore all this – or at least they have never
spoken about it to Jesus. We are told that they questioned 'one
with another what the rising from the dead should mean'. And
we learnt that 'they understood not that saying, and were
afraid to ask him'. But, although they were unable to talk
about such matters to the Christ, it was obviously very much
in their minds. In an oblique way, James's and John's request
was an assent of belief in this mystery. It was also a way of
joining in.

The sparsity of our knowledge about the disciples is pathe-
tic. But at least we know that James and John were the sons of
Zebedee, and that Zebedee was a man who had hired servants. It is possible that they came from a more privileged
background than the others, and perhaps – even in a minor
way – 'the insolence of wealth will creep out'. We also know
that Jesus nicknamed them 'the sons of thunder', which
implies that they were not renowned for their tact.

I imagine them running ahead of the other disciples, and
catching up with Jesus who was striding away in front of
everybody. But it may not have happened that way. In St
Matthew's version the request is made by James's and John's
mother – with the two sons standing by. But Mark – and Peter
– does not like mentioning ladies, and gives us little indication
of the crowd of relatives and friends who may have been
following with the disciples. Matthew writes: 'Then came to
him the mother of Zebedee's children with her sons, worshipping him, and desiring a certain thing of him.'

'Worshipping him' sounds like blatant flattery before asking
a favour. A huge, toothy smile . . .

'And he said unto her, What wilt thou? She saith unto him,
Grant that these my two sons may sit, the one on thy right
hand, and the other on the left, in thy kingdom.'

After this the dialogue is practically the same as in St Mark's
version.

Jesus distances himself from the two young fishermen. He seems jealous that they should claim any equality with him. He asks: 'Can ye drink of the cup that I drink of?' – meaning the cup of his life and experience; 'and be baptized with the baptism that I am baptized with?' – meaning the baptism of his suffering. And, with adorable pushiness, the sons of thunder reply, 'We can.' Then Jesus has to admit that he has no priority on experience and suffering. With a prediction, which turned out to be partly true, he allowed that they too would suffer. (In The Acts Of The Apostles 12: 2. it is written that Herod 'killed James the brother of John with the sword'.) But still Jesus couldn't promise them top seats at his table in heaven. That was his chosen father's province.

How did 'the ten' learn about this? I imagine that James and John, in their ingenuous way, told them. They probably said to Peter – in case he had any ideas of his own – 'Don't bother to ask for any favours! We've already tried!' And Peter told the others. And 'they began to be much displeased with James and John'. 'Much displeased' could mean 'indignant' as it is now usually translated, or even 'angry' – but I prefer to think of it more as 'outraged', which sounds better humoured. The other disciples knew James and John very well; they would have been accustomed to their artless behaviour. It would surely have been a case of 'Have you heard the latest about James and John? They actually went and asked Jesus if they could sit next to him in heaven!'

But whatever the strength of the disciples' reaction – whether it was anger or outrage – Jesus used the situation to teach them all a lesson. It was the same lesson he tried to teach before, with the child in the house in Capernaum after they had disputed among themselves 'who should be the greatest'. If Jesus returned today, he would still be teaching this lesson. This lesson is the core of Christianity; it is what attracts most people to the teaching of Christ; it is also the lesson which most of us blithely ignore.

'But Jesus called them to him, and saith unto them, Ye know that they which are accounted to rule over the Gentiles exercise lordship over them; and their great ones exercise authority upon them. But so shall it not be among you: but whosoever will be great among you, shall be your minister: And whosoever of you will be the chiefest,

42

shall be servant of all. For even the Son of man came not to be ministered unto, but to minister, and to give his life a ransom for many.'

Is it perhaps because, in this context, we are sensitive about being among 'the Gentiles' that some modern translators change this to 'the heathen' or 'the pagans' – which does not seem to include us? In The New English and The Living Bible the specification is avoided altogether: 'You know that *in the world* the recognised rulers lord it over their subjects . . .' 'As you know, the kings and great men *of the earth* lord it over the people.' Which sounds as if Jesus was teaching from another planet. It is an astonishing fact, as we have already noted, that the Christian faith was inspired by a carpenter from Nazareth, probably – as is hinted in St John 8: 41 – 'born of fornication', and dying the shameful death of a criminal. It is even more astonishing that this Jewish revolutionary was so eagerly adopted by the Gentiles as their Saviour, and that he is worshipped in churches and cathedrals from Halifax to Hong Kong and from Darlington to Dallas. In his ministry Jesus chiefly concentrated on teaching the children of Israel, and seemed – from the little evidence available – to have little time for the rest of the world. 'Let the children first be filled,' he said. In this lesson to the disciples about status and position, Jesus was talking in a critical way about the Romans and the Greeks; but he could also have been talking about *us today*. Although, officially, we call ourselves a Christian nation, the actual institution is a million miles away from the requirements of the Son of man.

Once again Jesus presented the disciples with a paradox: 'great' equals 'minister'; 'chiefest' equals 'servant of all'. There are no top places at the table. There can't be. 'For even the Son of man came not to be ministered unto, but to minister, and to give his life a ransom for many.'

The second half of this verse provokes controversy. Some people think that by giving his life 'a ransom for many' Jesus meant that he intended to atone for the sins of mankind. The word 'ransom' is difficult. I like to think that Jesus meant that he would give his life as an 'example' for many, or even as an 'inspiration' for many.

But Jesus may have meant that he would act as an intermediary with his chosen father; put in a good word for us, and plead with him on our behalf.

There is also some surprise that Jesus should have such a clear idea of the future. People wonder whether the words 'to give his life a ransom for many' may have been an invention of Mark's – or even whether they were written at a later date, when the church had been established, and the cross had been adopted as a symbol. But I think there is a natural progression in the verse from Jesus describing his ministering life of service, to his prediction of a sacrificial death. From the time of his baptism by John in Jordan – and possibly before – Jesus knew exactly how he was going to live his life, how he was going to die, and what would be the result of his death and resurrection. He believed that he would found a new faith. He was probably the most fanatical person who ever lived.

★

'And they came to Jericho . . .'

46

Only fifteen miles to Jerusalem . . .

'. . . and as he went out of Jericho with his disciples and a great number of people . . .'

Here, at last, is a mention of the accompanying crowds – probably swollen because of the approaching passover, and also because of curiosity about what would happen to Jesus in the Holy City. Imagine hundreds of people. Imagine men, women, children and dogs. And as they went along the road:

'blind Bartimaeus, the son of Timaeus, sat by the highway side begging.'

And now Mark tells us a wonderfully warm-hearted story.

'And when he heard that it was Jesus of Nazareth, he began to cry out, and say, Jesus, thou Son of David, have mercy on me. And many charged him that he should hold his peace: but he cried the more a great deal, Thou Son of David, have mercy on me. And Jesus stood still, and commanded him to be called. And they call the blind man, saying unto him, Be of good comfort, rise; he calleth thee. And he, casting away his garment, rose, and came to Jesus. And Jesus answered and said unto him, What wilt thou that I should do unto thee? The blind man said unto him, Lord, that I might receive my sight. And Jesus said unto him, Go thy way; thy faith hath made thee whole. And

47

52

immediately he received his sight, and followed Jesus in the way.'

Because of its position in the Gospel, some commentators think this is a symbolic story. I don't believe this. It seems perfectly logical that the incident occurred at this particular moment in the ministry. Jesus had just been teaching the disciples – for at least the third time – about their place in the new order of things. ('If any man desire to be first, the same shall be last of all, and servant of all.' 9: 35. 'But many that are first shall be last; and the last first. 10: 31. 'But whosoever will be great among you, shall be your minister: And whosoever of you will be the chiefest, shall be servant of all.' 10: 44.)

A beggar shouts at him.

Jesus is on his way to Jerusalem. He will soon be teaching in the temple. He will soon be face to face with the high priest. He will soon stand before the Roman Procurator of Judaea. He will publicly acknowledge that he is the Christ.

But, first, a beggar shouts at him.

He shouts at him with marvellous familiarity: 'Jesus!' And then adds – as a beggar might shout at a toff today: 'Guv!' 'Squire!' 'Y'r Grace!' – 'Thou Son of David!' This was the title of Israel's messiah. Then he peremptorily demands: 'Have mercy on me.'

It must have been a very noisy cry – so noisy that it upset some of the crowd. Perhaps the disciples tried to silence him – or perhaps it was some of the women who were accompanying Jesus – perhaps the ambitious mother of James and John, or our old friend Simon's wife's mother; perhaps the mother of Jesus . . .

'Shut up!' some of the people yelled at him.' (The Living Bible)

Bartimaeus did not shut up. On the contrary, 'he cried the more a great deal'. It was probably a shocking noise – like the howl of a child in pain; like the howl of anybody in need of love and attention – except that most of us are too polite to make it. 'Thou Son of David, have mercy on me.'

The beggar demanded attention from Christ. Christ obeyed the beggar. 'Whosoever of you will be the chiefest, shall be servant of all.'

'And Jesus stood still, and commanded him to be called. And they call the blind man . . .'

The crowd's hostility to the beggar changed immediately.

' "You lucky fellow," they said, "come on, he's calling you!" ' (The Living Bible)

Now there is another one of those eye-witness details which give this Gospel such reality. The blind man didn't want Jesus to see his dirty old robe. He was self-conscious about his appearance. It is described in the King James Version as if the beggar was a king. 'And he, casting away his garment, rose, and came to Jesus.' And it continues with a grand formality: 'And Jesus answered and said unto him, What wilt thou that I should do unto thee? The blind man said unto him, Lord, that I might receive my sight.' First, the beggar called Jesus by his name; then he called him 'Thou son of David'; now he calls him 'Lord'. Evidently the original word is 'Rabboni', which Marshall says was 'the highest title of reverence'. The beggar was taking no chances.

Jesus had not performed a miracle of healing since he came down from the mountain at Ceasarea Philippi; on that occasion he made a ruthless demand for belief, and reduced a man to tears. Now, in the middle of a huge crowd, on his way to Jerusalem, a beggar yells at him, rudely demanding attention. And something about this raw request appealed to Jesus. With no solemn provisions about belief; without – it would seem – having to spit upon the man's eyes or even touching him, Jesus gave the beggar his sight. In fact, he implied that the beggar had healed himself – like the woman 'which had an issue of blood twelve years'. He used the same words to the beggar as he did to the woman: 'Thy faith hath made thee whole.'

And he didn't send him away saying, 'Neither go into the town, nor tell it to any in the town.' He didn't charge him or the onlookers to 'tell no man'. He simply continued on his journey, and the beggar followed – without his old robe, no longer needing 'two coats'.

Placed as it is, after the teaching of the disciples in the house in Capernaum; the teaching of the Pharisees about marriage and divorce; the teaching about wealth with the rich young man; the teaching about the status of the true Christian after the request for preference by James and John, the story of blind Bartimaeus comes as light relief. It is as if Jesus suddenly remembered his power of healing; as if he felt the need to celebrate. And also as if he needed to illustrate his kinship with the poor, the afflicted and the undistinguished.

In St Matthew's version there are two blind beggars, and Jesus heals them both. But then St Matthew described two wild men coming out of the tombs in the country of the Gadarenes. Does it make either story more impressive? Surely 'less is more'. Let's stay with Mark.

And with this episode I have a feeling that Mark started writing independently – without relying solely on the memory of Peter. There is no actual evidence for this, but from now until the end of the Gospel the writing seems to have a new and reassuring authority. There is a fullness about it that has been missing up till now. It's possible that Mark was living in Jerusalem when Jesus arrived. It's most likely that he heard of the Galilaean, and was immediately attracted to him. Perhaps he got to know the disciples and the people who followed Jesus. Perhaps he cross-questioned them – not with any idea of writing an account of the ministry – but because everything about Jesus fascinated him. Of course it's not likely that he was in Jericho or witnessed the healing of Bartimaeus, but Jericho is very near to Jerusalem, and I feel an amateur detective has been at work. Note the specific naming of Bartimaeus: 'the son of Timaeus'; the reporting of the actual words of the crowd; the graphic description of the beggar casting away his garment. All this seems more detailed than one old man's memory.

I think it is possible that Mark joined Jesus and the disciples in Jerusalem; that he was present when Jesus taught in the temple; that he was an eye-witness to the crucifixion; and that he actually appears in his own story in the Garden of Gethsemane.

JERUSALEM

Now the Gospel takes a buoyant leap forward.

'*And when they came nigh to Jerusalem, unto Bethphage and Bethany, at the mount of Olives . . .*'

Only two miles to go . . .

'*. . . he sendeth forth two of his disciples, And saith unto them, Go your way into the village over against you: and as soon as ye be entered into it, ye shall find a colt tied, whereon never man sat; loose him, and bring him. And if any man say unto you, Why do ye this? say ye that the Lord hath need of him; and straightway he will send him hither. And they went their way, and found the colt tied by the door without in a place where two ways met; and they loose him. And certain of them that stood there said unto them, What do ye, loosing the colt? And they said unto them even as Jesus had commanded: and they let them go. And they brought the colt to Jesus, and cast their garments on him; and he sat upon him. And many spread their garments in the way: and others cut down branches off the trees, and strawed them in the way. And they that went before, and they that followed, cried, saying, Hosanna; Blessed is he that cometh in the name of the Lord: Blessed be the kingdom of our father David, that cometh in the name of the Lord: Hosanna in the highest. And Jesus entered into Jerusalem, and into the temple: and when he had looked round about upon all things, and now the eventide was come, he went out unto Bethany with the twelve.*'

This passage is a beautiful example of Mark's reporting. He does not explain; he does not comment; he simply and ruthlessly drives the story forward. Within eleven verses we arrive at Bethphage and Bethany outside Jerusalem; we are told a charming little anecdote about the finding and the borrowing of a donkey; there is the description of an unofficial procession;

there are the actual cries of the crowd. There is the arrival in Jerusalem; a visit to the temple; and, finally, at the end of a busy day, Jesus's return to Bethany with the twelve. Mark certainly doesn't let us hang about.

St Matthew takes a little longer . . . In the first place, he gives us another double-act. In this version Jesus says: 'Ye shall find an ass tied, and a colt with her: loose *them*, and bring *them* to me.' And the disciples 'brought the ass, and the colt, and put on them their clothes, and they set him thereon'. But the reason for this version of the story is not simply Matthew's liking for doubling characters; there is a more serious explanation.

The authors of the four Gospels tried to fit events of Jesus's life, and particularly the last days, to predictions found in the Old Testament. As the writer of the first Gospel, Mark is the least guilty of this. But in this episode with the donkey, Matthew actually admits that 'All this was done, that it might be fulfilled which was spoken by the prophet, saying, Tell ye the daughter of Sion, Behold, thy King cometh unto thee, meek, and sitting upon an ass, and a colt the foal of an ass'. This is a reference to Zechariah 9: 9. 'Rejoice greatly, O daughter of Zion; shout, O daughter of Jerusalem; behold, thy King cometh unto thee: he is just, and having salvation; lowly, and riding upon an ass, and upon a colt the foal of an ass.' Now it could be that Matthew's version with the ass and the colt was historically correct. It would obviously have been more persuasive to prospective converts if it was correct, but I think it is unlikely. The Jesus we find in St Mark's Gospel is more concerned with creating a new and original tradition, rather than troubling about other people's predictions.

Nevertheless, we are faced with a decision which illuminates an interesting aspect of Jesus's personality. At some point, Jesus decided to enter Jerusalem riding on a donkey. At some point, he decided that he would make a star's entrance. He didn't intend to sneak into the Holy City. He decided to signal the arrival of the Son of God. It would be an entrance fitting for a king; and it would cause confusion and controversy.

To most of us the donkey is a humble beast, apparently stupid, and mainly associated with reluctantly giving very small children rides along the sands. But, as the Rev. Marshall reminds us, 'in the east the ass is held in high esteem'. Jesus's decision to enter into Jerusalem in this fashion was not necessarily a 'humble' or a 'lowly' idea. Asses were used by great officials; 'it was the beast of kings'.

The actual arrangement of the borrowing of the colt is of course mysterious. As Manford George Gutzke says: 'It leaves me wondering; I am not worried about it, but I am recognising there is more here than is written.' But as we have accepted Jesus raising a little girl from the dead, controlling the weather, and walking on water, we may as well accept that he knew the whereabouts of a convenient colt, and was confident that the owners would be delighted to lend it. (The King James Version's 'and straightway he will send him hither' sounds like a reference to the owner. It is more clearly translated in the Revised Standard as 'The Lord . . . will send it back here immediately' – which allays our fears that Jesus simply appropriated the animal.)

Only in Mark's Gospel are we given the actual whereabouts of the colt. The description couldn't be more specific: 'Tied by the door without in a place where two ways met.' Either Peter was one of the disciples sent on the mission, or else detective Mark subsequently visited the spot to check his details.

'And they brought the colt to Jesus . . .' and suddenly the excitement begins. With the arrival of the colt, one idea leads to another. The crowd starts to improvise; the disciples make a saddle for the colt and Jesus sits upon him; people start spreading their clothes along the road as if honouring royalty; branches are cut from trees and doubtless waved in the air – as well as 'strawed' in the way. There is singing and shouting and laughter.

'And Jesus entered into Jerusalem . . .'
Did this cause a sensation?
No!
'. . . and into the temple . . .'
Did this provoke a confrontation?
No!
'. . . and when he had looked round about on all things . . .'
Yes?
'. . . and now the eventide was come . . .'

Yes?

'. . . he went out unto Bethany with the twelve.'

This is such an anti-climax, I think it must be true.

Honest Mark gives us the facts.

St Matthew describes: 'And when he was come into Jeru-salem, all the city was moved, saying, *Who is this?*' And both Matthew and Luke have Jesus immediately attack the money changers in the temple. This is much more impressive. It is what most of us would expect to happen, and what we would want to happen.

But, in Mark's version, nobody says *'Who is this?'* Nobody seems to take any notice of the newly-arrived Messiah. The crowd around Jesus seems to disperse. Perhaps, in the big city, it was not such an enormous crowd after all. Perhaps, in the big city, there were other interesting personalities and diver-sions. Perhaps Jesus changed his mind about the grand entr-ance, and joined the passover crowds sight-seeing. Nineham writes 'This visit to the temple seems entirely pointless, for the idea of Jesus 'seeing the sights' like some provincial tourist is entirely at variance with the spirit of the Gospels.' But it is not at variance with the spirit of St Mark. I think it is highly likely that Jesus was temporarily overwhelmed by the city and by the temple. There is a touching and believable humanity about Jesus looking 'round about on all things' – and then, when 'the eventide was come', leaving the city and returning to the quiet village of Bethany, perhaps returning the donkey to its owner.

There is a split in the personality of Jesus as he is described in the four Gospels. Mostly, we are presented with a completely authoritative and confident man. This would have been consi-dered necessary by the Evangelists and early Christians. But in Mark's Gospel, the first Gospel, there are times when we glimpse a less confident person. Here, after the grand attempt to enter Jerusalem like a king, Jesus retires to spend the night in the obscurity of Bethany. I love the superb arrogance of Jesus in St Luke's version of the entrance into Jerusalem. Some Pharisees meet Jesus and ask him to rebuke his disciples for making such a noise, and Jesus replies: 'I tell you that, if these should hold their peace, the stones would immediately cry out.' This is joyous stuff. But it is also wonderfully comforting to read Mark's version, and recognise a carpenter with stage-fright.

'*And on the morrow, when they were come from Bethany, he was* 12
hungry: And seeing a fig-tree afar off having leaves, he came, if haply
he might find anything thereon: and when he came to it, he found
nothing but leaves; for the time of figs was not yet. And Jesus 14
answered and said unto it, No man eat fruit of thee hereafter for ever.
And his disciples heard it.'

'This story is one of the most difficult in the Gospels . . .' (Nineham)

Is it?

'The whole story does not seem to fit Jesus at all.' (Barclay)

Doesn't it?

'Unless we realise that this was an acted parable of Israel, we shall be puzzled by all sorts of irrelevant questions.' (Cole)

Shall we?

'The fig tree was Israel which has not borne fruit at the appointed time . . .' (Crotty)

Was it?

'The precocious putting forth of leaves denoted that the tree was diseased and should be cut down. So the time of the abrogation of Judaism was at hand.' (Marshall)

Heavens!

This story obviously causes great embarrassment. Commentators search desperately for explanations to excuse Jesus's behaviour. They insist on symbolism. 'It is the condemnation of *promise without fulfilment.*' 'It is the condemnation of *profession without practice.*' Etcetera, etcetera.

I would like the story to be simply about Jesus being hungry; being nervous before his day in Jerusalem; fancying a nice fig; making a special detour from the road to the tree; discovering he had made a mistake; and blaming the tree instead of himself. I would like to be comforted by Jesus's cursing. I would like his company in the dozens of small curses that occur during a working day. I would like to feel he experienced the small frustrations and indignities that befall the rest of us – and that he occasionally blasted off with a natural loss of patience. I would like Jesus so much more if this was the explanation. I don't care for the abrogation of Judaism or parables of Israel. I would like to think that Jesus made a mistake about the fig tree. It would be nice to have him as an occasional colleague in incompetence.

There is a natural temptation for the commentators and the earnest Christians to find symbolic meanings in the few places in the Gospel that smack of frailty. Rather than accept Jesus as a fallible human being, they flatter him and Mark with a scholarly prowess which I find hard to credit. When Jesus called a Greek woman a dog: '*Symbolically* she stands for the Gentile world which so eagerly seized on the bread of heaven which the Jews rejected and threw away.' (Barclay) When Jesus failed to heal a blind man at the first attempt: 'The blind man is a *symbol* of the group of disciples . . . What takes place in the curing of the blind man parallels the process of faith taking place in the group of disciples.' (Crotty) And when Jesus curses a fig tree: 'The manner and place of its insertion strongly suggest that the story was intended to make a didactic point, the fate of the fig tree *symbolising* the fate that awaited Jerusalem and the Jewish people and religion.' (Nineham)

I do not find this search for symbols necessary or attractive. I would rather believe that Mark included these stories in order to illustrate the humanity of Jesus. He wrote his Gospel at least thirty years after the crucifixion. Already the carpenter was disappearing, and the Son of God – pure and without sin – was being bravely worshipped and adored. I believe that Mark determined that some glimpses should remain of the Man of Galilee. Although it seems that even *he* needed to verify his facts in this story of morning hunger. Detective Mark is in evidence again. After Jesus curses the fig tree – 'No man eat fruit of thee hereafter forever' – comes the tiny sentence: 'And his disciples heard it.' It sounds as if young Mark checked up with the twelve – just to make absolutely sure.

There is a refreshing reversal of events in this story. When Jesus overheard the disciples discussing the meaning of his parable, 'Take heed, beware of the leaven of the Pharisees, and of the leaven of Herod,' he turned on them in fury because of their lack of understanding. When he overheard them discussing 'who should be the greatest', he faced them with it later in the day and taught them a lesson. Here, the disciples overheard *him* in a moment of weakness, and as we shall see they didn't forget it.

Not altogether surprisingly, St Luke and St John omit this story. And St Matthew gives us a somewhat truncated version which takes place *after* Jesus had attacked the traders in the temple. But I think it is more believable that the fig tree incident happened immediately *before* the act of aggression, and, of course, this is how Mark reports it.

'*And they come to Jerusalem: and Jesus went into the temple, and* **15** *began to cast out them that sold and bought in the temple, and overthrew the tables of the moneychangers, and the seats of them that sold doves; and would not suffer that any man should carry any vessel through the temple, and he taught, saying unto them, Is it not written,* **17** *My house shall be called of all nations the house of prayer? but ye have made it a den of thieves.*'

When he first entered into Jerusalem, after the impromptu procession, Mark tells us that Jesus went into the temple: '*and when he had looked round about upon all things,* and now the eventide was come, he went out unto Bethany with the twelve.' I think this looking 'round about upon all things' is important. It was then that Jesus must have noted the moneychangers; the merchants selling doves – and other animals – for sacrifices at exorbitant prices; and the people using the temple as a useful short-cut – especially when carrying goods and shopping. It was probably then that he felt his temper rising.

One also wonders about the reaction of the people with Jesus; the innocent friends and relatives from Galilee; the women who accompanied him. Were they shocked by the trading and overcharging? Were they cheated or insulted? And did Jesus privately vow to return the next day without the encumbrance of so many loved ones?

If that was the case, there is a touching loneliness about his actions. One can imagine a sleepless night spent planning the assault; and an early-morning departure from Bethany – probably not waiting for any food. One can then more easily understand the behaviour with the fig tree. And one can then more clearly admire the great courage of the countryman in the big city attempting, single-handedly, to halt the desecration of the temple.

Why was he not arrested immediately? One can only suppose his actions were very popular with the passover crowds.

173

It is possible that they might have cheered him on, and assisted him to rout the merchants and moneychangers. And, when he began to teach, perhaps – on his instruction – members of the crowd obstructed those people who used the temple as a highway in their everyday business.

There are Old Testament allusions from Hosea and from Malachi connected with this story, and Jesus's actions have again been linked with prophecies. And, in Mark's brief summary of his teaching, Jesus's words are quotes from Isaiah and Jeremiah: 'for my house shall be called an house of prayer for all people.' (Isaiah 56: 7) 'Is this house, which is called by my name, become a den of robbers in your eyes?' (Jeremiah 7: 11) One only hopes that these are not inventions by well-meaning missionaries of 'the word'.

But *the action* of Jesus in scourging the temple is reported in all four Gospels; although, in St Matthew, Jesus manages a quote from Psalm 8, and in St John the disciples conveniently remember a quote from Psalm 69 . . .

18 *'And the scribes and chief priests heard it, and sought how they might destroy him: for they feared him, because all the people was astonished at his doctrine.'*

It certainly sounds as if he was immensely popular with the crowds – and an immense embarrassment to the scribes and chief priests. 'All the people was astonished at his doctrine' is variously translated as '. . . the whole crowd was amazed at his teaching'; (Good News) '. . . the people were carried away by his teaching'; (Jerusalem) '. . . all the multitude was so full of admiration at his teaching'; (Knox) '. . . the people were so enthusiastic about Jesus' teaching'; (Living Bible) '. . . the whole crowd was spellbound by his teaching'. (New English) This gives us – if only by repetition – a glimmer of their reaction, and explains the dilemma of the authorities.

19 *'And when even was come, he went out of the city.'*

Back to the quiet and safety of Bethany, and a well-deserved night's sleep.

★

He was in tremendous spirits the following day . . .

20 *'And in the morning, as they passed by, they saw the fig tree dried up from the roots.'*

174

Now, at last, the disciples have an opportunity to score against him. Who will be their spokesman? Well, of course . . .

'*And Peter calling to remembrance saith unto him, Master, behold,* 21 *the fig tree which thou cursedst is withered away.*'

It was probably carefully spoken . . . perhaps with a hand hovering to hide any hint of a grin. But there was no need for any nervousness.

'*And Jesus answering saith unto them, Have faith in God.*' 22

It is morning again. It is a morning like the one back in Capernaum at the start of the ministry when the disciples told him, 'All men seek for thee.' It is a morning 'fresh as if issued to children on a beach'. It is a morning when everything is possible, and when anything can be accomplished. It is a morning when the words of Jesus of Nazareth are buoyant and blithe, jocund, jaunty, joyous and jubilant.

'Have faith in God.'

What's it about?

What's this stuff – St Mark's Gospel, St Matthew, St Luke, St John, The Acts of the Apostles and all the rest of it – what's it about?

Why did it catch on?

'Have faith in God.' And now I need to write in capitals because it seems to me that Jesus was talking in capitals.

'*FOR VERILY I SAY UNTO YOU, THAT WHOSO-* 23 *EVER SHALL SAY UNTO THIS MOUNTAIN, BE THOU REMOVED, AND BE THOU CAST INTO THE SEA; AND SHALL NOT DOUBT IN HIS HEART, BUT SHALL BELIEVE THAT THOSE THINGS WHICH HE SAITH SHALL COME TO PASS; HE SHALL HAVE WHATSOEVER HE SAITH. THERE-* 24 *FORE I SAY UNTO YOU, WHAT THINGS SOEVER YE DESIRE, WHEN YE PRAY, BELIEVE THAT YE RECEIVE THEM, AND YE SHALL HAVE THEM.*'

Great events often spring from small, unimportant, insignificant things.

Life itself comes from a tiny seed.

St Peter's in Rome began with one piece of stone.

The first journey to the moon started from an undistinguished piece of scrubland.

The most positive and joyful speech of Jesus is triggered by a withered fig tree.

As the possible result of a childish curse, we are suddenly presented with the challenge of faith.

He challenges us to become Gods.

He provokes us to move mountains.

Belief is attainable to the poorest and meanest.

'. . . WHOSOEVER SHALL SAY UNTO THIS MOUNTAIN, BE THOU REMOVED, AND BE THOU CAST INTO THE SEA; *AND SHALL NOT DOUBT IN HIS HEART* . . .'

Jesus appeared to be without doubt that morning. This is the start of the most fully reported day in the ministry. If Mark's time sequence is correct, this is the start of a day which takes the next two and a half chapters to describe. Was Jesus charged with an energy released by his act of aggression? He had already reduced Jerusalem to a village, and the temple to his local synagogue. *He* had already moved mountains.

In the theatre, we talk about actors 'going over the top'. It means that they are guilty of over-acting, that they have lost reality, that they have become larger than life. It is regarded as a very bad thing. And yet . . .

And yet I find that my few treasured memories of great theatrical moments are of just such occasions. As a young man I saw Ralph Richardson as Falstaff. In the *Second Part of Henry IV*, when Doll Tearsheet reminds Falstaff that eventually he must die, Richardson seemed to stop the action. In my memory – which may be distorted – Richardson stepped right out of the frame-work of the play, and, taking pauses of unreal length, he looked out-front into space, and the lines came with uncharacteristic terror: 'Peace good Doll! . . . do not speak like a death's head: . . . do not bid me remember mine end.' For a few moments *Henry IV Part Two* was forgotten; the situation and the other actors were forgotten; Falstaff himself was forgotten; and there was a direct communion between the man on stage and the rest of us sitting in the audience. We all paused and considered our mortality. For a moment we were all united in consideration of the mystery of life and death. This was achieved by an actor 'going over the top'.

On the morning of the ministry when Jesus was walking

from Bethany to Jerusalem, and Peter pointed to a withered fig tree – which may or may not have died as the result of a curse – Jesus went 'over the top'. His words terrify the timid, and trouble the realists. 'Of course he didn't mean a real mountain . . .' 'Of course, moving mountains was a popular metaphor of the day for doing difficult things . . .' 'Of course he wasn't talking literally . . .'

I believe he meant a real mountain.

I believe Jesus was talking literally.

It was the natural exaggeration of an original revolutionary. And Jesus *was* an original revolutionary. And he meant what he said. And 'we petty men' are left with two alternatives: to accept his challenge; or to 'peep about to find ourselves dishonourable graves'.

Of course, it is dangerous stuff. 'What things soever ye desire, when ye pray, believe that ye receive them, and ye shall have them.' Does it include unlimited riches? Does it include unending sensual pleasure? May we simply desire eternal life? Presumably. But I don't think there is much likelihood of shortcuts.

The operative word is: 'Believe.' Compared to the *belief* of Jesus, the *belief* of most of us is a puny thing. Jesus believed he was the Son of God. He believed it with such fanaticism that millions of people today believe it also. The belief of Jesus has become an emotional substitute for many well-meaning simple people. Their faith gives them temporary status; momentarily they are also the sons and daughters of God. But *this* is often hysterical stuff. The belief of Jesus was like rock. It was hard, and real, and sure. It brooked no argument. It needed no church, no music, no protestations, no ceremony, no costumes, and no gush. It was a fact. And, at the end, it failed him. But the seed was sown – and it grew 'he knoweth not how'. And the fact of Jesus's belief remains. It provokes and inspires.

★

Now he proceeds to instruct the disciples on forgiveness. I wonder why?

'And when ye stand praying, forgive, if ye have ought against any: 25
that your Father also which is in heaven may forgive you your

trespasses. But if ye do not forgive, neither will your Father which is in heaven forgive your trespasses.'

What was the link between the subjects of belief and forgiveness?

Was it the very human link of a man suddenly catching himself talking with undue authority? Was it the link of a man who became aware that he had 'gone over the top'? What was he doing blasting fig trees, throwing the temple people out of their jobs, boasting about moving mountains? Was Jesus suddenly aware of bombast?

Was he even saddened by the fate of the fig tree? Many people would like him to be a sensitive, sentimental creature who wouldn't dream of kicking a mad dog, squashing a troublesome fly, or harming a single leaf or flower. Their dream Jesus walks suspended like a vapid fairy, unrelated to man, and remote from the dust of the world. Nevertheless, perhaps he was a *little* distressed by the result of his curse.

But surely, much more than this, Jesus was suddenly aware of arrogance. In fact, his words about moving mountains are thrilling 'beyond measure'. But – as with most ordinary human beings – moments of great certainty are often followed by great doubt. We have seen examples of this throughout the Gospel – from the beginning when Jesus heard the voice of God naming him his beloved son, followed by the forty days of doubt in the wilderness. I think that here, on the road to Jerusalem, Jesus was asking his chosen father for forgiveness in case his authoritative words to the disciples were offensive or overbearing. The emphatic repetition of the phrase 'your Father *which is in heaven*' is revealing. The man of Galilee was aware of priorities, and of his own place in the order of things.

★

'And they come again to Jerusalem: and as he was walking in the temple . . .'

'St Mark alone mentions that Jesus was "walking in the temple".' (Marshall) Was Mark there? I think he was there. I think he saw Jesus 'walking in the temple', and witnessed the following events.

'. . . there come to him the chief priests, and the scribes, and the elders . . .'

These were members of the Sanhedrin – who were legally entitled to examine the claims of a new teacher.

'*And say unto him, By what authority doest thou these things? and* ²⁸ *who gave thee this authority to do these things? And Jesus answered and said unto them, I will also ask of you one question, and answer me, and I will tell you by what authority I do these things. The baptism of John, was it from heaven, or of men? answer me. And they reasoned with themselves, saying, If we shall say, From heaven; he will say, Why then did ye not believe him? But if we shall say, Of men; they feared the people: for all men counted John, that he was a prophet indeed. And they answered and said unto Jesus, We cannot* ³³ *tell. And Jesus answering saith unto them, Neither do I tell you by what authority I do these things.*'

Good stuff here!

First, more cheers for the King James Version and its splendid repetition – four times – of the words 'these things' which makes a frame-work for the story.

What were 'these things' that the members of the Sanhedrin complained about? 'These things' were the content of Jesus's teaching, combined with his scourging of the temple. They ask Jesus, 'By what authority doest thou these things? and who gave thee this authority to do these things?'

The Rev. Marshall tells us that 'each Rabbi had his certificate or diploma, usually conferred by a distinguished Rabbi. Thus the question means: (1) Where is your diploma? (2) By whom was it conferred? They knew that our Lord could not produce one, so the question practically amounted to a repetition of a demand for a sign from heaven.'

Jesus counter-attacks – in the same disarming way that he has done in the past. He throws another name at them. Early in the ministry, in the confrontation with the scribes and Pharisees about the sabbath day laws, Jesus suddenly asked them, 'Have ye never read what *David* did . . . ?' Later in the ministry when he was questioned by the Pharisees about divorce, he sprang on them, 'What did *Moses* command you?' Now, he suddenly asks the group from the Sanhedrin about the baptism of *John*. Totally ignoring their attack on him, he asks them: 'The baptism of *John*, was it from heaven, or of men?' There was evidently a considerable pause in the proceedings, probably accompanied by protesting and wavering from the chief priests and the scribes and the elders, because Mark then reports Jesus as saying, 'Answer me.'

These two words are important because they give us a glimpse of the stubbornness of the Son of man. In the first miracle of the loaves and fishes when he asked the disciples, 'How many loaves have ye?', I imagined a pause in the proceedings while the disciples remonstrated with Jesus about the impracticality of his question. He then said, 'Go and see;' which might well have been belted out at them. The words 'answer me' to the group from the Sanhedrin could have been similarly delivered. If Jesus made a challenge, he could not be persuaded to withdraw it. Mark's versions of these stories are obviously drastically truncated, but the tiny phrases 'go and see' and 'answer me' remain as indications of the strength of Jesus.

The question about John the Baptist was unanswerable and embarrassing. Jesus knew that, if the chief priests and their party acknowledged John, they would also have to acknowledge *him*. It reads as if Mark watched them debating the question. They had hoped to trap Jesus into blasphemy. Now he has diverted them.

They dither.

He waits.

Finally, their answer is feeble. 'We cannot tell.' *His* answer to them comes crashing out: 'Neither do I tell you by what authority I do these thing' – and without pausing to let them retire in confusion, without allowing them to re-form and return to the attack, Jesus continues with electrifying nerve.

'And he began to speak unto them by parables. A certain man planted a vineyard . . .'

This is a devastating trick of clever speakers. Not satisfied with humiliating opponents, they immediately continue the attack by arresting their attention with a seemingly unrelated story. Jesus now does this to the unsuspecting group from the Sanhedrin. He tells a good story. It is not until more than halfway through the story – or even later – that they realise his intention. But by then it is too late. They are involved in a seemingly innocent tale of a vineyard and its owner – without realising that actually they are being accused of religious contempt and ignorance. And, of course, all this took place in front of huge crowds of people. Read on!

'*A certain man planted a vineyard, and set an hedge about it, and digged a place for the winefat, and built a tower, and let it out to husbandmen, and went into a far country. And at the season he sent to the husbandmen a servant, that he might receive from the husbandmen of the fruit of the vineyard. And they caught him, and beat him, and sent him away empty. And again he sent unto them another servant; and at him they cast stones, and wounded him in the head, and sent him away shamefully handled. And again he sent another; and him they killed, and many others; beating some, and killing some. Having yet therefore one son, his wellbeloved, he sent him also last unto them, saying, They will reverence my son. But those husbandmen said among themselves, This is the heir; come, let us kill him, and the inheritance shall be ours. And they took him, and killed him, and cast him out of the vineyard. What shall therefore the lord of the vineyard do? he will come and destroy the husbandmen, and will give the vineyard unto others.*'

The commentators whip themselves into a froth over this tale of the vineyard. Is it a parable? Isn't it really an allegory? Perhaps it's an allegorical parable – or is it a parabolical allegory?

Well, whatever we decide to call it, it is actually a greatly developed version of the song in Isaiah which begins: 'Now will I sing to my wellbeloved a song of my beloved touching his vineyard. My wellbeloved hath a vineyard in a very fruitful hill: And he fenced it . . .'

We are enthralled by details. The detailed description of the vineyard with its hedge (of prickly thorn to keep out wild beasts) and the place dug for the winefat (the winepress) and the tower (for the watchmen to guard the fruit). And then the description of the fate of the various servants sent to collect the fruit. The first beaten; the second wounded in the head by stones and sent away 'shamefully handled' the third killed; and many others . . . some beaten and some killed. And then, quite casually, Jesus mentions that the owner has 'one son' – whom he calls 'his wellbeloved' – and suddenly we realise that Jesus is talking of himself; and we realise, not only – as in the Isaiah version – that the vineyard is the Jewish nation ('For the vineyard of the Lord of hosts is the house of Israel'), and that the owner is God, but also that the husbandmen are the religious hierarchy, and the servants are the many prophets who through the years had received all kinds of ill treatment from them. (Of course, the Rev. Marshall gives us a list: 'Micaiah imprisoned . . . Zechariah stoned . . . Urijah put to death . . . Jeremiah put in the stocks . . . Isaiah sawn asunder . . . etc., etc.)

The story is a specific condemnation of the establishment, past and present. It is also an astonishing proclamation of divinity.

Two things especially appeal to me.

The first is the distance of God from humanity. We learn that, after letting the vineyard out to husbandmen, the owner 'went into a far country'.

This is a continual dilemma for men. God isn't actually *here*. We seem to be on our own. People seem to be able to get away with murder. Unfairness, injustice, and suffering abound. 'His eye' is not always 'on the sparrow'. His eye even seems to avoid the multitude of innocent people killed in war, starved by famine, or decimated by plague. Why does God have to be 'in a far country'? Why are we so lonely in the universe?

Jesus accepts this loneliness. Soon he will reveal to some of his disciples the extent of his acceptance; he will reveal, with harsh reality, the terrible fate of humanity. God *is* in a far country. But he is also our father which is in heaven.

If we choose to believe.

If we choose.

Jesus chooses to believe that God is his father and that he is in heaven. And the *distance* of God does not matter. In fact the distance of God is an exhilarating challenge. The God whom Jesus endeavours to obey is not some local deity who can be tamed and befriended like a domestic pet. The kingdom of God of Jesus is the Holy Spirit working for the general good of mankind. The kingdom of God of Jesus is a benign universe. The kingdom of God of Jesus is the triumph of belief.

If, as sometimes seems, life on earth is a careless heavenly experiment, then this experiment includes a distant God; a god who leaves us to our own devices; to all the natural dangers of the world; to extreme heat and cold, to hurricane and drought – as well as to dangers of our own invention. Seemingly we have permission to behave as badly as we wish – as long as we successfully evade the law. We can create or we can destroy. We can worship or we can desecrate.

Choice again.

Without a distant God, this choice would not be ours.

Perhaps, without a distant God, the genius of mankind would not have flourished.

It would not have dared.

★

The other thing that appeals to me in this vineyard story is the knowledge and blatant self-love of Jesus.

Among other things, Nineham tells us that 'the authenticity of this parable has been widely doubted . . . because it presupposes: that Jesus knew in advance about his death'. Haven't these doubters read the previous chapters of the Gospel? Don't they believe Jesus's many predictions to his disciples of his death and resurrection? These have become increasingly specific. '. . . the Son of man shall be delivered unto the chief priests, and unto the scribes; and they shall condemn him to death, and shall deliver him to the Gentiles: And they shall mock him, and shall scourge him, and shall spit upon him, and shall kill him: and the third day he shall rise again.' (Mark 10: 33, 34)

In the story of the vineyard the owner has 'one son, his wellbeloved', and when he sends him to the husbandmen he confidently says, 'They will reverence my son.' This is Jesus talking about himself. In the same buoyant way that early in the ministry he likened himself to a bridegroom at a wedding, Jesus now presents himself – obliquely – as the wellbeloved Son of God: a God – innocent simple old soul – who imagines that his son will be reverenced by men. Jesus not only thinks of himself as wellbeloved, he also presumes to know better than his father. He knows he will be killed.

Finally he challenges his audience – and, in particular, the hapless group from the Sanhedrin – 'What shall therefore the lord of the vineyard do?' In St Matthew's version someone answers for him; but in Mark's version, which seems to me more likely, Jesus answers his own rhetorical question. 'He will come and destroy the husbandmen, and will give the vineyard unto others.' This is certainly spoken by 'one that had authority'. The listeners were so over-awed that, according to St Luke, 'when they heard it, they said, God forbid'.

But is this the end of the matter?

No!

Jesus continues relentlessly.

'And have ye not read this scripture; The stone which the builders rejected is become the head of the corner: This was the Lord's doing, and it is marvellous in our eyes?'

Jesus's quote is from Psalm 118; a Psalm of effusive praise and defiance. These are some of the verses which lead up to it.

'The Lord is on my side; I will not fear: what can man do unto me?'

'They compassed me about like bees; they are quenched as the fire of thorns: for in the name of the Lord I will destroy them.'

'Thou hast thrust sore at me that I might fall: but the Lord helped me.'

'The Lord is my strength and song, and is become my salvation.'

'I shall not die, but live, and declare the works of the Lord.'

And so on till . . .

'The stone which the builders refused is become the head stone of the corner. This is the Lord's doing; it is marvellous in our eyes.'

The dazzling confidence of Jesus brings comfort to every underdog and nonentity; gives hope to every understudy and poor relation; warms the hearts of every second, third and fourth division.

It is no wonder that the disciples and the early Christians were fond of referring to these words.

It is no wonder that in the temple the chief priests, and the scribes, and the elders reacted in the following manner.

'And they sought to lay hold on him, but feared the people: for they knew that he had spoken the parable against them: and they left him, and went their way.'

Can we imagine a new man in Canterbury Cathedral, calling it 'a den of thieves', destroying every money-making device, smashing the gadgets for the mechanically guided tours, scattering books, postcards, and souvenirs, arguing with a deputation from the Archbishop, humiliating them in front of crowds of people, and hinting that he is actually the Son of God?

How would the deputation stop him, and get him outside the sacred precincts? Perhaps by inciting him to break the law . . .

'And they send unto him certain of the Pharisees and of the Herodians, to catch him in his words.' 13

Or as the Rev. Marshall puts it, writing as if for a silent movie: 'Two opposite political parties mutually hating each other combine in unholy alliance to entrap Jesus.'

'And when they were come, they say unto him, Master . . .' 14

'Hypocritical flattery.' (Marshall)

'. . . we know that thou art true, and carest for no man: for thou regardest not the person of men, but teachest the way of God in truth.'

(I like the New English translation: 'and truckle to no one, whoever he may be.')

The Pharisees and Herodians continue – casually, oh so casually!

'Is it lawful to give tribute to Caesar, or not? Shall we give, or shall we not give?' 15

('Tribute: the poll tax hateful to the Jews.')

'If Jesus said "Yes," the Pharisees would undermine his popularity with the people. If "No," the Herodians would denounce him to Pilate as a rebel.' (Marshall) Either way Jesus would lose.

Pause.

'But he, knowing their hypocrisy, said unto them, Why tempt ye me? bring me a penny, that I may see it.'

Pause.

Someone finds a penny.
'And they brought it.' 16

Pause.

Jesus examines the penny.
'And he saith unto them . . .'

(Looking at the head of Tiberius, the reigning Emperor.)
'Whose is this image and superscription?'

Pause.

What's he up to?
'And they said unto him, Caesar's.'

No pause.

17
'And Jesus answering said unto them, Render to Caesar the things that are Caesar's, and to God the things that are God's. And they marvelled at him.'

Everybody loves this story. Even people who do not care to have any truck with Jesus and his teaching love this story. We see Jesus threatened by two powerful factions, and masterfully get the better of them. And, as the inheritance of his answer, we are given a choice – perhaps too wide a choice – between what belongs to Caesar and what belongs to God. Ninety per cent Caesar? Ten per cent God? Fifty per cent Caesar? Fifty per cent God? Ten per cent Caesar? Ninety per cent God? Take your pick. It's a matter of opinion. Most of us are Caesar's men. After all, God is in a far country . . .

The Pharisees and the Herodians are beaten. What is the enemy to do? Send in fresh battalions . . .

18
'Then come unto him the Sadducees, which say there is no resurrection . . .'

That should do it!

'. . . and they asked him, saying, Master, Moses wrote unto us, If a man's brother die, and leave his wife behind him, and leave no children, that his brother should take his wife, and raise up seed unto his brother. Now there were seven brethren: and the first took a wife, and dying left no seed. And the second took her, and died, neither left he any seed: and the third likewise. And the seven had her, and left no seed: last of all the woman died also. In the resurrection therefore, when they shall rise, whose wife shall she be of them? for the seven had her to wife. And Jesus answering said unto them, Do ye not therefore err, because ye know not the scriptures, neither the power of God? For when they shall rise from the dead, they neither marry, nor are given in marriage; but are as the angels which are in heaven. And as touching the dead, that they rise: have ye not read in the book of Moses, how in the bush God spake unto him, saying, I am the God of

Abraham, and the God of Isaac, and the God of Jacob? He is not the God of the dead, but the God of the living: ye therefore do greatly err.'

27

Great story-telling!

First, the introduction: 'Then come unto him the Sadducees, which say there is no resurrection.' This is an outrageous description! The Sadducees must have said a lot more than *that*! But, for the sake of this story, it is all we need to know. They said, 'There is no resurrection.' Obviously this is going to be a resurrection debate.

Nevertheless it might just fill in the background a little to know that the Sadducees were conservative and traditional. They considered the Pharisees non-conformist. They hated innovation. They believed in the Pentateuch – the first five books in the Old Testament – and would only accept the written Mosaic law as the basis of life and belief; and Nineham tells us, 'Belief in resurrection or immortality is entirely missing from the Old Testament, which knows only of a shadowy existence – it can hardly be called life – which the departed soul shares in a gloomy and desolate region known as Sheol.'

The Sadducees' question is based on the rules of 'levirate marriage' which are found in the Book of Deuteronomy. These rules were made to insure that a family name and property did not disappear. The brother of a dead man was duty bound to marry the widow if she was childless: 'her husband's brother must marry her and sleep with her. The first son she bears to him shall be counted as the son of the dead brother, so that his name will not be forgotten.' (Living Bible) If the wretched brother refused to do this, he was brought in front of the elders, and 'the widow shall walk over to him in the presence of the elders, pull his sandal from his foot and spit in his face . . . And ever afterwards his house shall be referred to as "the home of the man who had his sandal pulled off."' (Deuteronomy, 25: 9 and 10.)

The Sadducees reduced this ridiculous situation to absurdity with a family consisting of seven fatally unhealthy brothers (seven was always a good round number) and a very game wife who, presumably, finally expired from exhaustion. They did this in order to catch Jesus out on the question of resurrection; and asked who would be married to whom in heaven.

12

They obviously thought that the carpenter from Nazareth was a push-over.

To the crowd the situation must have been irresistible. They would consider the Sadducees to be Jesus's most dangerous enemy. The High Priest was always drawn from their number. The Sadducees were the priestly aristocracy. But, as we know, it is a fault of aristocrats to underestimate their opponents.

Jesus simply mows them down. Not, I think, with anger, but with pity. Modern translators have Jesus answer: 'How wrong you are!' or 'You are mistaken'; but to speak aloud the King James Version's, 'Do ye not therefore err,' is by far the best. The word 'err' can be prolonged at the back of the throat, and outdoes any aristocratic drawl.

Jesus informs the élite of the religious hierarchy – in front of crowds of people, in their temple – that they 'know not the scriptures, neither the power of God'. He was not a timid man. Like a schoolboy teaching his masters the alphabet, or like a commoner instructing the royal family on palace etiquette, Jesus corrected the Sadducees and gave them a little scripture lesson. He told them, in effect, that their question was a total misconception of the scriptures; that death is not a literal continuation of life; and that there are no husbands and wives in heaven. Then he attacked at source – as he has done in the past. When the Pharisees accused the disciples of unlawful behaviour on the sabbath day, Jesus asked them: 'Have ye never read what David did . . . ?' When they asked him their question about divorce, he took them back to Moses, and then to Adam and Eve. Now, he teaches the Sadducees from one of their revered books of the Pentateuch. He attacks them on their own ground. He dares to ask, 'Have ye not read in the book of Moses, how in the bush' (or in that passage about the burning bush) 'God spake unto him, saying, I *am* the God of Abraham, and the God of Isaac, and the God of Jacob?' I think the present tense, 'I *am*', is important. God speaks of Abraham, Isaac and Jacob as if they are present with him – so they cannot be dead. They are all immortals.

To us, the argument seems remote, but it seems to have silenced the Saducees. Jesus then spelt it out: 'He is not the God of the dead, but the God of the living.' And then he summarised his opening admonition. He began with, 'Do ye not

188

therefore err.' He concludes with, 'Ye therefore do *greatly* err.' On this active day in the temple, he was certainly not a timid man.

With the passing years the importance of the Sadducees lessened. Alan Cole writes: 'Christian history is littered with groups that have ceased to respond to the continual stimuli of the Spirit of God.' But at that time they were still influential; and in The Acts of the Apostles there is a description of another argument about resurrection . . . 'there arose a dissension between the Pharisees and the Sadducees: and the multitude was divided. For the Sadducees say that there is no resurrection, neither angel, nor spirit: but the Pharisees confess both.' Their difference of opinion perhaps helps to explain the attitude of Jesus's next questioner. We might expect, believing in the continuity of St Mark's Gospel, that by now Jesus would have attracted a few tentative disciples from the establishment. Jesus's answer to the Sadducees probably gave pleasure to at least some of the scribes and Pharisees. And so it follows:

'And one of the scribes came, and having heard them reasoning 28 *together, and perceiving that he had answered them well, asked him, Which is the first commandment of all?'*

This was not a trick question. It was not another trap for Jesus. The relative importance of the various commandments was a popular debate. The scribe was just curious. He asked merely for information. Evidently 'Six hundred and thirteen commandments were given to Moses, 365 negative commandments . . . and 248 positive commandments.' (R. Simlai) David and Isaiah and Micah and Habakkuk had made suggestions for drastic reductions. But the question of priorities was still pertinent.

The scribe wanted the opinion of this new man who spoke with such impressive authority. At first, Jesus's answer was seemingly conventional.

'And Jesus answered him, The first of all the commandments is, 29 *Hear, O Israel; The Lord our God is one Lord.'*

Every Jew would agree with this. 'That single sentence is the real creed of Judaism.' (Barclay)

'And thou shalt love the Lord thy God with all thy heart, and with 30 *all thy soul, and with all thy mind, and with all thy strength: this is the first commandment.'*

Then, perhaps unexpectedly, he added:

31 *'And the second is like, namely this, Thou shalt love thy neighbour as thyself. There is none other commandment greater than these.'*

Both of these commandments are from the Pentateuch. The first commandment is from Deuteronomy 6: 4, 5 and the second from Leviticus 19: 18. They were well-known commandments. But perhaps combining them in this way was original. And surely Jesus intended the second commandment to be unqualified. In the original it is written: 'Thou shalt not avenge, nor bear any grudge against the children of thy people, but thou shalt love thy neighbour as thyself.' This would appear to limit 'neighbour' to the immediate children of Israel. Jesus surely commanded *all* men to love one another.

The reaction of the scribe is only reported in St Mark.

32 *'And the scribe said unto him, Well, Master . . .'*
or 'Well said, Master.' (New English)
'. . . thou hast said the truth.'
And then he repeats – or nearly repeats – Jesus's words.

33 *'For there is one God; and there is none other but he: And to love him with all the heart, and with all the understanding, and with all the soul, and with all strength, and to love his neighbour as himself, is more than all burnt offerings and sacrifices.'*

Why does he repeat Jesus's words? Or, rather, why does Mark report that he repeats them? It could be that Mark wished to emphasise the accord between Jesus and the scribe. It could be that he wished to emphasise the nearness of Jesus's basic teaching with Judaism. Here, in this moment of union, is a rare moment of simplicity which shames the absurd intricacies of organised religion. The scribe endorses Jesus. Jesus then endorses the scribe.

34 *'And when Jesus saw that he answered discreetly'* (or 'wisely', or 'sensibly') *'he said unto him, Thou art not far from the kingdom of God. And no man after that durst ask him any question.'*

Some people claim that here Jesus meant that the scribe was close to conversion. I don't think this is necessarily so. There is a kinship in the love of God and the love of humanity which can exist between any sect, cult, creed, or caste – religious or otherwise. Surely the Holy Spirit wouldn't make distinctions. Jesus said: 'For he that is not against us is on our part.' There need be no labels.

After the questions of the chief priests and the scribes and the elders; the Pharisees and the Herodians; the Sadducees; and the friendly scribe, Jesus appears to be left in peace. So he asks himself a rhetorical question.

'And Jesus answered and said, while he taught in the temple, How 35
say the scribes that Christ is the Son of David? For David himself said 36
by the Holy Ghost, The Lord said to my Lord, Sit thou on my right
hand, till I make thine enemies thy footstool. David therefore himself 37
calleth him Lord; and whence is he then his son?'

Although it obviously made great sense at the time, this is a very confusing little passage. Was Jesus talking of himself? Did he wish to disclaim any connection with the family of David? Was he solely the Son of God?

On the other hand, although Matthew and Luke include the story, they also include long genealogical lists to prove that Jesus *was* descended from David.

Help!

This is 'a polemical passage which has been much discussed without any very satisfactory conclusion being reached'. (Manson quoted by Nineham)

'. . . neither the problem posed nor the answer offered strike much interest today.' (Crotty)

Oh well . . .

Still, it went down all right on the night. Mark then tells us:

'And the common people heard him gladly.'

Although the commentators say that this line was meant to be attached to the *next* story – which is a more obvious crowd-pleaser.

But whichever story the line belongs to, and it really doesn't matter, the common people in the temple certainly heard him gladly – and Jesus became increasingly outspoken.

'And he said unto them in his doctrine, Beware of the scribes, which 38
love to go in long clothing, and love salutations in the marketplaces,
And the chief seats in the synagogues, and the uppermost rooms at
feasts: Which devour widow's houses, and for a pretence make long 39 40
prayers: these shall receive greater damnation.'

I don't think that Jesus meant his listeners to beware of *all* scribes; only *those* scribes who behaved in *that* manner; the ostentatious, extortionate and hypocritical scribes. Much of the description could apply to *many* groups of people; people who love impressive clothes, costumes or uniforms; who love their titles and insist on being formally addressed; who have to sit in the best seats at any function, and have the best tables at any restaurant. We all know *those* people. Some of us *are* those people.

But the accusations become more serious. 'Which devour widow's houses' is wonderfully evocative. The Rev. Marshall explains: 'Either as being made guardians of widows they managed to embezzle their property, or, by a show of piety, persuading devout women to bestow on them their houses or estates.' The scribes also took money from widows as payment for prayers on their behalf, and the last part of Jesus's attack could be related to this.

It is exhilarating to hear Jesus attack the scribes in this way, but it is not a typical piece of teaching. It is not constructive. But, at least in St Mark's Gospel it is contained within three verses. At this point in St Matthew there is a whole chapter of invective. As an actor, I find this thrilling stuff – comparable with the great tirades of Timon of Athens – but nevertheless I do not think that this personal attack in St Matthew's version – with the repeated cry of 'Woe unto you scribes and Pharisees, hypocrites!' – fits the Jesus we have met in St Mark. It is possible, as Christianity became increasingly anti-semitic, that these lines were invented, or at least extended, and put into the mouth of Jesus. It was the simplicity and joy of Jesus of Nazareth which was revolutionary; it was the rock-like faith of Jesus of Nazareth which impressed; it was his compassion and understanding which made men love him. He had no need to shout abuse. At least, in St Mark, Jesus's words about the scribes are cool and dismissive.

*

Now there is only one more story set in the temple. This story rings absolutely true. It is typical of the man.

'*And Jesus sat over against the treasury, and beheld how the people cast money into the treasury: and many that were rich cast in much. And there came a certain poor widow, and she threw in two mites, which make a farthing. And he called unto him his disciples, and saith unto them, Verily I say unto you, That this poor widow hath cast more in, than all they which have cast into the treasury; For all they*

41

44

did cast in of their abundance; but she of her want did cast in all that she had, even all her living.'

The Rev. Marshall tells us that the original word for 'beheld' implied that Jesus watched these goings-on for a considerable time.

'Two mites' is variously translated as 'two small coins', or 'two little copper coins'. I like mites. They sound smaller.

Did the widow ever know of Jesus's high opinion of her?

Did she need to know?

By giving her two mites she gained immortality.

CHAPTER 13

This is a mysterious chapter.

It is the most difficult section of St Mark's Gospel; it is also the most exciting. In this chapter, after a cue from 'one of his disciples', Jesus says something so provocative that a gang of four of his disciples get him on his own and demand an explanation. He gives them an explanation. It leaves them, and us, stunned and terrified.

'And as he went out of the temple, one of his disciples saith unto him, Master, see what manner of stones and what buildings are here!'

Why did 'one of his disciples' say this? And why does Mark not name him? I thought at first the disciple might have been Judas Iscariot. But perhaps the identity of the disciple does not matter. Perhaps Mark intended us to concentrate on the request.

The request seems to be a desire to persuade Jesus at least to acknowledge the past; his own heritage; and the present establishment.

We have had astonishing drama in the temple; a series of stories in which Jesus has written his own death warrant. He has begged his own death. He has given the chief priests no other alternative. He has publicly humiliated and insulted the hierarchy, and hinted at his own divinity.

He has done this, seemingly, without consulting anybody. As far as we can tell, the disciples have been silent. Now, one of them – or, perhaps, as reported in Matthew and Luke, a group of them – asks him to pause for a moment and consider the scene. 'Master, see what manner of stones and what buildings are here!'

A rare exclamation mark!

The disciples have been presented by Mark as foolish men; often confused and slow to understand. Sometimes they have 'reasoned with themselves', or 'questioned one with another', without daring to confront Jesus. But they have never ceased to care for him. They have been loyal companions. On the way to Jerusalem they lagged behind him on the road; they were afraid for him. In the temple, we have not heard from them, or about them. What did they think of Jesus's words and behaviour? We have not found them to be careful or diplomatic men, but I think it is likely that they were horrified by the recklessness of Jesus. Even if they agreed that he – and they – must confront the old order, and teach a new way of life and behaviour, it is doubtful that they agreed with the head-on public collisions with the chief priests, the elders, the scribes, the Pharisees, the Herodians, and the Sadducees. They may have been appalled by the unnecessary risks that Jesus took. Could they not teach in private? Could they not form a secret society in Jerusalem? Could they not enlist the support of influential people? Could they not avoid the enmity of prominent men?

These thoughts and feelings may have prompted the unnamed disciple to make Jesus acknowledge the temple; as well as a natural awe and respect for the grandeur of the buildings; as well as a sort of exhaustion caused by the energy and presumption of the carpenter. A need to grasp him by the sleeve, to stop him in his tracks, and make him face reality; to make him acknowledge the huge achievements of men; to prevent him from threatening his elders and betters with damnation.

'Master, see what manner of stones and what buildings *are* here!'

I think it was a desperate request, made in the faint hope that Jesus might turn back or turn away, and avoid the almost certain consequences of his words and actions. It was a last hope for life not death; for acceptance not defiance; a last attempt to rest content and let the world turn. Perhaps, sentimentally, a longing for Galilee . . .

Jesus's answer is ruthless. He displays no respect for the temple. He foresees no compromise. The Old Testament is demolished.

2

  *'And Jesus answering said unto him, Seest thou these great
buildings? there shall not be left one stone upon another, that shall not
be thrown down.'*

  I don't think these words have anything to do with the
eventual destruction of the temple. I don't think Jesus was
speaking historically. He was prophesying his own victory
over orthodox Judaism. He was 'speaking in parables'. He was
confident that the new faith would obliterate the old.

  When? Soon?

  How? By conversion? By conflict?

  Would there be magic? Would God appear? Would Jesus be
dressed in shining white? Would there be angels?

  The disciples – or at least four of the disciples – finally find
the courage to confront him.

  Would Jesus be king? Would they be the leading members of
his court? Would there be glory in their lifetime? Would the
chief priests, the elders and the scribes bow down before
them?

  These questions must have been buzzing in their heads.

  It was late the same day. Perhaps it was late at night. Perhaps
they were aware of the sky and the stars, of distant city lights
and sounds. Perhaps their voices were hushed. They might
never have the chance to speak with him again. He could be
arrested at any moment. They could be separated. Events
were moving very fast.

3
4

  *'And as he sat upon the mount of Olives over against the temple,
Peter and James and John and Andrew asked him privately, Tell us,
when shall these things be? and what shall be the sign when all these
things shall be fulfilled?'*

  Tell us!

  It was a desperate cry. The disciples needed the trust of
Jesus. They needed comfort. They needed factual information. They needed to be educated.

  Jesus's next speech, the longest recorded speech in St Mark's
Gospel, is an extraordinary combination of loving advice and
terrifying prophecy. It switches from one theme to another.
And yet, to speak, it is absolutely logical. The two sets of
brothers, the original disciples, the fishermen called by the Sea
of Galilee, sat on the mount of Olives outside Jerusalem in
sight of the temple, and asked their friend, the carpenter from

Nazareth, for enlightenment. What did the future hold for them? What help might they expect?

'And Jesus answering them began to say . . .' 5

This is a thrilling moment in the Gospel. We are about to learn the fate of mankind.

'Take heed lest any man deceive you: For many shall come in my 6
name, saying, I am Christ; and shall deceive many.'

His first thoughts are for them. He is well aware of their credulity; of their eagerness to please. They must retain their independence. They must not be led astray by charlatans. They are the guardians of Christ. The first warning is a desire to protect them and their special knowledge from corruption by men.

'And when ye shall hear of wars and rumours of wars, be ye not 7
troubled: for such things must needs be; but the end shall not be yet.'

The second warning is prompted by a desire to protect them from the corruption of the world. In spite of hostility, and the threat of hostility, they should never be tempted to think that God has deserted them.

And now a sense begins that Jesus is talking not only to Peter and James and John and Andrew on a hill outside Jerusalem, but to all of us. To all of us down the years. Especially to us! This is the genius of the speech. It has a timeless quality. It can work for and apply to the four disciples on the mount of Olives. It can also work for anyone who cares to study Jesus's words; for anyone who cares to listen or to read. It seems as if Jesus is talking into each individual ear. Slowly and carefully he breaks the news.

'For nation shall rise against nation, and kingdom against king- 8
dom: and there shall be earthquakes in divers places, and there shall be
famines and troubles: these are the beginnings of sorrows.'

In these lines there is an extraordinary sense that God has set the world in motion; that he takes the risk that men may destroy themselves; that there is, and always will be, danger. One feels that Jesus accepts this reckless state of things. Perhaps he wonders at the eccentricity of God; but he doesn't rage against it. Gently, but sadly, he accepts it.

Physically, it seems, we are alone. Jesus warns explicitly: there will be war, there will be natural disaster, there will be human failure, there will be no help. And then he adds: 'These are the beginnings of sorrows' – which presumably means 'And this is just for starters!'

Now, Jesus's concern is for his disciples in this haphazard state of affairs; for them and us.

9 *'But take heed to yourselves: for they shall deliver you up to councils; and in the synagogues ye shall be beaten: and ye shall be brought before rulers and kings for my sake, for a testimony against*
10 *them. And the gospel must first be published among all nations.'*

He is talking specifically to his followers. He is warning them what to expect when he has left them. His words apply to the early Christians. But the work of spreading the gospel did not end there. It still goes on. The followers of Jesus are still challenged to stand and be counted. They may not be beaten in synagogues, but there is still the risk of disparagement and mockery. It still takes courage to proclaim one's faith. (More than I possess.)

Did Jesus realise that his words were daunting? that the disciples – they and us – might easily be overwhelmed by the enormity of the task, by the difficulty of the work, by the potential dangers? With disconcerting understanding, he now speaks words of advice.

11 *'But when they shall lead you, and deliver you up, take no thought beforehand what ye shall speak, neither do ye premeditate: but whatsoever shall be given you in that hour, that speak ye: for it is not ye that speak, but the Holy Ghost.'*

These are wonderful words of comfort. They are also practical. Like a doctor instructing a patient on the quickest way to recovery; or like a barrister instructing his client on how to behave in court; Jesus instructs his disciples in time of trouble. 'Take no thought beforehand what ye shall speak, neither do ye premeditate.' What amazing advice! What a relief to the nervous and inarticulate! 'Whatsoever shall be given you in that hour, that speak ye: for it is not ye that speak, but the Holy Ghost.' Jesus takes the burden off our shoulders. Faith takes over. Whatever we speak will be right.

(When I have recited St Mark's Gospel before an audience, there have been many occasions when words have gone out of my head. I have had no idea what the next line might be. But, without thinking or premeditating, I decide to speak. And the words come from somewhere. They are given to me. It is a mystery. There has never been a crisis. There never will be.)

The tone of Jesus's speech switches again; from words of comfort to words of warning.

'Now the brother shall betray the brother to death, and the father the son; and children shall rise up against their parents, and shall cause them to be put to death. And ye shall be hated of all men for my name's sake: but he that shall endure unto the end, the same shall be saved.' 12 13

Consider the scene.

Jesus is talking to two sets of brothers. He is looking into the anxious eyes of Peter and Andrew, and James and John. He says first: 'Now the brother shall betray the brother to death.' Does this relate to *them*? Is he preparing *them* for the unthinkable? He continues: 'And the father the son.' *Could this possibly relate to himself?* Could he be preparing *himself* for the unthinkable? Jesus's words may be a general prophecy of the worst that could happen in the future. But Jesus's words could also be specific. These brothers had given up their work and left their homes to follow him. He is their life. Now Jesus warns that they could betray each other to death. It is unthinkable. But it must be considered. Jesus's ministry has been based on the premise that he is the Son of God. After his baptism in Jordan, Jesus heard God say: 'Thou art my beloved Son, in whom I am well pleased.' Could this father in heaven betray him? It is unthinkable. But it must be considered.

People feel guilt at 'bad thoughts'. Unprompted, thoughts of death and disaster come into our heads. Is it wish-fulfilment – or is it simply terror? I think that Jesus tells us that the unthinkable must be considered.

'And children shall rise up against their parents, and shall cause them to be put to death.' This is most horrible of all. This negates all effort for the future. A child can be without love. It is unthinkable. But it must be considered.

'And ye shall be hated of all men for my name's sake: but he that shall endure unto the end, the same shall be saved.' Jesus finally warns of universal hatred. Hatred from brothers, fathers, sons, all men. He envisages total exclusion from society – but exclusion with continuing faith. The outcast with faith who endures will finally be saved. These are challenges beyond the endurance of most of us. These are unthinkable challenges, but they must be considered. This is no dream world; no ideal planet.

Now Jesus stops talking of horrible possibilities, and embarks on what seems to be grim certainty.

'But when ye shall see the abomination of desolation, spoken of by Daniel the prophet, standing where it ought not, (let him that readeth understand,) then let them that be in Judaea flee to the mountains: And let him that is on the housetop not go down into the house, neither enter therein, to take anything out of his house: And let him that is in the field not turn back again for to take up his garment. But woe to them that are with child, and to them that give suck in those days! And pray ye that your flight be not in the winter.'

Let's not trouble too much with Daniel the prophet! (Look up Daniel 9: 27 if you wish – but it won't help. Later translations leave out this reference to Daniel.) According to the Rev. Marshall it is thought that 'the abomination of desolation' could be interpreted as a reference to the Roman occupation, and to 'the abominations practised by the Romans, on the place where the Temple stood'. It is also interpreted as a prediction of the excesses of the Zealots in AD 66. But what use are these interpretations to us? Once again, I don't think that Jesus was necessarily speaking literally or historically.

The small instruction in parenthesis, 'let him that readeth understand', has been re-translated in many ways. The translation I prefer is by Ronald Knox: 'Let him who reads this, *recognise* what it means.' Everyone can *recognise* what it means; everyone according to his place and time.

Through the centuries there have been many abominations of desolation – and they have often stood where they ought not. The greater the artistic and scientific achievements of man, the more horrifying are the accompanying crimes of humanity. The higher the standard of a society, the more appalling are government-instigated murders, massacres and acts of torture. In our own recent history, the bombing of Hiroshima, and the Nazi Holocaust were abominations of desolation brought about by highly civilised countries.

What the future may hold for succeeding generations is hardly bearable to consider. It could be that the abomination of desolation referred to by Jesus has not yet occurred.

'For in those days shall be affliction, such as was not from the beginning of the creation which God created unto this time, neither shall be. And except that the Lord had shortened those days, no flesh should be saved: but for the elect's sake, whom he hath chosen, he hath shortened the days.'

This is surely a description of even more horror than the Roman occupation of the Holy Land, or the excesses of the Zealots in AD 66 – terrible as those events were at the time. This sounds like the end of the world. This sounds like total ruin and desolation. 'No flesh should be saved' conjures up images of uncontrolled nuclear war.

But these words are also mysterious. *How* has the Lord shortened those days? Or how *will* the Lord shorten those days? Presumably only the Lord knows.

And *who* are the elect? Who has the Lord chosen? Or who *will* he choose? Today there is something unattractive about a reference to 'the elect' or 'the chosen'. It smacks of unbearable complacency. It veers in the direction of insufferable superiority; of societies who refuse to integrate; of people who hold themselves aloof and apart. Presumably the Lord will make his own peculiar choice. But it might be as well to remember the teaching of Jesus and the chosen. 'If any man desire to be first, the same shall be last of all, and servant of all.' And '. . . many that are first shall be last; and the last first.' It is not for us to choose ourselves. Indeed it is not safe for us to choose ourselves. The very act of choosing ourselves is an act of vanity which could rule out our chance of membership in the kingdom of God. On the other hand, of course, we should beware of having pride in our astonishing humility . . .

Now Jesus warns his disciples – and us – of the dangers and temptations of false gods in such a time of isolation and terror:

'And then if any man shall say to you, Lo, here is Christ; or, lo, he is there; believe him not: For false Christs and false prophets shall rise, and shall shew signs and wonders, to seduce, if it were possible, even the elect. But take ye heed: behold, I have foretold you all things.'

Jesus has reached the ultimate test for his followers. He has broken the news that they must live with wars and rumours of wars; with earthquakes, famines, and troubles; with persecution for their beliefs; with the risk of betrayal from brothers, fathers, and even their own children; with the hatred of entire populations; and finally endure 'the abomination of desolation' – however we may 'recognise,' and whatever he meant by, that terrifying phrase.

This speech started with a gentle warning: 'Take heed lest any man deceive you: For many shall come in my name, saying, I am Christ: and shall deceive many.' After the catalogue of calamities, Jesus returns to this again – but now the gentle warning has become a stern command: 'And then if any man shall say to you, Lo, here is Christ: or, lo, he is there; *believe him not.*'

When people are weak and morale is low, when men appear to have been abandoned, these are the times when new leaders emerge. These are the times when people willingly allow decisions to be made for them. The twentieth century is a text book on this subject. The hammer and the sickle, and the swastika, have been signs, and the dazzling riches of capitalism have been wonders that have seduced 'even the elect'.

It is typical of Jesus that he should think ahead in this practical way, and that he should emphasise the dangers of false Christs and false prophets. Perhaps, to his disciples on the mount of Olives, these words of warning of how to behave in times of extreme suffering seemed remote. *They* were not likely to desert or betray Jesus. *They* were not likely to endure such appalling fates. Why did Jesus predict these terrible things? The four fishermen were the first recipients of these words. Up till now the ministry had been concerned with joy, with a new simplicity. Jesus had taught that there was no sin and no blasphemy except against the Holy Spirit. He had proclaimed a benign universe, a loving God, and the gift of individual choice in behaviour. He had reviled the many rules and laws of the old order. He had asked people to examine their hearts and be concerned with the faults within themselves, and not be so anxious to condemn their fellow men. All this had been a glorious revelation. Now, on the hill outside Jerusalem, the disciples were suddenly asked to face the concentrated reality of history. They were suddenly faced with the horror of centuries.

Besides all this, they were soon to be left alone – and knew that God was 'in a far country'.

They probably looked dejected and appalled as Jesus

announced, 'Behold, I have foretold you all things.' Perhaps for the first time there was doubt in their hearts. Perhaps their discipleship was a terrible mistake. Perhaps they discovered a hatred for the Master.

Mark hovers . . .

But Jesus had not foretold them all things . . .

Now, quietly, he begins to speak again. This is one of the great moments of the Gospel. The astonishing words develop into an extraordinary paean of faith and joy. Mark bursts into uncharacteristic song.

It should be written as a lyric.

'But in those days, after that tribulation,   24
the sun shall be darkened,
and the moon shall not give her light,   25
And the stars of heaven shall fall,
and the powers that are in heaven shall be shaken.
And then shall they see the Son of man coming in the clouds with   26
great power and glory.
And then shall he send his angels, and shall gather together his elect   27
from the four winds,
from the uttermost part of the earth to the uttermost part of heaven.'

To analyse these words makes them prosaic. To re-translate these words also makes them prosaic. These words are like stumbling on a Himalayan mountain in the midst of the South Downs. Jesus has warned of many dangers and many trials of faith. He has described 'the abomination of desolation'; 'affliction, such as was not from the beginning of creation.' He has left us in a world totally ruined. He has predicted that we will be tempted by false Christs and false prophets. We are, it seems, abandoned.

And then he says:

'But in those days, *after* that tribulation . . .' although the sun is darkened, and the moon no longer shines; although the stars of heaven have fallen; although the universe itself is in a state of chaos; 'Then . . .'

Then he makes a crazy promise.

Then! – When all is lost, and there is no more hope.

Then! – Would you believe it?

Jesus arrives on the scene – 'coming in the clouds with great power and glory.'

'And then . . .'

Would you believe it?

No matter where they are – 'from the uttermost part of the earth to the uttermost part of heaven' – his angels shall gather together his elect . . . and everything will be all right!

Would you believe it?

Do you *wish* to believe it?

I'd certainly *like* to believe it.

But I hope I am never put to the test.

★

From being reduced to a state of despair, it is likely that the four disciples on the mount of Olives were now gazing at the Master in a state of dazed delight. But Jesus changes tactics again. He now becomes a simple teacher instructing a kinder-garten. As we have seen him do in the past – during one of the great mass healings when 'he spake to his disciples, that a small ship should wait on him because of the multitude', or when he commanded the astonished family of Jairus's risen daughter 'that something should be given her to eat' – Jesus now becomes absolutely practical.

The disciples' original question had been prompted by Jesus's prediction of the destruction of the temple. They had asked him: 'Tell us, when shall these things be? and what shall be the sign when all these things shall be fulfilled?' As we have read, Jesus warned them that there would be many more horrors and wonders than the destruction of the temple. Now he says:

28
29
'*Now learn a parable of the fig tree; When her branch is yet tender, and putteth forth leaves, ye know that summer is near: So ye in like manner, when ye shall see these things come to pass, know that it is nigh, even at the doors.*'

It is a very simple parable – nevertheless I'm not sure if Jesus was referring to the abomination of desolation coming to pass, or to himself coming in the clouds with great power and glory; probably he was referring to both. In other words, when trees start to put forth their leaves, summer is near: and, when human suffering seems unendurable, God is near. Only believe!

If one takes the next verse literally, as spoken solely for the benefit of the four disciples, it was a mistaken prophecy.

'Verily I say unto you, that this generation shall not pass, till all **30** *these things be done.'*

It was the same miscalculation that Jesus made at Caesarea Philippi when he said: 'Verily I say unto you, That there be some of them that stand here, which shall not taste of death, till they have seen the kingdom of God come with power.'

Unless these words were the invention of Mark or Peter – or some unknown contributor – it would seem that Jesus believed that the kingdom of God would come in the lifetime of his followers. It seems that he believed that his disciples would endure the wars and rumours of wars, the betrayal of all men, and the abomination of desolation; and that they would see him coming in the clouds with great power and glory. *In order to celebrate the faith of Jesus, in order to effect his resurrection, we must make these words timeless.* I believe they are timeless. I believe – for instance – that the abomination of desolation need not be a national or world disaster. It is possible that the abomination of desolation can exist in the head of a single human being – at any time and in any place. It is also possible that the Son of man could appear to that person; that he could 'send his angels' and bring comfort to whoever he or she may be. This, surely, is the message of Jesus.

Now, as if to confirm the timeless quality of his words, Jesus makes the most confident statement in the history of the world. The audacity of this is simply staggering.

'Heaven and earth shall pass away: but my words shall not pass **31** *away.'*

Consider this man!

Where did he get the nerve to make a statement like that?

Who was he?

Why was he born at that particular time, and in that particular place?

What was the reason for his genius?

Why is there such a gap between the genius of one man and the brutishness or mediocrity of others?

Etcetera, etcetera . . .

There are no answers. But the mystery gives salt to the whole adventure.

★

Now Jesus returns once more to his disciples and to their original urgent question. 'Tell us, when shall these things be?'

This time he is even more specific.

32 *'But of that day and that hour knoweth no man, no, not the angels which are in heaven, neither the Son, but the Father.'*

In other words, Jesus does not know the answer. Only his father, God, knows.

And now Jesus gives them – and us – a challenge. Out of our ignorance he gives us a purpose.

33 *'Take ye heed, watch and pray: for ye know not when the time is.*
34 *For the son of man is as a man taking a far journey . . .'*

(Like his chosen father 'in a far country.')

'. . . who left his house, and gave authority to his servants, and to every man his work, and commanded the porter to watch. Watch ye therefore; for ye know not when the master of the house cometh, at even, or at midnight, or at the cockcrowing, or in the morning: Lest
37 *coming suddenly he find you sleeping. And what I say unto you I say unto all, Watch.'*

It seems we are on our own. We must choose. We can ignore God; or we can prepare ourselves for possible inspection.

Jesus knew that he would soon be gone, and that the disciples would be left alone. He knew it would be easy for their faith and special knowledge to stagnate. It would be easy for them to become complacent and worship an undemanding father in heaven. With the last part of his speech on the mount of Olives, Jesus gave his disciples a challenge.

He gave them his authority. In a sense, he charged them to become the Sons of men and the Sons of God.

He charged them – and, of course, he charged us.

Choose.

★

How did this extraordinary speech survive?

Who wrote it down?

Did Peter remember it word for word and relate it to Mark? Or did Peter remember *some* of the speech, and did Mark fill in the rest?

Was the young Mark actually eavesdropping on the mount

of Olives? Or, soon afterwards, did he tap the memory of all four of the disciples?

Did Jesus really make the speech? Perhaps it's all an invention.

Apart from the Rev. Marshall, who is a friend, with this particular chapter I have not referred to any of the other commentators. I will look at them now.

It is evidently known as the Little Apocalypse.

I seem to have got 'the abomination of desolation' all wrong. Gerard S. Sloyan writes: 'The "abomination of desolation" is perhaps the best-known meaningless phrase in the Christian's vocabulary . . .' He explains: 'Actually it was a heathen altar built by Antiochus IV in the Temple precincts in 168 BC.'

Ah . . .

And evidently Jesus was predicting events that were to happen in AD 40 when the Emperor Caligula nearly had a statue of himself erected in the Temple.

Oh . . .

And, according to Alan Cole, Mark's wonderful lyric about the Son of man coming in the clouds with great power and glory is merely 'a jigsaw of quotations from the apocalyptic books of the Old Testament.'

Hurrumph!

And, about the whole speech, Robert Crotty writes: 'Mark has fused together various sayings that came from the general reservoir of Jesus's sayings on the last times with material that may have been in circulation . . .'

C. F. D. Moule writes: 'Very briefly, it may be said that some scholars think that all or most of this chapter came from some Christian prophet's tract, written after the death of Jesus . . .'

Sherman E. Johnson writes: '. . . a Palestinian Christian wrote the Little Apocalypse . . . It is probably the work of a Galilean.'

D. E. Nineham writes: 'With regard to the authenticity and integrity of the discourse, there is a wide variety of opinion.' But in a footnote he mentions a writer who *actually* attempted to show that it *'goes back to Jesus himself and may even have been delivered by him, in more or less its present form, as a continuous discourse*'. But Nineham crushingly concludes 'for all its acuteness and learning, his argument hardly carries conviction as a whole'.

Depressing.

I mean depressing for a naive pilgrim like myself.

Well, I'm with the writer in Nineham's footnote. I have no scholarly argument. I can make no points with acuteness or learning. I simply *choose* to believe that Jesus made this speech 'in more or less its present form, as a continuous discourse'. It's a wonderful speech, and I think it more likely that the words came from Jesus than from anyone else. How it got written down is a mystery. The survival of Christianity is a mystery. Jesus himself is a mystery.

This is one of the greatest speeches ever recorded. With brutal frankness Jesus reveals the worst that can happen. The rest of his teaching should be seen against the background of these grim words. Christians shouldn't think themselves immune to the follies of their fellow men, or to the indiscriminating carelessness of nature.

Rather than be crushed by commentators, I would rather join forces with St Luke. Although most of his version of this speech is written in different words, the meaning is the same. And there are two splendid additions.

In St Mark's version Jesus simply warns the disciples to beware of being asleep when the master of the house cometh. In St Luke's version Jesus warns them to beware 'lest at any time your hearts be overcharged with surfeiting, and drunkenness, and cares of this life, and so that day come upon you unawares'. This touches many more of us.

And in St Mark's version, when the disciples are brought before rulers and kings and expected to defend themselves, Jesus advises them: 'Take no thought beforehand what ye shall speak, neither do ye premeditate: but whatsoever shall be given you in that hour, that speak ye: for it is not ye that speak, but the Holy Ghost.' In St Luke's version Jesus says: 'Settle it therefore in your hearts, not to meditate before what ye shall answer.' And then he makes this wonderful promise: 'For I will give you a mouth and wisdom, which all your adversaries shall not be able to gainsay nor resist.'

That's it! 'A mouth and wisdom!'

What more could one ask?

Whatever the difference in the choice of words, I think that Jesus made this speech upon the mount of Olives – and, miraculously, the meaning has survived him.

Watch!

THE PASSION NARRATIVE

St Mark's Gospel has been described as 'a Passion narrative with an introduction'. We have now reached the Passion narrative.

Apart from one incident at the beginning, which appears at first to be anachronistic, the narrative now sweeps us along smoothly to the end of the story of Jesus. Sometimes the preceding chapters have seemed like patched-up jobs. There have been unspecified passages of time. Mark rushes his Gospel forward; he seldom elaborates; there are fewer incidents reported than in the other Gospels; there are fewer parables; there is, most sadly, less of Jesus's teaching. But for all its brusqueness and bluntness of style, St Mark provides the most believable biography of Jesus. This is mainly because of the undoubted continuity of the Gospel; but it is also because, as we have seen, Mark includes many human touches that are missing from the grander versions. We gradually recognise a passionate, compassionate, practical, impractical, moody, humorous, and fanatical man. We are aware of his magnetism and charm. We are wary of his impatience and sarcasm. It would be exciting to meet him – but, to be on the safe side, it might be as well to take along a small child.

People worry about the dates of the Passion narrative, and try to fit the days of the Passover rites to our own Easter week. They also worry that in the opening passage the chief priests and the scribes say that they will not arrest Jesus during the feast time, and then appear to do just that. I don't think that these are important worries.

More important – and certainly more interesting – is the argument that Mark has carefully contrived the opening section, by inserting a domestic story, which could have occurred earlier in the ministry, between two reports of the activities of the enemy. First, Mark tells us:

'After two days was the feast of the passover, and of unleavened **1**
bread: and the chief priests and the scribes sought how they might take
him by craft, and put him to death. But they said, Not on the feast **2**
day, lest there be an uproar of the people.'

Jerusalem was packed with visitors during the Passover. Because of his teaching in the temple and the sensational confrontations with the various members of the hierarchy, Jesus must have attracted many followers. Mark has told us that 'the common people heard him gladly'. So it would obviously have been foolish for the chief priests and the scribes to have Jesus arrested publicly at this time, 'lest there be an uproar of the people'.

And then, unexpectedly, Mark breaks off from this news of imminent danger, and tells one of the most delightful stories in the whole ministry. It is surprising and a little disconcerting to follow the 'Little Apocalypse' with a cosy domestic scene, but it is typical of Mark's style; and I think that it completes our portrait of Jesus.

'And being in Bethany in the house of Simon the leper, as he sat at **3**
meat, there came a woman having an alabaster box of ointment of
spikenard very precious . . .'

Variously translated as: 'an alabaster flask of ointment of pure nard' (Revised Standard), 'a pot of very precious spikenard ointment' (Knox), 'a small bottle of very costly perfume, pure oil of nard' (New English), 'an alabaster jar full of very expensive perfume made of pure nard' (Good News).

'. . . and she brake the box . . .'
or flask or pot or bottle or jar,
'. . . and poured it on his head.'
Consternation!

'And there were some that had indignation within themselves, and **4**
said, Why was this waste of the ointment made? For it might have
been sold for more than three hundred pence, and have been given to
the poor. And they murmured against her. And Jesus said, Let her
alone; why trouble ye her? she hath wrought a good work on me. For
ye have the poor with you always, and whensoever ye will ye may do
them good: but me ye have not always. She hath done what she could:

she is come aforehand to anoint my body to the burying. Verily I say unto you, Wheresoever this gospel shall be preached throughout the whole world, this also that she hath done shall be spoken of for a memorial of her.'

This is the last time we shall see Jesus in an ordinary situation. This is the final reported event before the Last Supper, the agony in the Garden, the arrest, the trial, and the crucifixion. This is the coda of the ministry; a very apt winding up of the teaching of the man of Galilee.

It was evidently a habit of the time to drop a little perfume on to the head of an honoured guest at a feast. But it was obviously unusual to do this with a very expensive perfume, and even more unusual to pour on the entire amount. Whether the action of the woman gave any great pleasure to Jesus is impossible to know. Dr Nineham remarks tartly: 'Our evidence does not suggest that Jesus is likely to have gone in very much for perfume . . .' And it is understandable that the disciples, whom we assume to be poor men, were shocked by the woman's reckless action. The King James Version's 'and they murmured against her' is rather tame. The exuberant Living Bible puts it more vigorously: ' "Why, she could have sold that perfume for a fortune and given the money to the poor!" *they snarled.'* But the King James Version's translation of Jesus's reply is perfect. The first three words have a startling contemporary ring: 'And Jesus said, *Let her alone*; why trouble ye her? she hath wrought a good work on me.' I would love to know the tone of his voice. Was it spoken with anger, disgust, or fatigue? Was it a loving admonition? Or was it spoken roughly? I think that Jesus would have been more concerned to comfort the woman than to rebuke his disciples; to reassure her that he appreciated her expensive gift. After reminding his disciples that they would always have to work for the poor, he refers to himself. With typical self-appraisal, Jesus – the bridegroom, the Son of man, the Son of God – implies that he is sufficient reason for the woman's action. And then he says the wonderfully simple words: 'She hath done what she could.'

This is one of my favourite sayings of Jesus. It makes everyday life possible. It is a mini-guide to behaviour. It prevents nervous breakdowns.

And, as related to the lady, it is an example for everyone not to judge the actions of their fellow men and women. The gift of the perfume was the woman's way of showing her love. The self-righteous might think that she would be better off giving to the poor, or doing practical good works. But Jesus judged her to be worthy, and he defended her. In fact his defence becomes almost disproportionate. This could have been because someone was protesting. Jesus went on to claim that she was symbolically anointing his body for burial – which was probably not in her mind – reminding his disciples again of his approaching death. And, if that was not enough, he then confidently bestowed immortality on the woman with a 'Verily I say unto you', – and the promise that 'Wheresoever this gospel shall be preached throughout the whole world, this also that she hath done shall be spoken of for a memorial of her'.

If someone was protesting, who was it? In St John's version of the story, Judas Iscariot is specifically named as the disciple who said, 'Why was not this ointment sold for three hundred pence, and given to the poor?' It seems to me likely that Judas was the spokesman for the grumblers, and it is likely that he went on protesting, causing Jesus to defend the woman with an extravagance which equalled her expensive gift. Although Judas is not mentioned in Mark's version of the story, we now learn:

'And Judas Iscariot, one of the twelve, went unto the chief priests, to betray him unto them.'

It is a believable piece of continuity. I do not think the story of the woman was an old tale inserted by Mark as an artificial bridge between the opening lines about the intentions of the chief priests and the scribes, and Judas's betrayal. I think that the story of the woman with her ointment or perfume happened at exactly the time that it is reported. Mark is not the sort of writer to construct his Gospel artificially. But also, I think that the attitude of Jesus to the murmurers or snarlers was the trigger which finally caused Judas to betray him.

It is in this episode that Jesus appears to some to go too far. The majority of us love him for his praise of the poor widow who gave her two mites. But his defence of this seemingly extravagant, thoughtless woman is harder to accept. But Jesus said: 'She hath done what she could.' And, by defending her, he defends all less than perfect people. This is Jesus's last attack on intolerance. It is a last example of compassion. It is a vital story in the ministry; so vital, in fact, that it caused the betrayal, trial, and crucifixion. For Judas, it was obviously the last straw. He could no longer endure the unconventional teaching and authoritative attitude of Jesus. He offered to help the chief priests.

'*And when they heard it, they were glad, and promised to give him money. And he sought how he might conveniently betray him.*'

'Conveniently' implies that Judas had to find a way for the arrest of Jesus to take place without causing 'an uproar of the people'.

'*And the first day of unleavened bread, when they killed the passover, his disciples said unto him, Where wilt thou that we go and prepare that thou mayest eat the passover? And he sendeth forth two of his disciples, and saith unto them, Go ye into the city, and there shall meet you a man bearing a pitcher of water: follow him. And wheresoever he shall go in, say ye to the goodman of the house, The Master saith, Where is the guest-chamber, where I shall eat the passover with my disciples? And he will show you a large upper room furnished and prepared: there make ready for us.*'

Jesus appears to give very vague instructions to the disciples. But it was evidently only women who carried pitchers of water, so the man – whoever he was – would certainly stand out in a crowd. Nevertheless, since no time and no place are mentioned by Jesus, the meeting seems chancy. The instructions to the two disciples sent to find the colt in the village outside Jerusalem were clearer, but in both stories there is a mysterious element which we will never understand. In this instance, Jesus may have made careful arrangements with 'the goodman of the house' ahead of time; or it is possible that Mark is being purposely vague. Was it an all-male household? Or was it, as some people claim, the house of Mark himself? Was Mark the man carrying the pitcher of water? This is all surmise. We must accept a mystery.

The next lines are a beautiful example of Mark's style in the King James Version. We naturally want to know what happened to the disciples after Jesus's vague instructions, and Mark compresses all the information into two lucid sentences.

The first sentence contains four pieces of information, staccato. The second sentence contains one piece of information, rallantando.

'*And his disciples went forth, and came into the city, and found as* *he had said unto them: and they made ready the passover. And in the* *evening he cometh with the twelve.*' 16 17

With the minimum of fuss, Mark has prepared us for the Last Supper.

The meal has started. Were the disciples aware of the significance of the occasion? Were they restrained and quiet? Were they awkward? Did they wish to avoid the subject on their minds? They were not allowed to . . .

'*And as they sat and did eat, Jesus said, Verily I say unto you, One* *of you which eateth with me shall betray me. And they began to be* *sorrowful, and to say unto him one by one, Is it I? and another said, Is* *it I? And he answered and said unto them, It is one of the twelve,* *that dippeth with me in the dish. The Son of man indeed goeth, as it is* *written of him: but woe to that man by whom the Son of man is* *betrayed! good were it for that man if he had never been born.*' 18 21

After his meeting with the chief priests; after his offer to betray Jesus, Judas returned to the group. He is sitting with them at the table, unsuspected by the others. But Jesus knows . . . The situation is dramatic. And Jesus makes his accusation. And the disciples 'began to be sorrowful'. And one by one they ask 'Is it I? and another said, Is it I?' Did Judas challenge Jesus with his eyes? Did he dare Jesus to denounce him? I don't think so. If Judas had offered to betray Jesus, and was now sitting with him and his fellow disciples at supper, he must have been a clever actor. If his fellow disciples did not suspect him, he must have acted as they did, distracted and with sorrow. He must also have asked 'Is it I?' (as reported in St Matthew). Surely, if the other disciples had suspected him, they would have torn him limb from limb. Instead, Judas calmly eats with them. He eats with them from a common bowl. 'He dippeth' with Jesus 'in the dish'. And he heard Jesus give the frightening warning: 'Woe to that man by whom the Son of man is betrayed! good were it for that man if he had never been born.' He heard this, and didn't give himself away. He was a clever actor.

And now there is a marvellous change of key. Now, at this

passover meal, which we know as the Last Supper, Jesus is inspired with a simple and heartwarming idea. He has revealed that he knows his betrayer. He has made them sorrowful by this knowledge. He has grimly warned that it would be better for the guilty one if he had never been born. The atmosphere of the occasion must have been uncomfortable and unhappy. And now . . .

I came to this Gospel innocently, with no knowledge and no training; with no habit of church-going, and no theology. I have had to look up the word 'eucharist' in the Encyclopedia Britannica, and found nearly eight pages of incomprehensible writing. If you are still reading this book, it is amazing. I am an ignoramus. I was drawn to the writing of Mark because of its clarity and lack of artifice. I have been increasingly fascinated by the words and behaviour of Jesus. Except for the inclusion of more teaching, I resent the complications caused by reading the other Gospels. I have sometimes been enlightened by the commentators, but more often they have depressed me. And now I choose to ignore them. I wish to retain an original conception.

When I first studied the account of the Last Supper in St Mark, it did not appear to me to be a solemn occasion. I had not read Paul's first Epistle to the Corinthians, Chapter II. I was not aware of its sacrificial nature. It seemed to be a celebration – perhaps more pagan than Christian. According to the personality of Jesus which emerged from the continuity of the Gospel, I found confirmation of joy; permission to live life more abundantly. Jesus was ordering us to celebrate.

Here are the words:

'And as they did eat, Jesus took bread, and blessed, and brake it, and gave to them, and said, Take, eat: this is my body. And he took the cup, and when he had given thanks, he gave it to them: and they all drank of it. And he said unto them, This is my blood of the new testament, which is shed for many. Verily I say unto you, I will drink no more of the fruit of the vine, until that day that I drink it new in the kingdom of God.'

Surely Jesus is saying, remember me when you eat – not only when you eat a piece of bread, but all manner of food – the more appetizing the better.

Surely Jesus is saying, remember me when you drink – not

216

only when you drink wine and water, but all manner of drink –
the more intoxicating the better.

Surely Jesus is ordering us to celebrate his life, to celebrate
his teaching, to celebrate his sacrifice, to enjoy without guilt.

Surely, in the last sentence, Jesus is vowing that he too will
celebrate his life immediately he gets to heaven. 'I will drink no
more of the fruit of the vine, until that day that I drink it new in
the kingdom of God.' Until I read the commentaries, it did not
occur to me that Jesus was talking of drinking new *wine* in the
kingdom of God. I thought he meant newly *arrived*. I thought
he meant that the first thing he would do when he got to
heaven would be to have a drink. I still prefer to think that. It
seems in character. In fact, it is my favourite verse in the entire
Gospel.

I'm sure, if my father ever got to heaven, it was the first
thing that he did.

I'm sure, if I ever get to heaven, it will be the first thing that I
do. Otherwise I don't much want to go.

★

As if to confirm the joyous nature of his words, Jesus and the
disciples then sang together. Except Judas. He couldn't have
been *that* good an actor.

'*And when they had sung an hymn, they went out into the mount of* 26
Olives.'

The next lines could have been spoken as they walked along.

'*And Jesus saith unto them, All ye shall be offended because of me* 27
this night: for it is written, I will smite the shepherd, and the sheep
shall be scattered. But after that I am risen. I will go before you into 28
Galilee.'

By 'offended' Jesus meant that the disciples would 'fall
away' from him or 'desert him'. 'Smite the shepherd, and the
sheep shall be scattered' is a quote from Zachariah 13: 7. It is
interesting that after his death Jesus arranges to meet the
disciples back in Galilee. In Jerusalem they probably all had
yearning thoughts of home.

'*But Peter said unto him, Although all shall be offended . . .*' 29

or although all shall desert you,

'*. . . yet will not I. And Jesus saith unto him, Verily I say unto* 30
thee, That this day, even in this night, before the cock crow twice,

31 *thou shalt deny me thrice. But he spake the more vehemently, If I should die with thee, I will not deny thee in any wise.'*

Peter's part in the Passion narrative is very prominent. In a sense, he speaks and acts for everyman, and subsequently takes all the blame. After he protested vehemently, 'If I should die with thee, I will not deny thee in any wise,' we learn:

'Likewise also said they all.'

But *'they'* are not named; and *'they'* do not stand specifically condemned.

What happens now is surprising and embarrassing. We become intruders. We are privy to a personal emotional scene for which we are unprepared. Nothing in the Gospel since Caesarea Philippi has led us to suppose that Jesus would ever try to change his destiny. Since he affirmed that he was the Christ, he has acted with complete authority. His faith seems so sure that we have accepted that he is the Son of God. We have accepted his eventual death and resurrection. He has taught us to accept these things. Now, the man – the superman – cracks.

And we are reminded that his father, which is in heaven, is, after all, only his *chosen* father. We are reminded that Jesus is a carpenter from Nazareth. We are reminded, forcibly reminded, of the fallibility of this dynamic, wilful human being. We realise this is only the story of one man's dream.

33 *'And they came to a place which was named Gethsemane . . .'*

This may have been a private garden; a place known to Jesus.

'and he saith to his disciples, Sit ye here, while I shall pray. And he taketh with him Peter and James and John, and began to be sore amazed, and to be very heavy; and saith unto them, My soul is exceeding sorrowful unto death: tarry ye here, and watch. And he went forward a little, and fell on the ground, and prayed that, if it **36** *were possible, the hour might pass from him. And he said, Abba, Father, all things are possible unto thee: take away this cup from me: nevertheless not what I will, but what thou wilt.'*

Does this sufficiently convey the agony of Jesus?

There is the Living Bible translation where 'My soul is exceeding sorrowful unto death' is given as 'My soul is crushed by sorrow to the point of death'; and the Good News: 'The sorrow in my heart is so great that it almost crushes me.'

There is St Luke's description: 'And being in an agony he prayed more earnestly: and his sweat was as it were great drops of blood falling down to the ground.'

There is the description in Paul's letter to the Hebrews: 'Who in the days of his flesh, when he had offered up prayers and supplications *with strong crying and tears* unto him that was able to save him from death . . .'

All this conveys some anguish; some evident, audible anguish.

'And he cometh, and findeth them sleeping . . .' **37**

But I don't think they were sleeping. I think they were hiding their heads in horror at what they had heard. I think they were afraid to look Jesus in the eye. I think they were ashamed. I think they feigned sleep in order to avoid contact with him.

'. . . and saith unto Peter, Simon, sleepest thou?'

But Jesus thought they were sleeping, and he called Peter by his family name as if to recall the way things were before he started on his ministry; as if to turn the clock back: 'Simon, sleepest thou?'

'Couldest not thou watch one hour? Watch ye and pray, lest ye **38** *enter into temptation. The spirit truly is ready, but the flesh is weak.'*

As well as Peter's seeming battle with fatigue, surely 'The spirit truly is ready, but the flesh is weak' is related to Jesus's own fear of pain. His spirit was willing to face death, but he was reluctant to suffer physically.

'And again he went away, and prayed, and spake the same words. **39** *And when he returned, he found them asleep again, (for their eyes* **40** *were heavy,) neither wist they what to answer him.'*

I think 'neither wist they what to answer him' was the gist of the matter.

D. E. Nineham writes: 'Opinions are sharply divided about the historical value of this section, and even as to whether it formed part of St Mark's narrative source.' The main argument against the historical value of the section is 'that no one could have known what Jesus prayed in private'.

As the story is reported, this is an understandable argument – unless we assume that the young Mark was eavesdropping again; or unless we assume that at least one of the disciples was awake. But it seems to me that the evident distress of Jesus, and his confession to Peter and James and John that his soul was 'exceeding sorrowful unto death' would have disturbed them greatly. I think they must have watched and listened to him while he prayed. Maybe some of the other disciples did sleep, but surely the three nearest to him would have been stunned by this sudden lack of courage, this request to his father – reported only by Mark in the original Aramaic, 'Abba' – to be released from his cup of suffering. And then there is the reluctant compliance: 'nevertheless not what I will, but what thou wilt.'

Even if the disciples have been represented as insensitive men, they were surely not so insensitive as to sleep through this show of agony. Surely their so-called sleep – 'sleeping for sorrow' St Luke calls it – was more a wish to avoid consciousness; to avoid reality; to search in their minds for some way to help. If Jesus was suddenly lacking in faith, then they were suddenly powerless.

The arguments *supporting* the historical value of the section are, to me, more attractive. Why should someone invent this display of weakness from the Master? It was not a good example for the courage demanded from the early Christians. And why has this story of the doubt and agony of Jesus survived? It must have been considered by Mark, not only to be true, but to be of vital importance. It is a certificate of humanity. Because of the display of weakness in Gethsemane – and because of the desperate cry from the cross – Jesus is a recognisable human being. More understandable than raising people from the dead, more believable than walking on the water, items which smack of magic, it is the humanity of the teacher which attracts the average seeker today.

But, that night in Gethsemane, the disciples were shattered by this break-down. And finally – although *they* were unable to comfort Jesus, 'neither wist they what to answer him' – *he* comforts them. Three times he went away and prayed,

41   *'And he cometh the third time, and saith unto them, Sleep on now, and take your rest: it is enough, the hour is come . . .'*

But there was no more time . . .

42   *'. . . behold the Son of man is betrayed into the hands of sinners. Rise up, let us go; lo, he that betrayeth me is at hand. And*
43   *immediately, while he yet spake, cometh Judas, one of the twelve, and*

with him a great multitude with swords and staves, from the chief priests and the scribes and the elders.'

In St Mark it is not clear exactly when Judas left the group. In St John's Gospel, during the supper, without the other disciples knowing why, Jesus actually orders Judas to leave with the words, 'That thou doest, do quickly.' Judas knew that later they would go to the garden in Gethsemane, and he knew this was a place where Jesus could be 'conveniently' betrayed, without causing any 'uproar of the people'. He must have planned with the chief priests and the scribes and the elders the best way for the captors to know which man to take in the darkness of the night – without causing undue panic and confusion.

'And he that betrayed him had given them a token, saying, Whomsoever I shall kiss, that same is he; take him, and lead him away safely. And as soon as he was come, he goeth straightway to him, and saith, Master, Master, and kissed him. And they laid their hands on him, and took him.'

44
45
46

I have learned a strange thing from William Barclay. The first Greek word for 'kiss' chosen by Mark when Judas plans to give them a token, or signal – 'Whomsoever I shall kiss, that same is he; take him, and lead him away safely' – means the respectful kiss given by a disciple to a Rabbi; or the customary greeting between oriental men. But, for the actual kiss given by Judas to Jesus, Mark uses a slightly different word, meaning 'as a lover kisses his beloved'. It was not a 'mere formal kiss of respectful greeting. It was a lover's kiss'. (Barclay then writes: 'That is the grimmest and most awful thing in all the gospel story.')

It is pointless to surmise whether there is any sexual inference to be drawn from this, but if the actual kiss given by Judas to Jesus was a passionate kiss, it might well have been a desperate entreaty for forgiveness. It might well have been given in love. It is possible that, by the time the arrest was made, Judas regretted his action. St Matthew reports that the next day when Judas knew that Jesus was condemned, he 'went and hanged himself'.

Also, only Mark reports that Judas asks 'lead him away *safely*'. Although he betrays Jesus, it seems he does not wish him to be physically harmed.

What did the other disciples do during the arrest?

47 *'And one of them that stood by drew a sword, and smote a servant of the high priest, and cut off his ear.'*

St John, who is unusually factual in this episode, tells us that the disciple was Peter. It is touching to realise that in the earlier Gospels it was still considered unwise to name him.

And St Luke tells us that Jesus actually found time to heal the unfortunate servant's ear; but this could be wishful thinking by the romantic evangelist to excuse the un-Christian act of violence.

48
49 *'And Jesus answered and said unto them, Are ye come out, as against a thief, with swords and with staves to take me? I was daily with you in the temple teaching, and ye took me not: but the scriptures must be fulfilled.'*

'Thief' can be interpreted as 'bandit' or 'brigand'; someone who is violently dangerous. Jesus mocks the great crowd of armed men sent to arrest him, and taunts them because they wouldn't have dared to take him in the temple – where 'the common people heard him gladly'.

And what did the disciples do now?

50 *'And they all forsook him, and fled.'*

Note Mark's impartial reporting. We have just had a similar example, also about the disciples, after Peter's protest of loyalty: 'Likewise also said they all.' The emotion behind these tiny lines is stronger because of the lack of comment. And the emotion in this instance must have been very strong, because it's likely that the author was a witness to this hurried desertion. In fact he might have been the last person to defend Jesus.

51
52 *'And there followed him a certain young man having a linen cloth cast about his naked body; and the young men laid hold on him: And he left the linen cloth, and fled from them naked.'*

Was it Mark?

Again we can only surmise; but this seemingly irrelevant story must have had some meaning to the author. It reminds me of the movie director Alfred Hitchcock's brief unnamed appearances in his films. There are many theories. The Rev. Marshall writes: 'Only one personally acquainted with the circumstances would have narrated an incident so slight and trivial. It has been suggested that the Last Supper took place in the upper chamber of the house of Mary, the mother of Mark.

If so, it is probable that the soldiers in their search for Jesus would naturally, under the guidance of Judas, go there first. Then Mark, roused from sleep, had hastily cast about him the loose linen wrapper and followed the soldiers to see what would happen.'

He might even have rushed ahead of them. Since he was wearing only a sheet it would seem that he left in a great hurry. One wonders how he got home again.

Despite its seeming irrelevance, the story fits easily into this Gospel, with its collection of miracles, historic confrontations, cosy domestic scenes, and tales of children and poor widows. Naturally Matthew, Luke and John do not include it.

And so, from this tiny drama of a young man stripped naked in the cold night, we proceed to the first trial of Jesus, the Son of God.

'And they led Jesus away to the high priest: and with him were **53** assembled all the chief priests and the elders and the scribes. And Peter followed him afar off, even into the palace of the high priest: and he sat with the servants, and warmed himself at the fire. And the chief priests and all the council sought for witness against Jesus to put him to death; and found none. For many bare false witness against him, but their witness agreed not together. And there arose certain, and bare false witness against him, saying, We heard him say, I will destroy this temple that is made with hands, and within three days I will build another made without hands. But neither so did their witness agree together. And the high priest stood up in the midst, and asked Jesus, saying, Answerest thou nothing? what is it which these witness against thee? But he held his peace, and answered nothing. Again the high priest asked him, and said unto him, Art thou the Christ, the Son of the Blessed? And Jesus said, I am: and ye shall see the Son of man sitting on the right hand of power, and coming in the clouds of heaven. Then the high priest rent his clothes, and saith, What need we any further witnesses? Ye have heard the blasphemy: what think ye? And they all condemned him to be guilty of death. And some began to spit **65** on him, and to cover his face, and to buffet him, and to say unto him, Prophesy: and the servants did strike him with the palms of their hands.'

The witnesses' reference to a threat by Jesus to destroy and re-build the temple within three days is puzzling. Was there a misunderstanding of Jesus's words: 'Seest thou these great buildings? there shall not be left one stone upon another, that shall not be thrown down'? Was this overheard, repeated and misinterpreted as a threat of an actual attack on the temple? Or did the witnesses refer to some other saying of Jesus in which he used the temple as a metaphor for his death and resurrection? Whatever was meant, their testimony did not agree.

There is doubt about the authenticity of this whole trial – much of which is conveniently constructed from Old Testament allusions.

How could it have happened so late at night?

How was it that the chief priests and the elders and the scribes were all assembled at such short notice?

How did they produce the witnesses to accuse Jesus?

I cannot answer any of these questions. One can only say tentatively that surely this was an exceptional circumstance concerning an exceptional man.

And all that matters is that, in St Mark, Jesus answers, 'I am,' to the high priest's question, 'Art thou the Christ, the Son of the Blessed?'

In St Matthew he says: 'Thou hast said.' In St Luke he says: 'Ye say that I am.' But, in St Mark, Jesus positively says: 'I am.' And it reverberates . . .

Jesus then continues, as we might expect him to do, and asserts that they will see 'the Son of man sitting on the right hand of power, and coming in the clouds of heaven'. These assertions provoke the high priest to tear at his clothes – which was a formal act signifying grief in the presence of anyone found guilty of blasphemy. And the verdict of the council was that Jesus deserved death.

★

Then the first humiliations begin; with spitting; and the cruel game of blind man's buff; and the servants striking him 'with the palms of their hands'.

Meanwhile:

'And as Peter was beneath in the palace, there cometh one of the maids of the high priest: And when she saw Peter warming himself, she looked upon him, and said, And thou also wast with Jesus of Nazareth. But he denied, saying, I know not, neither understand I what thou sayest. And he went out into the porch; and the cock crew.

*And a maid saw him again, and began to say to them that stood by,
This is one of them. And he denied it again. And a little after, they
that stood by said again to Peter, Surely thou art one of them: for thou
art a Galilaean, and thy speech agreeth thereto. But he began to curse
and to swear, saying, I know not this man of whom ye speak. And the
second time the cock crew. And Peter called to mind the word that* 72
*Jesus said unto him, Before the cock crow twice, thou shalt deny me
thrice. And when he thought thereon, he wept.'*

What can one say about this?

Admire the courage of Peter who alone of all the disciples
followed Jesus 'even into the palace of the high priest'.

Note the obviousness of the countryman in the big city,
easily recognisable by his accent. The Rev. Marshall says: 'The
Galilaeans pronounced the gutterals incorrectly.' (Jesus probably also spoke with this accent.)

And marvel that Peter confessed this story of ordinary
human failure.

The narrative races on . . .

★ 15

'And straightway in the morning the chief priests held a consultation 1
*with the elders and scribes and the whole council, and bound Jesus, and
carried him away, and delivered him to Pilate.'*

This consultation was probably called to decide what to do
with Jesus. The Sanhedrin wished to put him to death for
blasphemy, but it seems that, according to the laws of the day,
they were not permitted to do this. The death penalty could
only be executed by the Roman authorities. It is also likely that
they were still reluctant to risk 'an uproar of the people' and the
ensuing loss of popularity. It would be preferable if Jesus was
brought before the Romans on a political charge; as a poten-
tially dangerous leader of the Jews against the occupation. The
Romans would not be interested in blasphemy.

There now seems to be a jump in the narrative. It continues
baldly:

'And Pilate asked him, Art thou the King of the Jews?' 2

We need the help of St Luke's version to prepare us for this
question: 'And the whole multitude of them arose, and led him
unto Pilate. And they began to accuse him, saying, We found
this fellow perverting the nation, and forbidding to give

tribute to Caesar, saying that he himself is Christ a King.'
Then Luke also writes: 'And Pilate asked him, saying, Art
thou the King of the Jews?' This additional information
clarifies the reason for Pilate's question.

Jesus's answer is ambiguous and non-committal.

2   *'And he answering said unto him, Thou sayest it.'*

This could imply that, although Jesus didn't have any royal
pretensions, he thought of himself as King of the Jews in a
spiritual sense.

3   *'And the chief priests accused him of many things . . .'*

('He stirreth up the people, teaching throughout all Jewry,
beginning from Galilee to this place.' St Luke, 23: 5.)

4   *'. . . but he answered nothing. And Pilate asked him again,
saying, Answerest thou nothing? behold how many things they*
5   *witness against thee. But Jesus yet answered nothing; so that Pilate
marvelled.'*

And now the story takes a new and unexpected turn. Mark
has, of course, greatly compressed this trial, and gives us only
the bare essentials. Matthew, Luke and John give various other
snatches of dialogue; there is also an additional trial before
Herod in Luke; and an intervention from Pilate's wife in
Matthew. But Mark rushes on:

6   *'Now at that feast he released unto them one prisoner, whomsoever
they desired.'*

There is actually no historical evidence of this custom of
releasing a prisoner at the feast.

7   *'And there was one named Barabbas, which lay bound with them
that had made insurrection with him . . .'*

We do not know what insurrection.

'. . . who had committed murder in the insurrection.'

Barabbas was probably a popular nationalist hero.

8   *'And the multitude crying aloud . . .'*

The multitude? What multitude? This meeting with Pilate
obviously took place in public.

'And the multitude crying aloud *began to desire him to do as he
had ever done unto them.'*

(In other words, release a prisoner.)

9   *'But Pilate answered them, saying, Will ye that I release unto you
the King of the Jews? For he knew that the chief priests had delivered
him for envy. But the chief priests moved the people that he should*

rather release Barabbas unto them. And Pilate answered and said again unto them, What will ye then that I shall do unto him whom ye call the King of the Jews? And they cried out again, Crucify him. Then Pilate said unto them, Why, what evil hath he done? And they cried out the more exceedingly, Crucify him.' 14

Who was this multitude? Where did they come from? Where are the common people who heard him gladly? Where are his followers? Some commentators answer these questions disarmingly by claiming simply that 'this was a different crowd'. It is certainly possible that the chief priests brought along many supporters. It is also possible that the family and friends of Barabbas were present. But the unanimity of the crowd's wish to 'Crucify him' is suspect. Perhaps it was a very small crowd . . . Or perhaps we should take something else into account.

We should take into account the desire of the early Christians – and indeed the later Christians – 'to emphasise the wide and general Jewish responsibility for Jesus's death' (Nineham). I think it was this desire on the part of the Evangelists which explains the surprising unanimity of the crowd. It was also this desire – for an exclusive Jewish responsibility for the crucifixion – which makes them present Pilate in a fairly sympathetic light. He protests on behalf of Jesus. 'He knew that the chief priests had delivered him for envy.' He is not persuaded by the political charge. He offers to release Jesus instead of Barabbas. It is only finally, out of expediency or exhaustion, that he allows the crucifixion to take place.

'And so Pilate, willing to content the people, released Barabbas 15 *unto them, and delivered Jesus, when he had scourged him, to be crucified.'*

This seeming diplomacy of Pilate – 'willing to content the people' – is not seen sympathetically by the Rev. Marshall. In an unusually aggressive footnote he writes: 'He knew our Lord to be innocent but he dared not release Him, for his own cruelty and rapacity had made him so obnoxious to the Jews that he feared to face the consequences of a report to Rome.'

I think the truth of the matter was that the religious establishment were so terrified by the influence of Jesus that they knew it was imperative to silence him. I doubt the sudden

227

appearance of a multitude demanding the release of Barabbas, and the crucifixion of Jesus. I think that the chief priests made a convenient deal with Pilate. I think that they alone share the guilt.

Gradually, through the years, Jesus and the disciples have become less and less Jewish. They just happen to have lived in that part of the world. It just happens that the ministry began in Galilee. It just happens that Jesus grew up in Nazareth – and not in Rome or Tunbridge Wells. They appear like strangers in a hostile country. They belong exclusively to us.

This anti-semitism makes a mockery of Christianity, and a mockery of Jesus.

But at least the beginning of this anti-semitism is less evident in St Mark than in the later Gospels. St Matthew even has the crowd shout out the unlikely words: 'His blood be on us, and on our children.' I don't think they would actually have asked for all that persecution.

And at least the Jews cannot be blamed for the next sordid episode.

'And the soldiers led him away into the hall, called Praetorium; and they call together the whole band. And they clothed him with purple, and platted a crown of thorns, and put it about his head. And began to salute him, Hail, King of the Jews! And they smote him on the head with a reed, and did spit upon him, and bowing their knees worshipped him.'

Now comes one of Mark's incomparable verses – in the King James Version – echoing Jesus's prophecy of these things to his disciples when they were on the road to Jerusalem:

'And they shall mock him,
and shall scourge him,
and shall spit upon him,
and shall kill him.'

Now Mark writes:

*'And when they had mocked him,
they took off the purple from him,
and put his own clothes on him,
and led him out to crucify him.'*

★

The action moves forward:

'And they compel one Simon a Cyrenian, who passed by, coming out of the country, the father of Alexander and Rufus, to bear his cross.' 14

In his usual style, having reached a poetic formality, Mark is now gossiping again. He could just have written: 'And they compel one Simon to bear his cross.' Instead he gives us the additional information that Simon was a Cyrenian, who just happened – accidentally – to be passing by – coming out of the country – and who just happened to be the father of Alexander and Rufus. Were these boys contemporaries of Mark? Did they become friends? Years later, in Rome, did Mark decide to include them in his Gospel, and, hopefully, make them immortal? The other Gospels do not mention them.

The realism of this memory prepares us for the factual reporting of the crucifixion: a succession of sometimes unrelated memories, seemingly etched on Mark's mind.

'And they bring him unto the place Golgotha, which is, being interpreted, The place of a skull. 22

And they gave him to drink wine mingled with myrrh: but he received it not. 22

And when they had crucified him, they parted his garments, casting lots upon them, what every man should take. 24

And it was the third hour, and they crucified him. 25

And the superscription of his accusation was written over, THE KING OF THE JEWS. 26

And with him they crucify two thieves; the one on his right hand, 27 and the other on his left. And the scripture was fulfilled, which saith, 28 And he was numbered with the transgressors.

And they that passed by railed on him, wagging their heads, and 29 saying, Ah, thou that destroyest the temple, and buildest it in three days, Save thyself, and come down from the cross. Likewise also the 30/31 chief priests mocking said among themselves with the scribes, He saved others; himself he cannot save. Let Christ the King of Israel 32 descend now from the cross, that we may see and believe.

And they that were crucified with him reviled him.'

The writing is intriguing. It appears to be straightforward eye-witness reporting. It reads as if Mark was there, watching it all. One by one the memories are vividly recalled. And yet nearly everything that happens in the description of the crucifixion – including the offer of the wine, and the dicing for the garments – is a fulfilment of Old Testament scriptures. It could have been written solely to convince early Christians that the crucifixion fufilled prophecies made in the Book of Psalms, in Proverbs, in Isaiah and in Lamentations.

And yet I hear the authentic voice of Mark.

It would be usual for a man to be offered wine and myrrh before crucifixion as an aid to dull his senses. There were women who regularly performed this act of mercy.

It would be natural for the soldiers to divide his clothes.

It was the custom for the crime of a condemned man to be written and displayed.

It would be convenient to carry out more than one crucifixion.

It might be expected that someone would taunt Jesus about the rumour that he could destroy and re-build the temple in three days.

It is only difficult to believe that the chief priests and the scribes would behave in such a manner. Let us hope it was only the worst of them.

★

33
34
'And when the sixth hour was come, there was darkness over the whole land until the ninth hour. And at the ninth hour Jesus cried with a loud voice, saying, Eloi, Eloi, lama sabachthani? which is, being interpreted, My God, my God, why hast thou forsaken me?

Jesus warned the disciples of the abomination of desolation. The death on the cross was the abomination of desolation for the Son of man.

In this book the emphasis has been on the humanity of Jesus; the reassurance of his humours, the companionship of his frailty. Now we reach the cry from the cross, but this should be balanced with recollections of the whole ministry.

'Thou art my beloved Son, in whom I am well pleased.'

'The time is fulfilled, and the kingdom of God is at hand.'

'I came not to call the righteous, but sinners to repentance.'

'All sins shall be forgiven unto the sons of men, and blasphemies wherewith soever they shall blaspheme: But he that shall blaspheme against the Holy Spirit hath never forgiveness, but is in danger of eternal damnation.'

'For whosoever shall do the will of God, the same is my brother, and my sister, and mother.'

'with what measure ye mete, it shall be measured to you.'

'Why are ye so fearful? how is it that ye have no faith?'

'thy faith hath made thee whole.'

'Be not afraid, only believe.'

'and as many as touched him were made whole.'

'For what shall it profit a man, if he shall gain the whole world, and lose his own soul?'

'For he that is not against us is on our part.'

'Why callest thou me good? there is none good but one, that is, God.'

'But many that are first shall be last; and the last first.'

'FOR VERILY I SAY UNTO YOU, THAT WHOSOEVER SHALL SAY UNTO THIS MOUNTAIN, BE THOU REMOVED, AND BE THOU CAST INTO THE SEA, AND SHALL NOT DOUBT IN HIS HEART, BUT SHALL BELIEVE THAT THOSE THINGS WHICH HE SAITH SHALL COME TO PASS; HE SHALL HAVE WHATSOEVER HE SAITH.'

'The stone which the builders rejected is become the head of the corner.'

'Render to Caesar the things that are Caesar's, and to God the things that are God's.'

'She hath done what she could.'

'Heaven and earth shall pass away: but my words shall not pass away.'

'The spirit truly is ready, but the flesh is weak.'

'My God, my God, why hast thou forsaken me?'

★

'And some of them that stood by, when they heard it, said, Behold, he 35
calleth Elias. And one ran and filled a sponge full of vinegar, and put 36
it on a reed, and gave him to drink, saying, Let alone, let us see
whether Elias will come to take him down. And Jesus cried with a 37
loud voice, and gave up the ghost.'

The 'vinegar' was a cheap sour wine. It was offered in kindness. But Jesus had said: 'I will drink no more of the fruit of the vine, until that day that I drink it new in the kingdom of God.'

★

To match the moment of Jesus's death, Mark writes a wonderfully haunting line:

38 '*And the veil of the temple was rent in twain from the top to the bottom.*'

And he couples this with the homely information:

39 '*And when the centurion, which stood over against him, saw that he so cried out, and gave up the ghost, he said, Truly this man was the Son of God.*'

The tearing of the veil of the temple is interpreted symbolically: 'At the death of Jesus . . . access to the innermost shrine – to the very presence of God – was complete.' (Moule) (At the same moment St Matthew includes an earthquake, tombs opening, 'and many godly men and women who had died came back to life again'. (Living))

And the centurion's tribute is interpreted as an immediate affirmation of faith from the Gentile world.

*

Now, at last, Mark makes good an important omission:

40 '*There were also women looking on afar off: among whom was Mary Magdalene, and Mary the mother of James the less and of Joses,*
41 *and Salome; (Who also, when he was in Galilee, followed him, and ministered unto him;) and many other women which came up with him unto Jerusalem.*'

An image of twelve lonely celibate men is shattered . . .

James the less and Joses may have become more friends of Mark.

Salome may have been the mother of the disciples James and John.

Who the 'many other women' were, we do not know.

*

42 '*And now when the even was come, because it was the preparation, that is, the day before the sabbath, Joseph of Arimathaea, an honourable counsellor, which also waited for the kingdom of God, came, and went in boldly unto Pilate, and craved the body of Jesus. And Pilate marvelled if he were already dead: and calling unto him the centurion, he asked him whether he had been any while dead. And when he knew it of the centurion, he gave the body to Joseph. And he bought fine linen, and took him down, and wrapped him in the linen,*

and laid him in a sepulchre which was hewn out of a rock, and rolled a stone unto the door of the sepulchre. And Mary Magdalene and Mary the mother of Joses beheld where he was laid.'

47

After the concentrated enmity of the chief priests and the elders and the scribes, the servants striking Jesus with the palms of their hands, the soldiers mocking and scourging him, and the passers-by railing at him, the appearance of sympathetic Joseph of Arimathaea is a relief. He was evidently a man of considerable wealth and influence. He went straight to the top and got the permission of Pilate himself to take Jesus down from the cross. By Roman command, bodies were usually left to rot. Mark has already introduced the centurion; he now appears again. Mark has already introduced the women; two of them now appear again. The story moves smoothly forward. The centurion gives evidence that Jesus is dead. The body is taken down, wrapped in a shroud, and interred. The women note the place of the burial. Mark does his best to insure that there can be no argument about the death of Jesus.

Now it is the sabbath. After the shouting and turmoil, there is silence.

★

1   *'And when the sabbath was past . . .'*

The last chapter of St Mark's Gospel has been called the greatest of all literary mysteries. There are only eight verses. Twelve more verses describing encounters with the risen Jesus were added by an unknown writer at a later date. But as the Rev. Marshall writes – after his final counting job – 'There is a manifest change of style, and no less than twenty-one words and expressions occur, which are not used by St Mark elsewhere.'

Did Mark design his Gospel to end abruptly? Was there a longer ending which was lost or destroyed? Was there controversy about the interpretation of the resurrection? Certainly all four Gospels have important variations. Or did Mark simply intend a mystery?

'And when the sabbath was past, *Mary Magdalene, and Mary the mother of James, and Salome, had bought sweet spices, that they might come and anoint him.'*

From a reluctance to mention the women who followed Jesus throughout the ministry, Mark now mentions some of them for the third time. In fact they would appear to have replaced the disciples. Were the disciples hiding for fear of arrest? Or were the women naturally braver?

2   *'And very early in the morning the first day of the week, they came unto the sepulchre at the rising of the sun.'*

I like to think that 'at the rising of the sun' was intended by the translators of the King James Version as a pun.

3   *'And they said among themselves, Who shall roll us away the stone from the door of the sepulchre? And when they looked, they saw that the stone was rolled away: for it was very great. And entering into the sepulchre, they saw a young man sitting on the right side, clothed in a long white garment; and they were affrighted. And he saith unto them, Be not affrighted: Ye seek Jesus of Nazareth, which was crucified: he is risen; he is not here: behold the place where they laid him. But go your way, tell his disciples and Peter that he goeth before*

8   *you into Galilee: there shall ye see him, as he said unto you. And they went out quickly, and fled from the sepulchre; for they trembled and were amazed: neither said they any thing to any man; for they were afraid.'*

This is the end of St Mark's Gospel.

'They were afraid.' We are afraid. What does it mean?

★

One can question the reports of this scene in the other Gospels. St Matthew has yet another earthquake. St Luke takes a page out of St Matthew's book and doubles the cast with two men instead of one in the tomb. St John gives us two angels, and also claims that Jesus actually appeared to Mary Magdalene – who took him for the gardener.

One can ridicule the other translations. The command of the young man clothed in white to the terrified women is variously given as: 'There is no need for alarm'; 'No need to be dismayed'; and 'Don't be so surprised'. 'They were affrighted' is obviously much too difficult. Manford George Gutzke helpfully explains: 'That's an old English way of saying they were literally scared to death.'

One can despair of the pernickety commentators. Nineham writes of the women's early-morning worry about rolling back the heavy stone: 'It may seem strange that this question did not occur earlier seeing that two of the women had already watched the burial.'

One can mock the splendid theory that the young man in the tomb was Mark himself – making another guest appearance in his sheet.

One can argue that another man took Jesus's place. One can argue that the women went to the wrong tomb. One can argue that the body was stolen. One can argue that Jesus was not really dead. One can argue that he escaped from Jerusalem and is buried in Kashmir.

Or one can say that the resurrection was a decision, a calculated decision by a few inspired men and women. They were inspired by the faith of Jesus. And they made the faith of Jesus come true. The faith of Jesus *is* the resurrection.

William Barclay writes: 'By far the best proof of the resurrection is the existence of the Christian church.'

It is certainly one proof. I don't agree that it is the best proof.

Another proof of the resurrection is the creative energy generated by the faith of the man of Galilee: energy which has inspired painters, sculptors, architects, composers and writers.

Another proof of the resurrection is the *practice* of Jesus's commandments; particularly: 'thou shalt love the Lord thy God with all thy heart, and with all thy soul, and with all thy mind, and with all thy strength.' And: 'Thou shalt love thy neighbour as thyself.'

★

We are not all Catholics. We are not all Non-conformists.

Some of us are non-conformist Non-conformists.

Does my insistence on the continuity of St Mark's Gospel really matter?

It matters to me.

Until I could form an image of the personality of Jesus, I did not really care. Then it fired me to write this book.

★

Jesus believed that he had a father in heaven.

He believed that – if we choose – you and I have a father in heaven.

What a ridiculous idea! but also . . .

What a beautiful idea!

. . . and a necessary one.

9 Now when Jesus was risen early the first day of the week, he appeared first to Mary Magdalene, out of whom he had cast seven

10 devils. And she went and told them that had been with him, as they mourned and

11 wept. And they, when they had heard that he was alive, and had been seen of her, believed not.

12 After that he appeared in another form unto two of them, as they walked, and went into the country. And they

13 went and told it unto the residue: neither believed they them.

14 236 Afterwards he appeared unto the eleven as they sat at meat, and upbraided them with their unbelief and hardness of heart,

because they believed not them which had
15 seen him after he was risen. And he
said unto them, Go ye into all the
world, and preach the gospel to every
16 creature. He that believeth and is
baptized shall be saved; but he that
17 believeth not shall be damned. And
these signs shall follow them that believe;
In my name shall they cast out
devils; they shall speak with new tongues;
18 They shall take up serpents; and if
they drink any deadly thing, it shall
not hurt them; they shall lay hands on
the sick, and they shall recover.
19 So then after the Lord had spoken
unto them, he was received up into heaven,
20 and sat on the right hand of God. And
they went forth, and preached every
where, the Lord working with them, and
confirming the word with signs
following. Amen.

— . —

Patience — p. 28.